Hermaphrodeities:
The Transgender Spirituality Workbook

Raven Kaldera

Hermaphrodeities:
The Transgender Spirituality Workbook

Raven Kaldera

Hubbardston, Massachusetts

Asphodel Press
12 Simond Hill Road
Hubbardston, MA 01452

Hermaphrodeities: The Transgender Spirituality Workbook
Second Edition, Second Printing
© 2008 Raven Kaldera
ISBN 978-0-578-00791-5

Printed in cooperation with
Lulu Enterprises, Inc.
860 Aviation Parkway, Suite 300
Morrisville, NC 27560

Dedicated to all the people of my tribe
in all their ambivalent glory

and to my partners, Bella and Joshua
without whom I would never have known
what sacred love really is.

Acknowledgements

I would like to acknowledge all the people who donated their words to the book—and even more, all those who believed in this book and donated money for it, way back in the beginning. Thank you. You all made it real.

Contents

Part One: Divine Lessons

Part Two: Solid Visions

Introduction to the Second Edition

This book came about because of an angry exchange of letters long ago, back in the early 1990s. At that time—before the age of forums, email lists, and online blogs—the Letters section of a particular notorious Neo-Pagan magazine of the time bristled with disagreements over practices and policies and Who Was Right. In many cases, it was the only place that certain hard theological questions were being discussed in a public forum, where people who were new to all of this could watch and form their own (loud) opinions. The magazine itself was willing to tackle controversial ideas, and one issue tentatively touched on spirituality as it related to transgendered people, including images of Deit(ies) that were neither—or both—male and female.

It touched off a stormcloud of debate. The few hesitant transsexuals who bravely wrote in were shouted down by men and women who had a lot of opinions, but little in the way of experience. By the next issue, it had all quietly fallen away, but it still reverberated in my mind. "You're going to do something about this," several Voices told me, and I found myself driven to do it. I was desperately poor at the time, scraping change together in order to eat and feed my daughter out of dented bins in grocery stores. No publisher would take the book; its target market was too small and an unknown territory—people put out books *about* transgendered people, not *for* them!—and its subject matter was too controversial. The print-on-demand industry of the time was new and costly. I put a little box with a slot in the entryway to my house, with a sign begging friends and visitors to contribute to getting this book published. Eventually I put together enough and put it out independently.

The response was amazing. While I didn't make much money off of it, I did get a plethora of transgendered people writing to me in gratitude, telling me that my words had helped them—and in some cases, saved their lives. Up to that point, no one had ever told them that what they were doing was sacred, worthy, necessary to the development of the world. *Hermaphrodeities* was literally the first book of its kind, and from a distance I watched the dialogue develop.

That was over a decade ago. Today, many new voices have taken up the challenge of the Third Path and its spiritual ramifications. I was, myself, still very much a beginner on my own path. I didn't think so at the time, of course, but that's what we all think: *I know what I'm doing, I'm clear on where all this is going, why, I'm almost to the End of it!* Oh, if I'd known then what I know now. At any rate, this second edition of *Hermaphrodeities* is long overdue; I offer it up, as I offered up the last one, as a gift to my tribe, all of you in your gritty, seductive, annoying, glamorous, painful, powerful, ambiguous beauty.

Some of the words in the original text have been altered; most I have kept as they were, not only because they still ring true but because this book is, in its own way, a historical document of the words of the brave folk who were willing to speak up during that difficult time. I've also added more interviews and more material, because more keeps appearing. Threads of Third crop up again and again, every time a mythology is studied closely. There's also that I've learned a lot more about the spiritual nature of being Third since then—not just the cosmological theory but the down-to-earth practicality. I've met new people who have found threads I missed, and whose work I respect. I'm not the only one writing about this any more, and I'm grateful.

This book has grown, and not just due to the new crop of interviews of transfolk. It is now divided into two sections. The first section, Divine Lessons, is the bulk of the first edition with its workbook-style lesson chapters, slightly rearranged. The second section, Solid Visions, contains longer essays about various people's spiritual experiences and discoveries. Some things just can't be contained in a single interview, and they add depth to the book's high-flying breadth. The first essay is my own, cataloguing some of what I've learned in the intervening decade.

One of the things I did change, hesitantly, was the considerable number of third-gender pronouns. While I think it's good for people to see them in print, and get their brains used to them, too many folk seemed to find them so distracting that it detracted from the material. It's a hard thing for me because I really don't think that "he" or "she" do justice to many of these deities ... and those normally-gendered pronouns give people the impression that these gods are "really" male or female, when they're not. But with a heavy heart, I've normalized the pronouns in many parts of the book (although not, of course, the pronouns of beings such as Hermaphroditus and Agdistis who are inarguably halfway between genders). Please keep in mind, however, as you read through this book, that it's only a convention. Try switching some of them in your head to the other one as you read. It won't offend Them and it's good for you. In fact, that's really what this book was meant to be about … a world that stretches your brain, that changes you in subtle ways so that you will never be the same again. If I've done that, I've done my job.

For the future,

RAVEN KALDERA
DECEMBER 2008
HUBBARDSTON, MASSACHUSETTS
ERGI SHAMAN OF TRIBE OF THIRD

Preface
(Or Why I Wrote This Thing Anyway)

"Become the change you wish to see in the world."

–Mahatma Gandhi

Because androgyny—whatever that word means to you—isn't a theory for some of us. It isn't an abstract situation. It's a reality we live with every day, perhaps every time we look into a mirror. Girl or boy? Boy or girl? Must we all choose? What about those of us who can't?

Because of the books that kept coming out on "gay" spirituality from the academic community. Many of them were well-researched and concisely written, but the authors lumped in a few "mysteries" that were clearly transgendered in with the "gay and lesbian" stuff. All right, there is some overlap, both in community and spirituality. We are a continuum, not a little box that can be moved around as the lines are redrawn. But sexual preference is about just that, who you desire sexually—and what ramifications that has on your life and spirituality. Make no mistake, it does have ramifications; sexuality is one of the strongest forces in the universe. Being third gender is something else again. You can be third gender and desire men, women, other third gender people, all of the above, or nobody at all, and still be third gender. You can be third gender in a vacuum with no other human beings in existence. It's about who you are, not what you are or who you would be with. Both should be respected, but one should not be confused with the other, especially by scholars who ought to know better.

Because I saw the earth-centered spiritual community (consisting of Neo-Pagans, feminist witches, radical faeries, mythopoetic men, folk dancers, old hippies, would-be shamans, spiritual ecologists, and many other random unclassifiable but very fine people) dividing Deity up into rigid male and female, categories as dualistic and stifling as the Judeo-Christian division of Good and Evil. This simply does not work out in the long run. A spirituality centered on the sacredness of life in this world must acknowledge and hold holy all the ways of being alive in this world, and that includes us. We must have a seat at the table, or we'll starve. Millennia ago, there may have been some options.

Granted, it was no paradise, but if our ancestors managed to grudgingly give over some sacred space and roles and duties to people like us, certainly we of today can do at least that much and more.

Because once I started discovering the gender-transgressive gods, they began to hound and haunt me, demanding attention, demanding that their stories be told, and I need some bloody rest from their demands. Read on, and let me get some sleep.

Why? Because I never could leave well enough alone.

In this book I use a lot of terms that somebody is bound to dislike or find fault with. Labels are continually debated in the gender-transgressive demographic, and no matter what word is used there's bound to be controversy. However, I need to settle on some terms, if only for consistency and general understanding. That said: I use the word *transgender* as an umbrella term to describe anyone who deliberately crosses back and forth over the boundaries of what we call male and female in this culture. That includes drag kings and transsexuals and everyone in between, people who identify with their birth sex but play with gender roles, people who identify with the gender they've crossed over to, people whose identities fall in the middle. It includes some people who happily shapeshifted their fleshly bodies and some people who are horrified at the idea, people who do it for political reasons and people who do it because they simply can't do otherwise.

I use the term *transsexual* for someone whose discomfort with the sexual characteristics of their body is so deep that they are willing to physically alter it through hormones and possibly surgery in order to make it resemble what's inside their head. I do not make the mistake of assuming that what they want to change that body to is necessarily a perfectly polarized male or female one; nor do I assume that transsexuals all identify as a single gender (although some do) and you shouldn't either.

I use the term *third gender* more specifically. It describes a feeling more than an ideological stance—specifically that feeling that your soul, the deepest part of your being, is poised somewhere between male and female, partaking of both but creating something different in the process. If it confuses you, that's all right; you just may not be one. You'll just have to take it on faith that this is all for real and I'm not just making it all up. If you are one, I'm betting you'll know instantly what I'm talking about. You do, don't you? You're sitting here reading this and making little um-hum noises. I can hear you from where I'm sitting.

On occasion, some of my contributors will use certain Native American terms—namely the Lakota word *winkte* for male-to-female beings, the Yuma word *kwe'rhame* for female-to-male, and the Dineh word *nadle* for an intersex umbrella term. These words are not used to insult or steal from Native American spirituality; I'm one of those people who believes that if Native Americans feel that their worship is being stolen by white people who won't stand up for them in local and national politics, we should keep our hands off and look to our own past for inspiration, of which there is plenty if we're willing to do the legwork. However, for some transgendered people, they've become common ways to refer to people for whom English has no good terms. I also object to the word *berdache*, which is a Persian/Spanish term referring to a kept catamite. I don't feel that word has any business describing transgender spirituality. Some Native Americans that I've spoken to about such things seem to feel that any real Native American word, from any tribe, is better than a conqueror's insult. Others are divided on the issue.

The term *two-spirit* is an ambivalent one for me; on the one hand, it is used by some Native American tribes to refer to *nadle* people, but in others it is a term for a half-breed, and has a very negative connotation. However, there are numerous ancient European legends that refer to a gender-crossing individual as being "two-souled" as they were thought to be male and female twins who spontaneously combined in their mother's womb. So I use it with that in mind.

I use FTM as a contraction of "female-to-male", and sometimes the word *transman* as an alternative. Likewise, I use MTF as a contraction of "male-to-female", and the complementary word *transwoman*. I use the terms butch and femme in order to refer to people of whatever sexual configuration at birth who choose to live in gender roles that strongly resemble those of traditional males and females.

The myths and archetypes herein are mostly, with a few exceptions, from European sources. This is simply because my religious background is modern

Neo-Paganism, which has a European bias. If anyone wants to write a companion volume to cover traditions I missed, I'd love to see it in print!

One thing that you won't see in this book is a lot of discussion about how to deal with those mainstream—or not so mainstream—religious persuasions that firmly believe we are evil, satanic, perverse, or just ought not to be the way we are. There's a whole lot of discussion on that subject in other areas, and since I'm not part of such a tradition, I don't feel qualified to go into depth about it. I have chosen instead to devote this entire book to the idea that we are sacred and spiritually worthy people, and to recount traditions that reinforce this paradigm. However, I will say two things on the subject, and then I will let it drop.

The first thing is that everyone deserves the right to pick and choose among your religious beliefs. Always fight for your right to pick and choose the things you like and dislike about any faith. After all, the heads of denominations do that; why should you have fewer rights? It's true that sometimes picking and choosing means that you select yourself out of a particular religious community, but you can bet that there are other like-minded people out there, waiting to connect with you. It's worth it to go looking for them.

The second thing is a little less compassionate. When you are abused by your parents as a child, but plead to stay with them anyway, people say you are codependent, and might suggest that you be taken away for your own good. When you are abused by your spouse or partner as an adult but refuse to leave because you love them, it is called codependence and you are strongly counseled to leave. Yet when your church or religious community treats you in ways that can only be called abusive, people say, "Oh well, that's the way it is." No. That is not the way it is. A codependent relationship with your church or faith is just as self-destructive as one with your parents, spouse, or partner, and all the same advice applies. Enough said.

This book is structured like a workbook for a reason. I wanted to write something more than an academic research tome; there are enough of them on the market already. This is not a research book. I wanted to write the book I wished someone else had already written, a book that would be used alone and in groups, shared and passed around; that would be the book to open for an activity when a support group was at a loss for a topic or a spiritual group needed inspiration for a ritual ... and that would be simple to read and easy to follow. Toward this effect, I have left out the encyclopedias full of data and details that might clutter its immediate usefulness. If this makes you bridle, because you want to see my sources, well, they're out there. If you bother to look, you'll find them. You can also check the bibliography in the back. But if you're primarily looking to write a research paper, you're not my target audience.

Each chapter has a guiding spirit, and a controversy as well. Each chapter also contains discussion topics, personal and political activities, and ritual pieces that can be combined and recombined in any way you like. Many of my own people as well as many others may well have problems with all the directions I explore as related to transgendered spirituality. Certainly I would not expect anyone to serve every god/dess in this book, directly or figuratively, but if you can't find what you want, let it spur you on to create that for yourself!

My credentials? Well, I'm medically intersex, raised female, transitioned to a male somatic physiology and (sort of) role. I've been—or tried to be, at least—a female housewife and mother, a lesbian-feminist, a butch dyke, a bisexual male Pagan priest, and a bi-leatherfag. I now see myself as exactly what I am—a bigendered being who prefers a masculine body but who has no illusions about being anything but intersex where it matters. I've been a Gardnerian Wiccan, a feminist Dianic, a tie-dyed-in-the-natural-fibers granola pagan, a student of Umbanda, an astrologer, and I find myself now an eclectic Pagan minister and transgender activist in the First Kingdom Church of Asphodel. I am also a Northern Tradition shaman, and this is my primary personal practice. I've been bringing both spirituality and transgender to groups that have distrusted it for decades, and I see no reason to stop now.

And one more thing: This book could not have been written without the help of all the brave and wonderful people who shared their stories and personal triumphs and tragedies in its pages. You are all my brothers and sisters, and I am honored to be among you. We are a bright and magical community, and we will flourish. My heartfelt thanks go out to Drey, Robin, Zot, Libby, Arthur,

Dawn, Gary, Henry and Julian, Julia, Zoltana, Max, Maureen, Halley, and most especially my beloved Bella, best friend and lover, muse and pillar of support. It could not have been published without the help of all the people who donated money to see it happen in print. Thank you, every one. I was blown away by the outpouring of aid and assistance. You are all wonderful.

May this be a work of the God/dess, and may S/He flow through me and into all who will receive Hir bounty and love.

Peace and blessed be,
Raven Brangwyn Kaldera, 2001

Part One: Divine Lessons

Chapter 1
Agdistis: the Bringer of Chaos

So, do you fear me?
(look me in the eye, you bastard—
I dare you—
look me in the eye—)
Do you fear me then?
Good.
You should.
I'm about to hurt you bad
with the greatest gift
anyone ever gave anyone else
ever
ever
in the history of the universe—
I'm about to wake you up
I'm about to change your world.

The Myth

Once, in the land of Asia Minor that was long ago ruled by the Great
Mother Goddess Cybele, a wild and laughing creature was born. Hir name was
Agdistis, and Agdistis was a hermaphrodite, being of both sexes. For a long
time Agdistis roamed free in the land, sleeping with whosoever s/he wished,
until the gods took notice of hir. They became frightened, feeling that such a
creature would eventually become accomplished in the magics of both maleness
and femaleness, both the giving forth and the taking in, and thus be more
powerful than any other. They resolved that such a creature must not be
allowed to exist, lest it become a force to reckon with.

So they went to Agdistis and spoke to hir. "Agdistis," they said, "you must
choose what you will be. If you choose to be female, we will cut off your male
parts. If you choose to be male, we will sew up your female parts. Choose,
Agdistis."

And Agdistis said, "Fuck you." And split.

And the gods became very paranoid, and they resolved that Agdistis must be forcibly gendered or killed. But none of them wanted the blood of the hermaphrodite on their hands, for what cursed powers might that blood have? So they went to Dionysus, who was a very young god, wandering adolescent through Asia Minor, not yet acknowledged by his Greek father Zeus, and he did not know about Agdistis. And they told him what to do, and he lay in wait for the wild laughing one.

Some say that Dionysus got Agdistis drunk, others that he merely crept up on hir, but either way he cut Agdistis's male organ off, and s/he screamed and bled and almost died. The blood splashed on Dionysus, and he was never the same again, but his story is another chapter. Where the organ fell, there grew a beautiful pomegranate tree (some say an almond) with tempting fruit.

The first to eat of it was Nana, a nymph of the river Sangarius, who found herself suddenly pregnant. Angered, she left the male infant to be exposed, but he was saved and suckled by a male goat. In adulthood, named Attis, Cybele the Great Mother Goddess of Anatolia saw his beauty and wished to have him as her consort.

In the meantime, Agdistis had become somewhat soured, and resentful, and bitter, for such is the lot of one who is different, alone, looked at askance; not to mention having gods trying to maim and assassinate you. And s/he saw Attis, the young man who was to be the consort of the Great Mother Cybele. Realizing that he was born of hir lost part, with which s/he wished to be reunited, s/he seduced him. Realizing what he had done, Attis fled in disgust, but then at a later time he fell in love with a young girl and decided to marry her against Cybele's wishes. Cybele sent Agdistis to disrupt the wedding and punish the unfaithful Attis; the hermaphrodite worked magic to inflict madness on all present. The bride cut her own breasts off and bled to death; Attis tried to commit suicide by castrating himself.

Realizing what hir power had done, Agdistis pleaded with Mother Cybele to restore Attis, and she agreed to keep him in a state of permanent sleep, never decaying, forever.

Some Native American tribes called us sacred people. In some northern Eurasian ancient traditions, we were shamans by default. The ancient Greeks considered us dangerous, since by being of both genders we had too much magical power. Modern medicine uses such labels as: congenital deformity, psychological imbalance, gender dysphoria. No matter where we are, our mere existence is cause for such controversy that we cannot help but polarize people, and make many of them profoundly uncomfortable.

We are androgynes, hermaphrodites. Some of us show it physically, some psychically. Third-sexed, two-souled. Not quite like most everyone else. We are living proof that gender is not a two-sided coin as some would claim, but a continuum; that there is a middle ground and that to inhabit it is not unhealthy, unwholesome or impossible. It is, however, a place of great power and transformation, a place that does not leave you the privilege of remaining an unaware being. We are not men. We are not women. We are both, and sometimes we are so much both that we are neither.

There are many levels of androgyny: genital, endocrinal, and psychological, to make large, sweeping generalities. People with visible physical signs of what used to be called "hermaphroditism" or "pseudohermaphroditism" now may prefer the words *intersexual* and *intersex*, or the even more recent and blander terminology *Disorders of Sex Development (DSD)*, a term invented because intersex was becoming associated with, well, with the sorts of things that this book is about, and some intersex activists were worried that parents would choose mutilation for their children out of fear that they would be queer "like those people". The term "hermaphrodite" is a powerful one, with many connotations, but unfortunately one of them seems to be a mythical nature, and intersexuals generally want people to know that we aren't a myth but a medical condition.

There are many, many forms of intersex; too many to list here. Genital hermaphroditism is evident at birth; the child has "ambiguous" genitalia ... some combination of both (or neither) male and female. In almost all cases, the child is immediately surgically altered to a gender chosen by the doctors and parents, even if the altering leaves genitals that are cosmetically acceptable but offer little chance of sexual pleasure. (This is especially common when there is a useful vulva and the "penis" is an enlarged clitoris, which is usually amputated or resectioned.) Endocrinal hermaphrodites look normal at birth, but at puberty frequently manifest the hormones and the secondary sexual characteristics of both sexes—boys who grow breasts, girls who grow body hair and whose voices lower. Usually they are put on hormones for the rest of their lives in order to be "normal".

There are women who discover at puberty that they have XY chromosomes, and no uterus; instead a pair of internal testes. Their body is simply immune to the male hormones that would otherwise have masculinized them, and they are women—who are often encouraged to get their gonads removed for fear of a tiny likelihood of future cancer. Some AIS (androgen insensitivity syndrome) women have started getting tattoos of orchids—the word "orchid" comes from the Greek word for testicle—to reclaim those lost parts of themselves. A partial form of AIS (PAIS) can result in a boy child who feminizes at puberty. Then there's Klinefelter's Syndrome, in which the individual has XXY chromosomes and which also sometimes results in a feminized boy.

The reaction of the medical profession is almost exactly like that of the gods' reaction to Agdistis—wipe it out, make it go away, cut it off, sew it up. Infants are mutilated to make them seem "cosmetically normal" to their parents, with little thought to the fact that many end up with no sexual sensation in adulthood. Many of these mutilated intersex adults are angry and traumatized by their experiences, and many are fighting back, trying to stop these disfiguring surgeries from being performed on infants who cannot consent, or even give an opinion.

In some endocrinological manuals, doctors are told to consider the birth of an intersex child as an emergency, not just for physical reasons in case there is a rare chemical or functional problem, but the idea that a gender must be established immediately and the child "corrected" to look like it or it will "interfere with parental bonding". A chilling phrase, that ... the idea that parents couldn't love a child if it wasn't exactly a boy or a girl. Perhaps some couldn't, which is an even more chilling thought, but what's the possibility that things might go a little easier with immediate referral to support groups and therapists? To this day, however, the medical profession, with only a few exceptions, will not allow small copies of Agdistis to run around.

The irony of the situation is that one never knows how an intersex child is going to turn out. Some are happy with the sex assigned them; some aren't and get sex changes. Some would simply prefer to live as both and be unmolested. Some are actually heterosexual; most of the ones I know are bisexual, with lesbianism (most IS people are assigned female for reasons of ease of surgery) in second place. So the idea that careful and stereotypical rearing will automatically create a normal heterosexual adult happy with their gender is utter fallacy. Of course, telling parents that you have no idea what their child will turn out to be isn't an easy task, and certainly isn't what they want to hear, but it's better to deal with the truth than to hide behind pretty lies.

Androgynes who are strictly psychological are an even thornier problem. This manifests as varying levels of the phenomenon psychiatrists call "gender dysphoria"—dissatisfaction with the gender of one's birth gender. Some go so far as to become transsexuals, some do not. Not all transsexuals consider themselves androgynes, however; many have bodies squarely on one end of the gender identity spectrum and identities squarely on the other end.

Some work by Drs. Pillard and Weinrich suggests that gender identity is formed by the "proper" combination of hormones affecting the fetus *in utero*. Nonstandard sexes and genders are formed by a "nonstandard" dose at a given point in fetal development. The causes are varied, sometimes chromosomal disorders (XXY, XO, etc.), sometimes autosomal genetic traits that skip generations. The genitals differentiate first, before the brain, at three months gestation. If the glitch occurs here, the genitals will be mixed. A week or so later, the adrenals, pituitary, and parts of the hypothalamus controlling pubertal hormones differentiate; glitches become more common and thence originate endocrinal hermaphrodites.

The last bit to differentiate hormonally is the part of the hypothalamus that directs sexual behavior and gender identity. Don't ask me why God/dess did things in this order; it mystifies me too.

Transgender is not about sexual preference; it is separate from sexual preference. Most lesbians consider themselves women; most gay men consider themselves men. Many, if not the majority, of admitted androgynes are varying levels of bisexual, as one might logically expect. When you move into the middle of the gender continuum, there comes a point where labels like "gay, lesbian, straight" are irrelevant; all sexual interactions become somehow queer.

The point of all this scientific prevarication is that we are here, and we are not making this whole thing up. Our nontraditional gender is not theoretical or abstract. We didn't choose to be this way for political purposes. In many cases, it drove us near to madness, confused our relationships, cast us out of peer and interest groups, and left us bereft of any kind of meaningful role, political group, or community. We live it. We have no choice but to live it. We can deny it and stay in the closet in spite of the ever-present feeling of incompleteness, or we can cease to hide our two souls and be what we are. We must believe that God/dess did this for a purpose.

In one issue of a recent publication in my religious demographic, a third gender person put forth the question as to whether there was a special role for two-souled people in their small religious community. An incoming flood of fairly hostile letters drowned out the original question in the argument as to whether we exist or not in the first place. Some people came at androgyny from a man-or-woman standpoint, in terms of "getting in touch with your feminine/masculine side" so that you can then become more comfortable with your birth gender. Some accused us of taking an abstract idea too far, of trying to obliterate all gender differences and deny manhood and womanhood, to step around the gender issues at war in our society. One angry letter said that creating a special social role for us would be "impossible". It was as if Agdistis hirself had thrown down the gauntlet, and the gods were having inappropriately hysterical reactions.

It's almost fashionable to speak of "male and female sides", "anima and animus", etc. as if it were all an intellectual idea that, of course, doesn't affect "real" or "actual" gender. However, for some of us, there's nothing abstract or symbolic about it. We look in the mirror and see it every day as a concrete reality. For those of us who have certain intersex condition, we've experienced it as a concrete reality since childhood. It is what is real for us.

The lesson of Agdistis is the first transgender mystery. We are all, every one of us, catalysts. We change people, and we don't even have to work at it. All we have to do is stand around, and people have to struggle with their world views just to cope with our very existence. This can have quite a few negative ramifications when you're the two-souled person taking the brunt of someone's painful struggle. Most people would secretly prefer not to have to bother with continually upgrading their headspace, and would rather let things rest in a rigid stasis than have to do the work. If they haven't done it in a while, it might even end up being pretty painful for them, especially if it involves letting go of cherished ideas about themselves and their place in the order of things.

There is a shadow of madness over Agdistis; infectious magic; s/he is said to be able to inflict madness on anyone. This "madness", similar to that of the Greek god Dionysus, tends to take the form of mutilation of the primary and secondary sexual characteristics; Attis castrates himself and his bride cuts off her breasts. There seems to be an undercurrent of fear that gender-crossing and the eventuality of body modification is somehow contagious, that anyone who has contact with an avatar of Agdistis will somehow "catch" transgendered behavior from them.

At one spiritual gathering I attended, the catalyst theory was driven home. One afternoon was set aside for discussion groups on "gender mysteries". Since the demographics of the gathering divided themselves into one-third female, one-third male, and one-third other-please-describe, we divided up into three groups. The male and female groups asked that members have lived at least one year full-time in that gender to be included. Our group figured that nobody in their right mind would claim to be third gender unless they were, and screening wasn't necessary.

We spoke on various things, and ended up talking a lot about how other people reacted to us. It was then that we came up with Agdistis' mystery, that of catalyst and generalized boat-rocker. We also discussed the fact that s/he suffers horribly from the transphobia, if you will, of the other gods, and also the ramifications of this myth.

Afterwards, I wandered over to where the rest of the gathering had rejoined the singing campfire group. Before I'd gone off with my own people, I'd had a discussion with the leader of the male mystery group, a large, friendly gay bear I admired. Since I was transitioning from female to male at the time, I asked if they would be interested, some time in the future, in doing a transition ritual for me—sort of showing me some of the male mysteries. When I checked back with the leader (after all this talk about being a catalyst), I discovered that their entire talk had centered on me and my request. After some arguing, they agreed to do it, but then realized that in order to create such a ritual, they would have to define those "male mysteries" more clearly and in a way that was not connected to a male upbringing or an ability to procreate. In arranging my own personal quest, I had helped them to define their own.

If you're a third gender person taking the brunt of someone's struggle with themselves, remember the reason the gods killed Agdistis—s/he had too much power! Imagine that. S/he could access parts of both male and female that others couldn't have at once. When faced with such angry and violent reactions, you might consider that they may simply be, on some level, afraid of your immense power. It might allow you to have a little more patience and compassion—while you're taking care to protect yourself, of course. You might not, at that moment, feel particularly powerful, but remembering this myth might change that.

Of course, we must not sidestep the terrible and ugly truth that there are people out there who think we need killing merely for being what we are, who so fear Agdistis' power that they must obliterate it in any way they can. "People want to see us dead close up," says Riki Ann Wilchins of *Transexual Menace*. She points out that one common feature of the murders of transgendered people is multiple stab wounds, multiple blows to the head, and other indicators of general hysterical overkill. Our very existence can make some people seem to lose their minds.

Discussion questions

Talk about what it would be like to have been born with a perfectly hermaphroditic body. What would growing up have been like? What about growing up in a permissive and non-dysfunctional society? Would you have enjoyed your body, or wanted it changed? How would sex have been different for you? Your choice of sexual partners? Your family? The social roles you might have taken on?

Talk about the many ways in which "male" and "female" physical characteristics can be combined. On your perfect theoretical hermaphroditic body, how would you have combined them? Facial and body hair or smooth skin? Breasts or a flat chest? Wide childbearing hips or narrow ones? Penis or clitoris, vulva or scrotum? Tall and muscular or slender and delicate? What would you want people to "see" when they looked at you? How would you dress and move this body? Would you have wanted to bear or sire children, or do both?

Would you still have been who you are now?

Inner world activity

Create an image of the body you've just explored with your mind—paint, draw, sculpt, collage from bits of magazines. Hang your image together with other people's images to compare the many and myriad forms of God/dess, and then take yours home for inspiration.

Outer world activity

If a child is born today in a modern hospital looking like Agdistis, s/he is mutilated just like in the myth. Intersex children are carved up in infancy and forced onto hormones in adolescence, all without their consent. This strikes at the very heart of our rights as third gender people. In the Appendices at the back of this book, you'll find resources for intersexuals and their families. You'll also find a flyer for would-be parents, with more basic information about intersex conditions and how real intersexuals would like them to be handled. Create an act of gender terrorism. Copy this flyer and distribute it to anyone you know who might have a child, or is currently pregnant. Leave piles of them in obstetrician's waiting rooms, where expectant parents can see and read them. If they throw them out, leave more. We can't change the minds of the doctors until we change the minds of the parents. So make sure as many people as possible get this information.

Even the most homophobic parents have to be made to understand that the current treatments for intersex children are often cruel and harmful, however well-intentioned. They also have to understand that such "fixing" of a child into one gender does not guarantee that the child will stay there, or be heterosexual. Intersex children who have been mutilated or pumped full of hormones in adolescence may have trouble if they later wish to change genders, or live (yes, they might, many do) as exactly what they are.

If you're the parent of an intersex child who has already been mutilated, what's done is done. You may not have had sufficient information to make an informed choice. Understand that many, many intersex children with such surgery do not have enough sensitive tissue to have adequate sexual relations, and they are very angry about this. Start a support group to give out this information, and make sure that parents realize that they can't really control the sexuality or gender expression of their child, however much they want to.

If you've just been informed that your newborn is an ... ah ... well ... er, you know—don't agree to any cosmetic sex-changing surgery! There are a very few intersex conditions that create actual health hazards that require medications, but unless your child has an actual health difficulty such as a blocked urethra or bowel, there's no need to bother with anything else. You may give them a male or female pronoun for the sake of the childhood years ("it" is such an awful pronoun), but don't channel them into traditional male or female things just because they go with that pronoun. I actually don't believe any child should be forced into that, but with intersex children it may well be wasted effort that may actually hinder their self-exploration. They may decide, sometime around puberty, that they are one gender or another, but adulthood is the time for surgery, when the genitals are adult-sized and there is a better chance of retaining sensitive nerve endings, and they can take responsibility for their own decisions. Don't pressure them. Honor their decision.

Be honest with them about what they are, and let them know that you think it's just fine and love them the way they are, regardless of what anyone else may think. Stand up for them and be prepared to do a lot of education. If you can't handle this, arrange for them to be adopted by someone who can. Harsh as it sounds, you have to love a child for what they are, not what you'd like them to be.

The Ritual: Chakra Self-Blessing

In a quiet, peaceful place, center yourself until your energy runs straight and unhindered up and down your spine. Then speak the following lines with the following gestures:

By my mind I be human
(touch third eye chakra on forehead)
By my heart I be divine
(touch heart chakra)
By my words I be a changer
(touch throat chakra)
By my will I be changed
(touch solar plexus chakra)
By my beginnings I take in
(touch navel chakra)
By my endings I let go
(touch top of head chakra)
By my living dying body I am a child of earth
and kin to all earth's children
(touch root chakra at genitals)
By the Powers above and below
(cross arms and put one hand on each shoulder)
I be strong
I be magic
I be blessed.

Interview with Drey Fisher (2001)

(Drey Fisher is an intersexual living in the Baltimore/Washington area, and is truly one of Agdistis' trickster children, being the creator of the ISNA T-shirt which reads: "Sugar and spice and puppy-dog tails: IMPROVED RECIPE"!)

How would you describe yourself and your gender?

Drey: Technically, I have congenital adrenal hyperplasia—this means a lot to doctors and other intersex people who know all these numbers and terms. I actually identify my gender in many different ways. I am an intersexed female (female because of my XX karyotype) and I identify as a transgendered stone butch. I was assigned as a girl at birth, although I had no surgery, and my parents basically assumed that I would grow up to be a "normal" girl and reared me as such. I'm transgendered because both hormonally and in personality and interaction style I'm closer to a male than a female. I have considered transitioning completely to be a man, but for now, that would just be spending a whole load of money, time and effort to become something else I'm not. Nature did a pretty good job with me, really; my mostly-male-with-a-touch-of-female brain goes quite nicely with my mostly-male-with-a-touch-of-female body.

How would you describe your spiritual path?

Drey: I had pretty much written off spirituality until about four years ago. I was raised by reform Jewish parents, and religion and spirituality were not a big part of their lives, and everything about the religions that I had been exposed to seemed condemning—who needs something else to make them feel like crap? And my friends who were raised Christian had it worse—they couldn't breathe without the threat of going to Hell. Then, with my ex-girlfriend, I discovered Wicca and Paganism. Fascinating! I attended a Beltane retreat with Candice, and it was, literally, the best weekend of my life. Here were these people, so happy, so free, and so willing to love and accept all: gay, straight, man, woman, intersexed, transgendered. During the full-moon ritual, I felt my spiritual self for the first time. In temple as a kid, I simply grew bored and restless at the few services a year I attended with my parents. But there at the retreat, I actually felt what the High Priestess was saying; I participated and felt so light and airy afterwards. I was really blown away. So I'll admit it—I'm hooked on Pagan spirituality.

How does your gender fit into your spiritual path?

Drey: Okay, here's the part I feel kinda funny saying, because traditionally-gendered people get so riled up when they hear it. I feel that my intersex was a gift, and a quest—and the ordeal is just part of it. As a child, my dad used to say that I had "super powers" and that's why I needed blood tests all the time. (Besides that, I loved superheroes as a kid!) Compared to other girls, I was physically stronger and faster (gotta love testosterone!) and my dad was so proud of that. In a way, sometimes I feel like a superior being—a "divine androgyne", if you will. I just think about how much power I have just being what I am—I singlehandedly (along with my intersex brother/sisters) break down the human notions of gender, sexuality, and nature vs. nurture. I really do feel like I was put here to do just that, and I feel a very strong duty to work hard to make it easier for other intersex children born in the future. Of course, being intersexed is harder and more complex than being traditionally gendered, but that's just because of the ignorance of those traditionally gendered people. So, here's the quest part: if, in my world, I can eliminate this ignorance, then, in turn, I make my existence, and that of all other intersex, transgender/transsexual, and gay and lesbian people, easier and more pleasant.

To represent this quest, I just got a new tattoo. It is the god/dess Baphomet—a masculine hermaphrodite, god/dess of wisdom and lust. The Christians took this image and called it evil out of fear and ignorance, much the way intersexuality is treated by mainstream society today. So when people ask me about this mysterious image on my shoulder, I'm proud to tell them just what it is and educate those curious enough to ask.

What do nontraditionally gendered people have to offer the rest of the world?

Drey: We have a whole new world to offer all sectors of spirituality. For the majority of Americans, who are Christian, we can help return them to the original teachings of Christ before ignorance and stupidity mauled it to the hate-filled institution it is today. Christ preached love and tolerance and celebration of differences. He preached that we act as upstanding citizens: no lying, stealing, killing, cheating, etc. For people who have not discovered their spirituality, or who are feeling rejected by the religion they were raised in, we can open their eyes to other religious choices.

Interview with Max Beck (2001)

(Max Beck is an intersexual, in the process of changing from a female social role to a male one. Max's struggle of healing has taken many years; some of it is chronicled in Silence = Death, *an essay by Tamara Alexander, Max's partner; it is published in* Trans Forming Families: Real Stories About Transgendered Loved Ones *by Mary Boenke, Arlene Istar Lev, and Jessica Xavier.)*

Could you describe yourself and your identity?

Max: Even as I "transition" into a "male gender role", even as I trade one set of exogenous hormones for another, even as I grow a beard at 32 and use the men's room, I am no more "male" than I was the day I was born a tiny, helpless almost-boy. Along with the medical trauma that this "almost" status engendered, 30-odd years of socialization as an almost-female have shaped me in ways that leave me decidedly Other. I refuse to relinquish such hard-won honorifics as "Ms.", "dyke", "butch", "queer", "herm", "sir". And I look forward to earning others: "husband", "daddy", "grandpa", "crone".

Tell us about your current spiritual path.

Max: Lately, I'm reading and thinking a lot about the idea of being awake. I'm practicing meditation, breathing, digging in therapy, and writing a lot, all focused on the idea of being in the here-and-now. The traumatized body doesn't want to be in the here-and-now, for obvious reasons, so while I am infinitely creative, flexible, and Aquarian, I have a hard time Being Present.

I believe I chose the body I was born into, chose my intersexuality, my parents, the place of my birth, the whole catastrophe. And I don't think it was because I felt I needed to learn about ambiguity and shades of gray; I think it was because I needed to learn to Be. So my spirit (rather perversely) chose a state that it would virtually soul-annihilating to Be in, recognized that if I could learn to Be in that state, I would have mastered that which I set out to master.

How does being nontraditionally gendered affect your spirituality?

Max: A blessing, a burden, heaven, hell, and purgatory. Being intersexed is black, white, and every imaginable shade of gray. It is the central, defining aspect of my Self and the core of my spirituality. Before I am pagan or Buddhist, before I'm a shaman or a sham, I am intersexed. There's no getting over, under around, or through that—it simply is.

That inexorable fact—that daily, felt experience of ambiguity, paradox, suffering and pride—shapes my understanding of everything, not just the Sacred. (But then, the Sacred is everything.) In learning to embrace myself, I have learned to embrace all the shades of gray, all the fuzziness, the mixing and swirling. Discarding dichotomies, the mountains are delightful, the ocean breathtaking, but I am nowhere more at home than in marshy wetlands.

So yes, I feel all of this makes me a sacred person. No more or less sacred than any other person, just sacred in my own, unique, beautiful, embarrassing, chosen way.

What do you think nontraditionally gendered people have to offer the rest of society?

Max: That's a hell of a good question. I bridle at the suggestion that I am an "enlightened being" because I have "two spirits". I put those descriptors in quotation marks because I've actually had folks tell me such things. Hogwash. I'm not some New Age fetish—I'm just intersexed. That doesn't mean I've been elevated to some higher path; in this time and this place, it means I've been subjected to a horrific series of medical and psychological traumas, just like other nontraditionally gendered people in this time and in this place.

So if there's something to offer, it's not some hokey message of "get in touch with your masculine/feminine self". Rather I feel it is a message of self-realization, identity, and acceptance: we must, each and every one of us, be allowed to discover and express who we are, and we must learn to not only value but honor and worship our diversity.

Interlude I: Hermaphrodeity Ritual

(This ritual was created by Q-Moon, our queer pagan group, for the third in a series of gender rituals. The first ritual was women's mysteries that all were invited to; the second men's mysteries that, again, all were invited to, and this was the third. The five participants wrote their own recitations. Thank you Zot, Bella, and Ilyn.)

You Will Need: a cauldron, large pot, or punch bowl; a large jug of water; a box of dry ice; several crystals; cups, one for each participant; a large conch shell, usable as a trumpet; sacred third gender objects (these ranged from carved figurines to shells to Radio Shack "gender changers"); four people willing to portray deities, and their costumes.

Four people representing the gods Lilith, Dionysus, Shiva, and Aphrodite Urania enter in procession. Lilith carries the cauldron, Dionysus the jug of water, Shiva the box of dry ice and several crystals, and Aphrodite Urania a great conch shell made into a trumpet. An altar has been prepared with many sacred objects and a variety of cups. They set the cauldron down, put in the dry ice, pour in the water, add the crystals, and recede to the edges of the circle of people as the mist billows out.

Lilith comes forward from the northeast, dressed in draperies of tan and brown and burnt orange, the sand colors of the desert. Lilith's feet are goat or donkey hooves and her legs are furred, and she wields a curved sword, which she swings about herself like a dervish. Her manner is taunting and sardonic.

Lilith: Do you know me? My name is Lilith, and they tell many horrible tales about me. The people of Babylon said I lived in a huluppu tree, between a dragon at the roots and an eagle at the height, between earth and air. Then the tree was cut down and I was banished to the desert.

And now I live there. I am the goddess of the sandstorm, the scirocco, the whirling winds of barrenness.

To the Hebrews, I was the first wife of Adam. I would not agree to be subservient to him in the garden, so I left, and at the gates I turned and called back to him, "I will be complete without you!" And so it was granted. I mated with demons and bore a thousand children, the succubus who comes to men and makes them spill their seed in their sleep, then turns into an incubus and lies with women, making them claw at the air and moan. I am the mother of wet dreams and fantasies, the goddess of lust.

I am the Queen of Sheba who came to Solomon to ask him the hard questions about his beliefs, He made me walk across a mirrored floor that he might see what truly lay under my skirts. And what does lie under them, boys and girls? Do you know? Do you want to know? I am called the hairy goddess—my hairy thighs, my hairy breasts, male lusts and female capacity for pleasure. I am the shapechanger, part female, part male, feet of a goat or ass, tail of a serpent, wings of an owl. I am the Sphinx in the desert, and I ask the hard questions. This is my gift to you.

They call me slayer of infants, baby-killer, bringer of infertility. They say I slip into the house at night and lie between the man and wife and make love to both of them, striking them barren. Do you know me now, children? I carry the fear of the breeders—that if sex is solely for pleasure, no one will have any more children, and the human race will cease. I am the voice crying in the wilderness, the interface between earth our body and the theory of our minds. Too long have we let our theories, our politics, dictate our sexuality! We must let our sexuality dictate our politics! Spirits of the northeast, come with the scirocco!

Lilith goes from person to person, sprinkling them with sand and asking them hard questions: "What do you really want? What sexual things do you want that you'd never tell anyone? What is your most politically incorrect fantasy?"

Shiva comes forward from the southeast, dressed in saffron-yellow robes. His skin is painted blue and snakes wind about his neck. His hair hangs long on one side of his head and is brought up in a bun on the other side. His manner is solemn and intense.

Shiva: Om Namah Shivayah! Gurur Devo Maheshvara, Tasmae Srii Guruve Namaha. I am Shiva, Lord of the Dance, and I bring you finality in all you do—and are. I, like Kali, come to you from a Tantric tradition, then became included in the Hindu trinity, serving the necessary if feared function of clearing the cosmos between creations. When it was noticed that I appeared to be without consort, I manifested Shakti as half of my own form.

Many of my priests marry me as priestesses, castrated and unshorn; other worshippers roll in ashes until they are covered. I loathe halfway measures; when you are trying to find the right distance between the heat of the fire and the cold beyond it, you may know me as the solution which urges, "Leap directly into the flames!" Worlds upon worlds are destroyed with each step of my dance, Tandava. Spirits of the southeast, arise as flame and smoke in our presence!

Shiva takes a skull in each hand and does the Tandava dance, kicking high in the air with alternate feet with arms outstretched. Then s/he goes around the circle, daubing the forehead of each person with ashes and saying, "You have a husband or wife in Shiva."

Dionysus comes forward from the southwest. He is dressed in a Greek women's chiton of purple, and possibly fawn or panther skins. His hair is long and flowing, and wreathed in grapevines or ivy. He carries the thyrsus, a long wand with a pine come on the end of it, and also a drinking horn or wine cup. His manner is wild and manic.

Dionysus: Dionysus I am, and you know me too well ... and fear me for it. This earth was made for my dominion from the beginning, though Titans rent me asunder; though kings may persecute my Maenads, and proscribe my holy rites and sacred dances, my worship shall never cease, for I am within all humankind and to deny me is to deny the Spirit which animates and transforms all that it contacts.

I am the Dying and Reborn, I am the Womanly One who gave himself to the Mother Goddess to transform. I am the Thyrsus carrier, the invoker of madness. I cut Agdistis' phallus from hir and paid with my own. I am beyond all reason. I purify with catharsis and bless with transcendence; I am the Lord of the Dance and all ecstatic states are my tools of destruction and transformation. Every wino and every whisky-sodden politician is Mine, as is every acid-head and every junkie. My name has been reviled by hypocrites even as they worshipped me and prudes have denied me even as they bring me new converts.

I have returned; I never left you. I am wherever you turn, no one escapes me. Surrender and be one with the Cosmos through me.

Dionysus goes from person to person around the circle, offering them either a drink from the horn, or else a tap on the head with the thyrsus.

Aphrodite Urania comes forward from the northwest. She is dressed in beautiful flowing robes or gown of aqua, and much gold jewelry. S/he has eye makeup, hennaed fingers, and a full beard. Her manner is sweet and seductive.

Aphrodite Urania: I am Aphrodite Urania, the bearded love god/dess of Cyprus. I am the avatar of the unconventional love. I symbolize love in all its many forms, between men, between women, between too young and too old, between beautiful and plain, rich and poor, love that is asexual and platonic, love that is kinky, perverted, and queer. No act of love or pleasure is ugly to me. I blossomed from the sea and the severed genitals of my sire, Uranus. I am healing and codependence, joy and obsession, silk and lace, whips and chains. I am the love that plays havoc with family ties, social rules, bigotry and preconceptions.

You think of me as beautiful, as feminine, and so I am—part of the time. But I submit to no one; all kneel before me. And one day I saw that Hermes, that youthful deity, did not kneel before me because he preferred men. So I drew out my male side, grew a beard, and had him for a time. Love passes all boundaries, love transforms all, love brings out sides you never thought you had. Our child, of course, was Hermaphroditus.

I tear down the walls of fear, of caution, of social boundary, as if they were the thinnest tissue paper. None of you can stand against me. I am the bridge between the sweet waters of the heart and the earthy depths of the body, the mud that first you crawled out of, the love that you will always turn back to, the quicksand that mires you, your tears crashing against the rocks like tides. Powers of the northwest, we step forth on your primordial shore.

Aphrodite Urania goes around the circle, marking each on the palms of their hands with henna mud, saying, "Love and be loved."

Dip into the cauldron and ladle out the now mineral-rich and carbonated water into the conch shell. Each person takes a drink from the shell to celebrate femaleness, and then turns it around and blows a blast to celebrate maleness. People may pass it back and forth, or honor only one, or do it in any combination. Then a speaker cries: "The woman knows the secret of the circle. The man knows the secret of the fast-racing line. But we, we celebrate the spiral!" All join hands and end in a spiral dance, and then dole the mineral water into cups and drink.

Chapter 2
Lilith: Pure Lust

I am come
I am come like the scirocco
I am come dancing in a dervish whirl
I am come again

You say I am barren and I say
I am truth stripped of frippery
You say I am death and I say
I am change
You say I am animal and I say
I am nature's child
You say I am lust and I say
I am lust for life

now come dance with me
on the cutting edge
of answers

The Myth

There are two tales told of Lilith, one an old Hebraic -legend, and the other told by the Babylonians that is shorter and more mysterious. It tells of Inanna, the Queen of Heaven, who eyed a great *huluppu* tree growing on the edge of the desert and coveted its wood for her new bed, or throne, or some other piece of furniture. However, there was a problem; the tree was occupied. A great blind dragon (named by some Tanin'iver) lived in its hollow, cavelike base and an eagle nested on its peak. In the middle, poised between earth and air, lived Lilith, a shapeshifting deity who often took on the forms of serpent and owl and goat and ass, Lilith the hairy goddess, the dark one.

But Inanna's wishes would not be denied, and she asked Gilgamesh, that great hero, to cut down the tree and drive out its occupants. This he did, forcing them to flee and take refuge in the desert.

The Hebrews tell a different tale, but it too is one of sadness and exile. They claim that Lilith was the first wife of Adam, made not from his flesh but from the dust, like him, so as to be his equal. However, she objected to Adam taking the superior position during sex, wishing to be his equal in this area as well, and she turned away from him in anger when he refused to compromise. The Hebrew God, Jehovah, ordered her to submit to Adam, and she fled the Garden and went to live in the wilderness. As she left, she called out to him that she would be complete without him, that she would become all that was needed to bear children herself.

Three angels pursued her, but when they found her she had undergone a strange metamorphosis. She had become as hairy as an animal and was birthing thousands of children, sending them out into the world to lie with men and women. Her children were called succubi in their female form; they would lie with men and steal their seed, and then shapeshift into a male form—incubi— and fertilize women with it. They were said to be far better lovers than any mortal, and to feed off of the souls of those they lay with. Where they swarmed, wet dreams thrived and women did not know who had sired their children. Lilith herself was said to steal into houses at night and lie with both husbands and wives, making them sterile.

Lilith makes a shadowy appearance in other myths, too; the Sphinx who asked lethal questions of passersby was said to be one of her children, or perhaps a by-form. She is associated with the Biblical Queen of Sheba who came to question King Solomon. Legend has it that he was not sure as to the reality of her body—how much of it was female and how much male, how much was animal and how much human—and he had a floor of mirrors (some say glass over a pond) installed into his throne room so that she would be forced to walk over it, and he could find out what was under her skirts. Whatever he saw, he became her lover for a brief time.

Lilith is a god/dess of lust. She is said to have an overwhelming libido; the satyrlike quality of Lilith's sexual nature has been reviled for centuries. Her association with the desert (the scirocco is said to be Lilith dancing) and her tendency to create barrenness paints a picture of her as symbolizing sex which is specifically nonprocreative, utterly unlinked to physical fertility. Lilith does bear children—the thousands of incubi/succubi "lust-children"—but these can be taken to represent sexual dreams and fantasies that "proliferate" in the minds. They are the devas of masturbation, of wet dreams.

Lilith is a shapechanger, often shown as part animal, with the legs of an ass or goat, the wings and claws of an owl or bat, and any other forms. She is occasionally shown as hermaphroditic, and is referred to frequently as "the hairy goddess". What can we learn from this particular set of physical attributes? On the one hand, we can see the ancient association of lust as an animal nature, and lusty deities as being drawn as half-animal. Hairiness, too, is an attribute of animal nature and therefore animal lust.

There is something else that we can recognize in Lilith, however. As any female-to-male transsexual can tell you, a "female" body that is hairy, infertile, and has an extremely high libido is evidencing a larger-than-normal production of androgens. Even before the introduction of artificial hormones, there were intersex conditions that created these symptoms in women, such as the primary (evident at birth) and secondary (appearing at puberty or later) versions of congenital adrenal hyperplasia.

In some populations, such as the Inuits of Alaska, intersex conditions that masculinize females appear at a higher rate than normal. The Inuits actually have many legends about such masculizined women, who are often shown as being lovers of women and taking on the male (hunter) role in the tribe. Some of them seem to have a "tall tale" dimension, such as the female hunter whose "clitoris was so large that a fox fur would not cover it"!

Androgens, when introduced to a female body, induce the following changes: The voice deepens permanently, and hair growth ensues all over the body, including facial hair. The clitoris can swell to a length of from one to two inches. Fertility is impaired, often stopping menstruation, and the libido increases.

The object of that libido can vary as well. In two studies performed by Dr. John Money on intersex children with congenital adrenal hyperplasia who were raised female, only 22% preferred only men as sexual partners and identified as heterosexual. A sizeable percent were bisexual or preferred women, and many had come out of a "tomboy" childhood, transgressing gender at an early age. And many, of course, despite what doctors say, eventually apply for sex reassignment. Does the myth of Lilith carry an ancient shadow of these hormonally intersexed women? And is it surprising, given the intervening centuries of gender fear, that a goddess based on such individuals might have been demonized as a "Queen of Hell"?

One example is the curiously ambivalent social attitude towards women who actually grow beards for whatever metabolic reason. These women, who visually embody Lilith for the masses on a daily basis, meet with shock, ridicule, and discomfort in the buses and on the grocery stores. Yet in her book *Freaks*, Leslie Fiedler writes: "...in actual history women with beards have attracted rather than repelled husbands and lovers." Bearded ladies in sideshows throughout the centuries, however else they were exploited, never lacked for suitors and spouses.

If the four archetypal elements (earth, water, fire, and air) are taken as to their folklore symbolisms (earth as physical body, water as emotions, fire as will and energy, and air as mental powers) then Lilith's place on the elemental wheel—between earth and air, dragon and eagle, dust and wind—indicates that she is a bridge between the body's desires (earth) and the intellectual, abstract mind (air). In our culture, our bodies and minds are not infrequently at war with each other. We restrict our physical desires, repress them, rationalize our way around them, and are bewildered when they bypass our minds—and occasionally our permission and judgment—and leap out in a blaze of lust and trouble. Even in politically progressive circles, there are often a great many rules around how much sex, and what sort, and with whom, is socially acceptable. Theories are introduced, and people are encouraged to conform their actual libidos in an act of sheer mental will. And, of course, it never works for long. Lilith swoops down with a scream of triumph and reclaims us, and we lie in lust or tears or both, beating off to things we're afraid of.

Lilith also carries the onus of being the one who asks the hard questions, as her association with the Sphinx and the Queen of Sheba indicates. The position of "devil's advocate" is often a thankless one, although it was sometimes a sacred role in ancient religions. As transgendered persons—who have often been forcibly separated from a traditional worldview by our condition—we often find ourselves asking questions like "But why?" and "But why not?" Many of these questions are about the intersection of the flesh and the mind. Is there a theoretically acceptable way that a body should appear, or will the body have its own way? Is a sex change a matter of the body being shaped by the power of the mind, or a prenatal hardwiring of the physical brain tormenting the more malleable mental process? Do transgendered people who alter their bodies do so for social or physical reasons—i.e. are they more attached to the role and the body it symbolizes, or the actual physical form, regardless of role? Is there a right and a wrong way to have consensual adult sex? Is there such a thing as an unacceptable desire? Can you change your desire to conform to your politics, or should your politics change to conform to your desires? Do we own our bodies, or does the state own them—and should the state be able to tell us what modifications we can make to them?

This brings us to another hard question. Lilith's darker and more horrifying side is Lilith the baby-killer, who not only brings infertility but slaughter infants in their cribs. Setting aside the issue of superstitions surrounding medieval infant mortality, Lilith is an aspect of the Dark Goddess, the Lady of Death. In a way she is the Death Crone's transgendered side, and like a good gardener who weeds out the seedlings, she has an element of implacability to her nature. In this era of overpopulation, Lilith the baby-killer, patron deity of abortion, can be seen in a different slant. "Once you've made the decision that the time is not right for bringing new life into the world," says Lilith, "do what you have to. Just do it—with respect, with compassion, but without swaying in your judgment that you have chosen rightly."

Many transgendered people will not produce genetic offspring of their own, especially as sex reassignment becomes more available and young transsexuals refuse to go through the denial period of attempting to be "normal" and denying their feelings. As a largely barren population, we are able to provide resources (if not of money, then of time and attention) to other people's children, and yet the public refuses to let us near children as a rule. This is different from other cultures, where transgendered people made good foster or stepparents. Among the Lakota Native Americans, *winkte* (male-to-female transgendered people) were often encouraged to wed widowers with children, as they would take care of the family without bringing in any new mouths to feed that might take priority. Many other Native American tribes see their transgendered members as having special talents with regard to teaching children, especially older children and teenagers. Their homes are havens for disgruntled adolescents, and they often adopt orphaned children or children from overcrowded families.

Today, if you are visibly transgendered in any way, your fitness to work with children or even be allowed near them is questioned. Although many people resurrect the tired old excuse of the fear of child molestation (a fear that is statistically unfounded) some are more honest; they simply don't want to have to explain us to their young ones. Children will, however, ask questions and attempt to satisfy their insatiable curiosity, and they will find out sooner or later.

At a recent gathering, one of the families consisted of two transgendered people living as a couple, and the young daughter of one of them. After being asked repeatedly about her parent and stepparent by the other children, the young girl finally held a "conference" of kids while sitting in a tree, explaining to them all about the situation in simple terms they could understand. When the parents of the other children found out, many were glad that it had been taken care of by someone who could do a better job of explaining, but many were upset that their children had to be exposed to this reality at all. (Remember Agdistis and the "infection" idea?)

Of course, some transgendered people do breed, and they have the strange and marvelous experience of being men who have borne and women who have sired children, of being male mothers and female fathers. They can have a unique perspective on childrearing that is less likely to produce children preprogrammed into stereotypical gender roles.

The women's movement has been instrumental in bringing the issue of abortion on demand to the forefront of political issues, with the underlying concept that women's bodies are their own and not to be mandated by the state. It's not too far a jump to see this concept applying not only to the politics of abortion, but also to those transgendered people who do want to modify their bodies, and who do not want others to judge their right to do this. Today, someone who wants to get a part of their body enlarged, reduced, pierced, tattooed, or otherwise changed, no one regulates them or tests their sanity. The only obstruction is money—unless, of course, you want to modify a body of one gender into a body of another one. Then society, with its front man the medical profession, gets into the act with reams of (often arbitrary) rules.

It's almost as if the state thinks it some kind of vested interest in keeping individuals locked into their gender roles of birth. Well, of course, it does! The third gender person turns a huge set of social assumptions on its head, rearranges it, shows that it's not such a rigid boundary after all. If such fundamental rules are questioned, what will be next? Think about that one. In a sense, society is protecting its members from having to think about Lilith's hard questions, from having to face the depredations of the Hairy Goddess on their delicate world views.

Discussion questions

What do you really want sexually that you're not asking for? Why aren't you getting it? How would you need to restructure your life in order to be able to get it?

What is your current theory of sexual morality? Has it changed over the years? Is it likely to change again? Is it based on what you want, or what you think you should want?

What gender are you when you have sex? Is it a different one than what you are when you're say, taking out the garbage? What gender are you in your sexual dreams and fantasies?

If you have children and you're transgendered, are you out to them? If not, why not? Will they really be that traumatized? If you have children and you're not transgendered, what do you tell your kids about transgendered people? Do you keep silent, allowing harmful stereotypes to be absorbed? Do you teach your children how to act courteously and effectively when confronted by someone whose gender they're not sure of? What would you do if one of your children turned out to be transgendered? What do you think that third gender people have to teach children?

How do you feel about the rules and regulations surrounding sex reassignment? Is it too much? Not enough? Do you think that people should be allowed to make any modification to their body that they like, on demand? If not, why not?

Do you own your body, or not?

Inner world activity

List all the sexual items you do that you enjoy. Now list all the ones that you do but don't enjoy, and think about why you're doing them. Now list all the ones that you'd like to get but can't, and consider the reasons why. Ask yourself: What would my life be like if I made a commitment to do only those sexual things I enjoy, and to try to get as many of those as possible? If I chose never to settle only for what I could get?

Outer world activity #1

Get information from one or more of the following organizations: Feminists for Free Expression (2525 Times Square Station, New York, NY, 10108), the National Coalition Against Censorship (275 Seventh avenue, New York, NY, 10001), or the National Campaign for Freedom of Expression (1402 Third Avenue, No. 421, Seattle WA 98101). Lilith despises censorship and will not be silenced.

Outer world activity #2

Volunteer your time with a pro-choice organization, even if you'll never have children and you think the whole situation has nothing to do with your life. If they ask you why you're there, explain the vested interest third gender people have in eventually acquiring legal control over their bodies. Draw the parallels so that they can understand, and then get down and help them.

The Ritual: Truth Or Dare

Lilith's ritual is a form of the old childhood game Truth Or Dare. No one needs to bring anything but themselves. Lilith sits in the center of the circle and chooses people. S/he should wear a skirt in desert colors and have a lot of body and/or facial hair. (We had a bearded butch woman play Lilith, in a skirt and leather "hooves".) Each person is challenged to choose to speak a hard truth or take a dare; both the truths and the dares should be sexual in nature. This is a dangerous game, and Lilith should be completely ruthless in hir questions and hir orders.

Interview with Robin Sweeney (2001)

(Robin Sweeney is a writer, editor, and gentleman butch dyke living in California.)

Describe your current gender identity and expression.

Robin: I experience my gender in the same way I understand astrology—there's the way I appear to others, the way I experience myself, and how I feel, emotionally and spiritually. I am a butch woman, with inner boy rising, and my spirit in masculinity. My gender and my spirituality are much intertwined.

The way the world experiences me, and the way I primarily walk in the world, is as a butch woman. Like most of the butches I know, I struggle to feel as comfortable in my skin as I can. I have a female body, and now I actually like it.

It took me a long while to get here. Along the way, when many of the female-bodied, masculine-spirited people I knew starting to transition and live as men, I needed to decide, for myself, if I wanted to take that path. I couldn't. I appreciate the reasons people transition to live fully in the gender of their perception, and I do my own untangling of those issues. Who am I? How do I want to live, and move in the world, and how do I want people to perceive me? Am I a woman, a man? None of the above? Just as I needed to undertake a process of discernment about a spiritual vocation, I needed to do the same process with gender. (Gender ended up actually being easier than a vocation. Go figure.)

I need to have this female body. I need to live in and treasure the body I have, now, in order for me to feel my own spiritual power. Being butch is part of that power, for me. Being a masculine woman is how I find that power.

I am a gentleman butch, and for me that is as much about being gentle as being a man. A lot of that is staying in a sort of "Dad" space. (Not necessarily Daddy as a sexual or role play thing, although that's an awful lot of fulfilling fun.) Where, traditionally, the path is from Maiden to Mother to Crone, I was a lousy Maiden, and have not grown into a Mother. I am the Mother's counterpart, the Father.

Most of the way I perceive myself is masculine—an internal counterpoint to my external way of being butch in the world. I let my inner kid out, and that kid is a boy. Where I hear my trans friends talk about knowing they were boys or girls when they were very young, and explaining that to the adults in their lives, I explained in great detail to my mother, when I was about four, that I didn't mind being a girl, but I didn't want to be treated like one. I still pretty much feel like that.

Describe your current spiritual path.

Robin: I'm a Heathen, a follower of Asatru, the Norse tradition of pre-Christian spirituality. Asatru can be conservative, with an emphasis on family and tradition. I personally put a high value on those sorts of beliefs, albeit in queerified and different ways. But that also means there's an emphasis on doing the right thing, which I value, and being truthful, which I need.

I do solitary meditations and solo ritual. I do daily devotions to the Norse gods, weekly rune readings to practice that skill, and a lot of my day to day is infused with behavior that is very spiritual for me. Most of the time, sweeping the kitchen is just a chore, but when I can really be present and in tune with my faith, it's performing housekeeping in a way that celebrates house and home and hearth and heart, that is an offering of service.

I have grown my hair as part of a spiritual commitment, as part of my service to one of the Norse goddesses. My hair is halfway down my back, much longer than I've ever had it. I've learned how to feel like myself, still feel butch. I have done that, and it is a great relief. So much of my identity has been freed by growing my hair and finding a way feel about myself that is more truthful, and much less appearance-driven.

How does your gender expression intersect with your spirituality? Would you have come to the place that you are in if you had been more traditionally gendered?

Robin: Second question, first. If I had been more traditionally gendered? I probably would have never left the Christian church. I had a very positive experience with Christianity, and with the mainstream Church. I converted as an adult, felt very welcomed, up to a point. That point was where I started feeling like a "bad gay," like I was too weird, too queer, too open about being a pervert, and celebrating being a leatherperson as part of my identity. (I have always believed that sexuality is a great and strange gift from God. Here I use God as short hand for "some force greater than ourselves that is really happy we humans are here and helped kick-start our creation.")

The feedback I got from other lesbian and gay folks was to tone it down, and not rock the boat. Stop being so weird, so, well, queer. Between that, and the heresy trials of the officiants who were ordaining gays as priests, I left the Church.

Fortunately, I was able to find Pagan folks around me who made it possible to me to shift to a spirituality that was more able to accept weirdness as a gift; that emphasized being closer to the planet, and to the Gods, and where my psychic skills and abilities were an asset, and where I could live closely to my truth. So the upheaval and upset I felt in leaving the Christian church—which had very little to do with deity, and a whole lot to do with people—was actually a gift.

My gender identity is very accepted among the people I am most connected to in the tradition. It's very accepted, and expected, that magically and energy-wise, I'm masculine/male; that I'm not a girl when I'm working with the Gods. Some of it is that I don't think, spiritually, the Gods give that much of a hoot about gender and body parts. But most of it is that one's energy, one's Spirit and emotions, can be very different from the way one's Mind or Body appear.

What's the spiritual aspect of butchness, of masculinity in a female body, to you? What is its place in spiritual community?

Robin: I think that butchness is a path to masculine energy in a form that challenges some of masculinity's shortcomings. If I'm doing sex magic, and the phallus is a blessed instrument of pleasure—and oh, honey! It is!—the fact that I get to go pick my blessed instrument, perform some sort of trade (even if it's folding paper money) and go home and strap it on changes that energy, changes that magic. It makes it more intentional, and by making masculinity intentional, I feel like it actually gives it more power. (It's that assumption challenging thing, again.)

Being butch makes me treasure the ways my masculine energy can work, magically and spiritually. I guard the circle and the door, I move the energy in a joyful and downright penetrative fashion. I take the North, the aspect of the Earth, and I get to be a big strong oak tree, with big strong roots and big strong hugs. I bring the energy of big strong and scary bears and dogs that protect and guide and challenge. (And I appreciate extensive feasting and belly scratches, too. Masculinity, for me, is not all grim and serious.)

What do you think the traditionally gendered masses out there have to learn from us?

Robin: I think us genderfreaks provide a great lesson in not judging a book by its cover. We can challenge ideas of what is "real," which I believe is the basis of a lot of personal discovery. We also clearly challenge folks to get over their preconceived notions about other people, which I think is a huge part of growing as a person.

I also think that the basic separation of the idea of biological sex, gender identity, social identity and sexual identity are all separate pieces of self. What pieces a person is born with, whether they feel masculine or feminine (and to what degree, or not), whether they want to use the men's or women's bathroom, and who they want to have sex with doesn't necessarily have much to do with each other. For some people, all those pieces fit together, like a tidy package. For many people, it doesn't, and not fitting that normative package causes a great deal of upset and suffering. Folks like us, who challenge that puzzle and celebrate our lives that are not those categories? We have a lot to teach and offer about living truthfully.

Interview with Jake Lasalle (2009)

(Jake Lasalle is a self-proclaimed "butch dyke with attitude", and a great deal of thoughtfulness about the nature of butchness.)

Describe your current identity and expression.

Jake: The name you're printing here for me is Jake; that's what everyone knows me by. The name on my driver's license is Jacqueline. As a child, my parents called me Jackie, and I was happy because I thought that was a boy's name. Then I found out that my mom was actually thinking about Jackie Kennedy when she called me that, so I changed it to Jake, at the age of six. I walked into first grade, and the teacher asked us what we wanted to be called, and I realized that I had the power to name myself for the first time. So I became Jake—not a boy, but a girl with a boy's name. That's somehow indicative of the convoluted nature of my nature, as it were. I wish that I could say that I was a butch dyke, pure and simple, but it isn't pure and it damn well isn't simple.

I'm not a transsexual and will never be one, although don't think I've never thought about it. I have. I'm not entirely free from dysphoria, but there are reasons that I will never cross that line. Why? Well, one of the defining characteristics of having "transgender" as the first word in one's gender identity, rather than as a mere refining adjective further on, is that your gender identity is not dependent on your sexual preference. My trans brothers and sisters are who they are first and foremost regardless of desire choice; who they want to be with is all over the spectrum. It doesn't change who they are.

For me, that's not true, and I think that's really the dividing line between butch and FTM. I love women. I lust after femininity. I have friends who are male or masculine, and while I love them like brothers, they just don't ring my chimes. I've loved women since I was a little kid mooning after Jenny Lee in the second grade, and I'm also very masculine ... but I'm not a man. The energetic niche I fit into is that interplay of opposites and sameness. The women I'm lovers with—and I am polyamorous and have two long-term partners, Joanna and Pearlie—are both the same sex as me and a different gender. That's where I find home, that's where the defining characteristics of my identity are. My sexual preference is of equal weight with my personal proclivities in defining that identity.

If I were to cross the line into manhood, I believe that I would lose that space. I like being a dyke. I like dyke culture and community, even when it galls me. I like the subversiveness of a female body with a masculine gender, a female body that lets its hair grow freely (including that bit of chin hair!), that proudly sports muscles, that moves like a man's body, and yet is clearly woman. I love with a deep and abiding passion the connection that I have with my female lovers, even across the huge gulf of our different gender expressions, that comes of us both being women. I believe that if I changed my body and stepped over that line, I would lose that, and that would kill me. Not to mention that I really don't want to be a heterosexual male! I've seen a lot of young butches transition and desperately identify as gay men even though they preferred (and continued to chase) women, just because they didn't want that label.

Some might say that to define one's self by one's romantic relationships is a female trait. Well, so be it.

Describe your current spiritual path.

Jake: I work with the Hunter. I wear leather for him, I do actually go hunting with a real gun and occasionally actually shoot something. (Defending hunting, meat eating, and all that to my lesbian friends is interesting, let me tell you. But it's something that the Hunter requires of me.) Sometimes he comes to me as the Wiccan Horned God, sometimes he's Herne or Cernunnos, sometimes Ull. Always a male hunting god, though. I don't pretend to understand the nature of God/Gods. I just know him when I see him.

I work with the Warrior. Sometimes he is Mars, or Ares, or Hanuman, or Cuchulain, or any number of warriors. For him, I protect my lovers, I practice martial arts, I escort my friends through bad places in town.

I work with the Corn God, the sacrificed one. Sometimes Dumuzi, sometimes Frey with his huge phallus. I own a lot of phalluses, and they are sacred to me. They are the magic wands of masculinity, the wand on my altar whose magical power is the giving of pleasure. I'm not stone, but sometimes I am stone for purposes of embodying these divine powers. The Warrior is stone because nothing touches him, he is dominant and takes what he wants. The Corn King is stone because it is all about giving, about the other person's pleasure ... and when he's not stone, it's about his surrender and sacrifice, the intensity of it slays him and then rebirths him again. I can be any of these things and more, depending on the phase of the moon, the whim of my lovers, anything.

I don't work with the Goddess, I worship her, in ritual and through the bodies of my lovers. It has always been the male gods who came to me; I'm their son who happens to have a woman's body, and they don't care. I am always aware that I am dependent on the Goddess for my connection to Love, to the Earth, and I appease her through doing right in relationship to women. My lovers embody many goddesses just as I can embody many gods. I used to hate my menstrual cycle, but I've come to terms with the fact that it is my connection to the moon, my sacrifice to the Goddess in her various forms.

How does your gender expression intersect with your spirituality? Would you have come to the place that you are in if you had been more traditionally gendered?

Jake: No, never. My spirituality is bound up with who and what I am just as my identity is bound up with my sexuality. Each is a link in the chain attached to the last link; you can't separate them. I was pretty chuffed that you wanted to put this interview in the Lilith section, because Lilith came to me once, embodied in one of my lovers, and she asked me those hard questions, which I in turn went out to ask other lesbians—about just how much desire defines our natures. I think there's a lot of rejecting the body's desires now, in order to look politically cleaner, like who we are isn't based on anything to do with grunting and oozing and yelling "Fuck yes!" in the darkness. That's undignified, so let's talk about how it's about culture or some such. Well, for me, all the grunting and oozing is part of why this is sacred for me, thank you very much. My body wants to be a masculine woman entangled with the flesh of a feminine woman. It wants it very much, and for me to deny that those bodily urges define me in a lot of ways would be a lie.

What's the spiritual aspect of butchness, of masculinity in a female body, to you? What is its place in spiritual community?

Jake: While I do not fuck men, I do go out of my way to have friendly relations with them, because I am a bridge. I'm not a "safe" piece of partial maleness that women can wrap up and keep on their side of a huge divide. I'm a bridge for both parties. I explain men to women. I explain women to men. I can talk about a menstrual cycle to a man in a way that makes him get it, and not think that it's strange or mysterious. How cool is that? Yes, some men are homophobic or overly competitive and are lousy to me, but some aren't. I have a lot in common with them, though not everything by any means. Men are torn between valuing women first, as much as their hearts want to value them, and valuing the male bonding group which pulls them away from that and puts other things first. I am a walking example of how to do the first one. Maybe that's not entirely right for them, or for all of them (gay men, for example, are a separate mystery), but when they want to do it I'm there to show them how.

I'm a bridge, a woman's man, a subversive conundrum, someone who can do the Great Rite and not get a woman pregnant with a physical baby, but I can give her a different kind of child. One who will grow in her and burst out as some kind of inspiration. That's a sacred act that only a butch can pull off. I've learned how to be a femme's muse, that's one of the butch mysteries.

What do you think the traditionally gendered masses out there have to learn from us?

Jake: How to love each other in ways that don't stifle each other. We are in the privileged position of being able to learn that so beautifully ourselves. We can teach that, too, if they'll listen. That's the tough part, getting them to listen.

Chapter 3
Shiva: The Burning Ground

It took me five years to figure out a mildly adequate definition of Tantra. It's been described as finding a briar patch in the middle of one's metaphoric spiritual path. While some people try a little and give up, others change paths, and most paths-or-prescriptions advocate some form of negotiating around the brambles, Tantra says to trust the placement and delve straight in, disentangling and inviting injury as you go directly. That which can be scratched should be scratched right off, and why delay? Another picture was a laundress on a river, stretching clothes on a frame to beat them clean on wet rocks. The rocks, river, frame, and her arms are what we know of the world. She is Parama Puru'sa, the Supreme Consciousness, and her actions are Tantra Yoga. We are the cloth, but the self we think we are is the dissolving dirt.

-Zot Lynn Szurgot

The Myth

Shiva, Mahadeva, Great Destroyer God of the Hindus, is one of a Trinity including Brahma the Creator and Vishnu the Preserver. Shiva, however, is far, far older than his "brothers", coming from the older Tantric tradition where he was the dying-and-reborn androgynous consort of the Great Mother Kali. The Destroyer's greatest weapon is the fire of his Third Eye, which can devastate whatever it looks at. When closed, it is shown as three vertical stripes on the forehead, which his followers mark on their own foreheads with ashes.

Yet Shiva is known as the Lord Who Is Half Woman, whose bilaterally hermaphroditic image, Ardhanarisvara, shows hir as one with Shakti, hir mate and other self, who is also Uma the maiden, Parvati the mother, Durga the virgin warrior, and Kali the Destroyer. To this day his priests wear the traditional hairstyle of Shiva—one side long and the other in a roll above the ear—signifying their sacred androgyny. Many of them are also required to have wives, so that they may never remove themselves completely from feminine energy and forget their middle path.

(In an interesting aside, which shows how symbols can crop up in different parts of the world and mean the same human experience, there is a famous myth about a Hopi warrior named He'e, who loved to cross-dress in secret. He was afraid of the responsibility of taking on a sacred androgyne role in the community, so he confined his cross-dressing to going to a cornfield with his apparently understanding wife and swapping clothing. Once, when all the men were off fighting a neighboring enemy tribe, he sneaked back to the village to engage in his favorite pastime. When the enemy suddenly attacked the pueblo, he rushed out of the cornfield in women's clothes, one side of his hair braided into half of the double bun Hopi maidens wear, and one side still hanging down. He fought off the enemy singlehandedly, as they saw him as a two-spirited and therefore magical being, but the onlooking villagers then forced him to take on the role he had been destined for. His *kachina*, exactly like Shiva's priests, wears its hair up on one side and down on the other. He'e also traditionally wears women's clothing and carries both a "masculine" bow and arrow and a "feminine" rattle. Shiva probably approves.)

Great Shiva spent long years on top of a mountain, learning the ascetic austerities of yoga, honing his willpower into a weapon with which to fight demons. His mind is powerful and his heart is strong, and he will aid you in your war with the devils within you. Unlike Brahma and Vishnu, who rule those with importance and position, Shiva is the ruler of people without status, such as vampires and demons, and those who reject society, the ascetics and hermits. Like Dionysus, Ariadne, Lilith and Athena, he is shown wreathed in serpents; like Dionysus also s/he is known as Lord of the Dance, wears a tiger-skin, and his hair is shown as long and tangled. The Ganges River is said to flow from its long locks. And, like so many dying-and-reborn deities, like Dionysus the wine-god, Ing the beer-god, Patecatl the *mezcal*-god, Shiva is associated with hemp-smoking as a method of achieving altered states.

The Great Work of Shiva is the Destruction of Illusion, but this is not a path of sadness but joy. As Lord of the Dance, Shiva teaches us that this Great Work is like a dance, one whose steps are difficult to learn but allow one joy in the mastering of it. Shiva's dance, *Tandava*, which is performed by kicking the feet high into the air with a skull clasped in each outstretched hand, can both destroy worlds and bring new ones into being.

Skulls and death are also the symbols of this Destroyer, consort of Kali, the Death Mother, and who shares with her the cremation ground as a sacred place. The burning ground symbolizes the heart, which must be put through the fires of purification on order to purge it of illusions.

When the gods tortured the great serpent Vasuki and it poured out so much venom that it threatened to poison the world, Shiva was the one who drank and transformed it with his own body. His throat is still burnt blue from this ordeal, but the world was saved.

Shiva had many different relationships with the goddesses that are both his lovers and other half. Parvati, the sensuous goddess of love and fertility, desired Shiva, but Shiva would not yield to Parvati's desires until she had learned also the ascetic path and earned Shiva's respect. Kali is the Destroyer of Shiva, for one well versed in the path of destruction of others' illusions must also humbly submit oneself to the hand of a greater power.

The lesson of Shiva is that of necessity. Everyone carries within them cherished illusions that support a particular comfortable and valued world view, and often these illusions have little resemblance to the outer reality. Giving up these illusions is often a painful and emotionally arduous process, one that can feel like death and the burning ground. It is no accident that the Destroyer of Illusions is often shown as an androgynous figure. Leaving aside the more familiar idea that one sees more clearly when one's masculine and feminine natures are in harmony, the transgendered person's frequent position as "professional outsider" can allow them to be the child pointing out the Emperor's lack of clothes.

Of course, we as transgendered people are no stranger to illusions. Many of us have stereotypical or idealistic ideas about what is appropriate for the gender we were not raised, and what it would be like to be a member of that gender. These illusions may be one of the reasons for the rather scary post-surgical suicide rate, when transsexuals realize that changing their genitals does not guarantee happiness in society, relationships, or other areas of interpersonal life—in other words, it only fixes one problem, not all of them. To be fair, the suicide rate of post-transition transsexuals, whether or not they get surgery, is far lower than that of closeted ones, and poor surgical results may also contribute to that number.

Directly after a full-time transition, either from one gender to another or to full-time "bi-gendered" behavior, it's almost a cliché to find the individual going through a so-called "teenage" phase. This is characterized by hypermasculinity or hyperfeminity, indulging in stereotypical behavior (often an exaggerated version of that of one's parents and role models while growing up), and a valiant attempt to ignore as mythical all the very real obstacles that transgendered people face in this society. There may also be an attempt to shun other transgendered individuals who are currently struggling with just these problems. The "teenage" phase is spiritually akin to walking straight into Shiva's cremation ground of the soul with one's eyes closed.

Pulling up the long tap root of an illusion almost always results in finding a seed of fear at the bottom, an internal demon kept in check by that delusion's defense mechanism. And, appropriately, Shiva (as well as his consort/otherself Durga) is known as Destroyer of Demons. Discipline, says Shiva's message, can give the courage needed to face those fears.

Discipline is a word with a variety of connotations. It can refer to self-control, and "a" discipline can also refer to a series of structured activities that teach and maintain self-control. Shiva's lessons do not merely suggest that one take up a traditional discipline, be it yoga, T'ai Chi, or Tantra; Shiva's underlying point is that awareness itself can be a discipline—constantly expanding it, digging out what is hidden, battling the internal demons and silencing the voices of fear that would turn your eyes away. It is, in fact, the ultimate discipline—exploring the perceptions of others and balancing them with your own feelings, visions, and intuitions, leaving no stone unturned in the search for inner truth, no matter where it may take you or how it may change your existence. Shiva's ascetic isolation implies that that although what one learns from others may be a useful source of inspiration, the truth can only be found within.

The prayer to Shiva in the rosary of the Order of the Horae is "I will strive always for mindfulness and clarity of soul." While this is useful advice for anyone, it is particularly important for a transgendered spiritual path. If one looks at the Universe and human life from Shiva's point of view, then part of the karmic task implicit in being assigned a life where one cannot take one primary cultural assumption for granted is to become someone who thoughtfully questions all of them. Having the outsider perspective in one area is a gift that makes it easier to loosen up one's thinking in other areas. We walk about all the time, taking things for granted that we ought to be mindfully considering, from where our food comes from to where our waste goes to how we treated that service person. Shiva's lesson is to develop a discipline of mindfulness, so that nothing we do is unconscious, or even semi-conscious, but is a deliberate action done out of a well-considered set of ethics and a deeply thoughtful view of the world ... and that means a serious inconvenience to us. The main reason for unquestioned behavior is convenience, and convenience is the enemy of the Mahadeva.

Think about this, perhaps, the next time that someone (transgendered or not) does any action that makes you reflexively think, "That was gender-inappropriate," in a disapproving way. Stop yourself and ask: Gender-inappropriate for whom? Why? Where did that behavioral expectation come from, and what purpose did it serve then? Is that purpose still useful today? More to the point, is it useful for that person? For you? What was the result of that person's putatively inappropriate behavior? Were they ostracized? Why? Was it due to other people's unquestioned issues? Might it not be good for people to see that behavior challenged? Or perhaps no one noticed or cared except you, and what does that imply? Did it bother you because it embarrassed you to be seen with that person, or as someone like them? How committed are you to really gaining freedom around stifling cultural gender norms? Committed enough to stay the course in the face of embarrassment? And so forth. As you can see, Shiva's road leaves no stone unturned, and is not for the easily discomfited or those who are emotionally dependent on an unquestioned life for mental survival. It is also vitally important if we are to live fully and not like automatons, easily programmed by anyone with the right codes.

An FTM friend of mine came to me with his first syringe of testosterone, wanting me to inject him in a sort of initiatory ritual. He was an animal lover, and knew that the original source of his medication was processing byproducts of the slaughterhouse industry, which he found repellent ... but he wanted that testosterone. I created sacred space for both of us, and spoke to him about snake medicine, the idea that one can take poison into one's body and transmute it into something harmless, or even helpful. What can kill, can cure; that was the old adage of the herbalists. "You'll take this into you, with all its karmic pain and debts," I told him, "and you'll be mindful of it, all the time that it's in your body. And you'll live a life where you make choices that offset the kind of thinking that created the suffering you abhor. Perhaps you'll eat only organic cruelty-free meat. Perhaps you'll support organic farming. Perhaps you'll take in other people's abandoned animals. It doesn't really matter which choices you make, so long as they are part of the solution, and they are done in honor of what flows in your veins. Then the evil will have created more good than it did evil, and you will have transmuted the poison."

The serpent wends its way through many myths of androgynous mythic figures, associated with the earth and the underworld beneath it. It was once thought to be immortal and holding the secret of regeneration, shedding its skin every year and becoming fresh and new again. It is also very difficult to sex a snake, and it has symbolized both the long, narrow phallus and the "writhing" female genitalia. Snakes can be poisonous, and the legendary "snake power" is the ability to eat poison and transmute it into something harmless with one's own body and soul. Shiva shows this ability in the legend of the serpent Vasuki, whose vomiting of venom threatened to poison the entire world.

This brings up another parable of Shiva as third gender role model. What poisons threaten to consume the world today? One might consider the "war of the sexes" and many other areas of human suffering, and ask ourselves if we as the third gender have the power to consume and transmute these poisons. Certainly those of us who "do" gender, who twist it and play with it and transform it into something quite different from what society intends, have learned something important that could be of use to women and men everywhere.

We also understand non-physical death in a direct way that most single-gendered people don't experience. "I had to give up everything I had," one FTM friend recounted to me, "in order to get everything I ever wanted." We don't get the privilege of living an unquestioned life. Even if we go through a "teenage" phase, sooner or later we fall on our faces—and find there is no way to turn back.

In *Iron John*, Robert Bly speaks of the *katabasis*, the point in a life catharsis when one hits the very bottom, and associates it with ashes, the delicate grey dust that is the only thing left after everything has been burned away. Shiva, marked in ashes, is the deity of the *katabasis* point. He is the deity of the southeast, bridging fire and air, the purifying flames and the bitter wind that blows away the ash and lifts the now feather-light soul.

Discussion questions

What things have you believed in that you no longer see as true? What changed this? What do you think you life would be like if you had been born and raised a different gender? If you did change, was it what you thought it would be? What illusions do you think people who have never had this experience are still holding on to? What would be the best way to help them understand?

What was the worst day in your life? Have you experienced a *katabasis* yet? How would you feel if you got a glimpse of your future and discovered that it was yet to come?

What's the worst poison that saturates this world? How can you eat it and transform it into something harmless?

Inner world activity #1

Create a discipline of awareness. This will have to be custom-built just for you, but one suggestion for starting is as follows: Carry a notebook. If at any time during the day you have a fleeting feeling of discomfort over a personal subject, note it down and save it before the inner censors take over and divert your train of thought. Later, set aside a time in a quiet, private place to concentrate on that thought and fight through your defenses. You might begin by drawing a magic circle around yourself and formally declaring it "censor-free". Explain to your internal guardian that you understand and respect hir job, and that anything discovered in this circle will be gently integrated into the outer world consciousness so as not to impair functioning (which is what your guardian is there for) but that s/he is not needed here. Then do your best to trace the source of your discomfort, and don't be satisfied with the easiest explanation. Useful tools to bring into the circle with you are: drawing or art equipment (in case your verbal function goes out on you), dolls or finger puppets to symbolize different voices or urges, or Tarot cards or other divinatory methods. On the way out of the circle, acknowledge the guardian again and do something to distract yourself from what you've just learned; obsessing on it will simply make your guardian clamp down harder out of fear.

Create this circle of self-awareness a few times a week, until you can get that guardian to relax a bit and let you apply short-form, more mental techniques to your everyday life. Eventually, you will want to use what you're learning about yourself to change your behavior. This is where you have to be strict, and not let yourself slide back down into laziness. Self-honesty is Shiva's ultimate goal. Treat it as sacred, and as a life-long process of discovery and maintenance.

Inner world activity #2

Find a deep poison inside you. It should be one that is so intertwined with your being that "casting it out" it out of the question. Think about the part of you that has been "twisted" or "spoiled" by this poison. What was it before that happened? What would it have grown up to be otherwise? Now think about a way to reclaim it, just as it is.

For example: You may have been raised in a gender role with varying degrees of rigidity, which may have been painful and limiting. As a transgendered person (or indeed as any gender-aware person) you are no longer required to mentally confine yourself to any role except as you consciously choose to do so, but old "programming" may still dog your footsteps—and more importantly, your reactions. What good qualities do you retain from growing up in this role? Celebrate them. What use can you put these skills to, especially around mutual understanding of others? Look at the most frightening things about each gender role. Where did they come from? Why were they originally written into the script? Is there a particular social or survival necessity behind them that, if we honor it, will allow us to dispense with the harmful structural trappings? Get together with other people— especially ones who were raised in a different role than you—and discuss your perceptions of what it's really like to live those roles.

Outer world activity

The first step of the medical control process over transgendered people is seeing a therapist. Many therapists, however, know very little about what really goes on in a transgendered person's mind, and a few are actually exploitive of this "captive population". If you are a transgendered person who is seeing a new therapist, you unfortunately may need to do more work than the average client. If your therapist knows nothing about how to treat the special needs of TG-continuum people, give them a reading list, perhaps taken out of the bibliography at the back. Therapists who have already dealt with transgendered people may actually have a sheaf of papers for you to fill out, loaded with personal questions. Some of the questions may seem insulting or inappropriate to you, but instead of the unhelpful reactions of a) passively submitting, b) lying on your questionnaire, or c) leaving to try again elsewhere, assume for the moment that your therapist really wants to be effective. Many mental health professionals turn to the Big Professional Microscopic Observers Of Us and Creators Of Unquestioned Assumptions About Us largely because they may have no other resources.

Look at the questionnaire and fill it out—but include a critical commentary about the appropriateness of each question. If you feel things have been left out, indicate them; if you feel that questions could be phrased better, do so. If you're up to it, create an alternative questionnaire for suggested use. Make sure that your answers are heartfelt, articulate, and helpful for the therapist.

For example: The questionnaire may ask how the client's parents feel about their gender change, and how the client relates to hir parents. Preface your answer by pointing out that most transgendered people are well past the age of consent, and the relationship with their parents is probably not their most important one at this time. Suggest that it might be more appropriate to start by asking them to describe their social support system—lovers, friends, family, etc., and then perhaps ask if there are important people in their life who may not handle the change well, and how they intend to manage this. Then answer the questions for yourself in this way. Another question may ask how they intend to reconcile being transgendered with the religion of their upbringing, without taking into account their current spiritual beliefs. Point out this omission, and then enumerate your current beliefs and how they developed.

The most insulting questions asked are usually ones of a sexual nature. For a long time, social scientists tried to parcel out the different sorts of transpeople by the nature of their sexual activity. For example, a male-to-female transsexual was not supposed to have any enjoyment during anal sex; if they found it pleasurable, they were reclassified as "gay drag queens" and denied hormones. The sanity of those who admitted to having sexual fetishes was called into question. It is only recently that transsexuals have been "allowed" to be gay or lesbian after transition. Suggest that more useful questions about sexual behavior might be phrased with regard to how the person sees themselves mentally during the activity and how that affects their feelings, not what is actually being done.

You may also want to discuss the nature of gender in general, and how you feel about it; if you consider yourself a third gender person, stand by that fact, while showing that you are open to realistically exploring how you intend to live honestly and healthily as one.

Discuss the amended questionnaire with your therapist; if they refuse to take your suggestions, that's when you should leave. Always go into the situation with an attitude of teamwork, not an adversarial one. A good therapist is eager to learn more and able to admit to ignorance.

The Ritual: Ashes

Lay an altar facing southeast, draped in orange. Light as many candles on it as you can get your hands on, and incense. Sit in front of it for as long as it takes to feel calm and peaceful, If you like, recite *Om Shiva Shakti, Mahadeva-Mahadevi*.

Make a list of everything you used to believe on paper, and then draw several blank lines below it to symbolize those things you still believe that may be illusions. List below that all the fears that you would be rid of. Then burn the paper until it is entirely ash, and draw three lines on your forehead. If there are ashes left, wipe them on doorways, so that whenever you go in and out you will pass under Shiva's influence.

This ritual can also be performed for the benefit of someone else who you believe is mired in illusion. However, remember the Law of Karma, which states that what you do will come back to you. Another way of describing the Law of Karma is, "as ye sow, so shall ye reap." Still another is, "For every action there is an equal and opposite reaction." If you direct this energy at someone else, it will also rebound upon you, and making it basically the same for you as if your name had been on the paper as well. Shiva believes in even-handed treatment; what is good for the Destroyed is good for the Destroyer.

Interview With Zot Lynn Szurgot (2001)

(Zot Lynn Szurgot is one of those magical people living between genders; born and raised a boy, s/he lives part of hir life as a masculine union-supporting electrician and part as a feminine spiritual being. S/he is also, among other things, a former Shivaite monk. "Cross-dresser" is far too limited a term for a being like Zot Lynn. I have kept her self-referencing pronouns as lower case by her request.)

How do you describe yourself and your current spiritual path?

Zot Lynn: First and foremost, i am a servant; hopefully serving Gaia in all her biological splendor, if i'm not lost here. Difficulty with self-description led me to ask my lover to describe me, and she says; "Zot Lynn is an explorer, patient and courteous, and she knows how to mourn. She is committed to social change to extremes; she refuses to pay federal tax for war, and refuses the economy based on new purchases and its glamour-draw. She is so bedazzled by thoughts and dreams that she finds it hard to operate in this world."

In my natal astrological chart, Venus and Mars are conjunct on either side of my dawn rising sign, marking equal influences from masculine and feminine, and from the same direction. As with many other transgendered people, the asteroid Pallas is placed notably.

My home culture (media-drenched USA) is both somnambulistic and amnesiac. Because it has forgotten my gender exists and has forgotten the sacred roles we once filled, there is no plug-and-play religion for me. It has sent me farther afield, and into syncretism. i inherit from the Catholicism of my birth its crowded pantheon, its use of ritual, pomp, theater, and props, its use of fasting and repetitive chanting as technologies of consciousness change, its sense of being watched by those in other world(s), and its attraction to gore. From Buddhism i learn to cleanly strip to bare essentials, and a developmental map with a psychological flavor. Taoism reinforces my seeing out through the eyes of animals, and links the natural world to a terran harmony the translators misleadingly called Heaven. Native Americans open the idea of spirit warrior, recognize *nadle'eh* as sacred, and introduced me to powerful experiences in sweat lodges. Animism links all Life as holy, transcends talk, and places the sacred right here, where it is! Tantra puts the total in total transformation, demands that i do so to society and self alike simultaneously, admits no concession, and heals the illusory split in immanent transcendence. Paganism offers forms that feel right, are not stolen, are usable without leaving out these other traditions, and are open to improvisation and reinterpretation, even to inclusion of us.

What do you think about the spiritual nature of being transgendered?

Zot Lynn: i should talk about the chameleonic nature of the bigendered. We are strong in the ability to identify with other people and creatures, to relate to and empathize with them. This develops our compassion, and may help us bring one point of view across to someone holding another point of view. This same trait often has us losing ourselves in our current context (as chemicals, we're highly soluble) and removes the "not-that" next to those we'd rather not be. For example, while i am highly conscience-driven, i cannot reject anyone for moral failings, since i can find some version of the same inside me; and the empathy is stronger than comparisons on a scale of evil, or i have the thought and i just don't act on the same urges. i'm just like everybody else, only more so.

These gifts didn't come on the backs of astrologers' camels while i lay around in the straw; they accreted while i flopped around, earnestly struggling with being transgendered, with having a hunger for the divine, with being the kind of animal we are. Much of what has accreted is baggage, a spiritual junk shop. Sometimes i hid from the struggle, sometimes i sought a spirit-centered life in one *sangha* or another. Repeatedly, i made impractical choices as i tried to integrate spirituality with eating, sex, making a living, being a member of my family of origin, and talking in a way that made sense to those around me. This past-tense talk makes it sound like i'm the wise crone, done with flopping and struggling and learning, and that's hilarious. It's OK; laughter's the essence.

What do you see us as having to offer to the world?

Zot Lynn: While i associate being transgendered with having a spiritual assignment, i would have come to this level of spirituality were i not transgendered, but not this form. It's not that i think the poor monogendered nontrans ones (impoverished as they may seem to us) do not have their assignments; it's more like ours are special to us, and have a gender-transcending flavor. i also don't think we have a choice. Maybe it's like this: There is disagreement in the world over whether the Divine is one or many, female or male, loving or judgmental, parental or faceless. We answer, "Yes." Maybe you have to get your own binaries burned off to approach the numinous closely.

Chapter 4
Dionysus: Madness and Ecstasy

IO Dionysus
I called upon the God
the Womanly One
child of Zeus and Semele

I drank from his cup and joined
the maenad train—in the cup I gained
escape from care
ecstasy in the vine
god's blessing under which
the sacred and profane became one
and the gods' wedding party never ended

Our clothes tore off our bodies
we were uncaring, drunken
our mad hunt coursed the hills, unstoppable
we'd tear apart our meat, raw
our feast
with raw hides we adorned
our wild woman maenad bodies
we went beyond all boundaries
desperate to escape the confines
the expectations of others
the strictures of class bigotry convention
too much to bear
drink the wine and goodbye to care

Until all our former selves
were washed and danced away
we collapsed into the arms of God
when we awakened reborn

former lives cast away, refuse
wake us back to sobriety
Twice-born, we will give thanks
we'll tell our stories again and again
of running with maenads
and the gift of the gods
we'll testify
to the gift of the Womanly One
Dionysus.

-Bella Kinney Kaldera, 1999

The Myth

Dionysus was the son of Zeus by a mortal mother, Semele. Zeus' wife Hera, in a jealous rage, had the pregnant woman killed. Zeus managed to rescue the child's beating heart and enclosed it in his own thigh, bringing it to term again in his own body. In order to hide the baby from Hera, he was fostered out and raised as a girl. Hera, however, discovered him in adolescence and drove his caretakers mad, forcing him to flee. He ended up on Mount Nysa for a time, where he learned the secrets of wine-making from the aged Silenus, a tipsy old man.

Then, somewhere along the line, he was tricked by the other deities into murdering the wild hermaphrodite Agdistis (see Chapter 1). Agdistis' blood was said to have some sort of strange curse on it, which no one spoke of openly, but hir touch induced Attis to castrate himself. What happened to Dionysus, at first, was that he went mad, and wandered all over the countryside spreading madness in his wake. Violence and inadvertent murders and suicides followed him, until finally he made his way back to the temple of Cybele. There he was initiated into her mysteries and became a *galla* (see chapter 10, The Gallae), castrated and dressing in women's clothing. In repentance of the havoc he had caused, he traveled all over the lands spreading the culture of the vine.

After that Dionysus was referred to as "the womanly one". In later times, the Romans attempted to masculinize him again by fusing him with their very male bearded fruit-tree god Bacchus, but the true Dionysus was spoken of as wearing a woman's *chiton*, having long, flowing hair, and acting feminine. In the Greek play "The Bacchae", Pentheus mocks him as being a man-woman. In order to sneak into the ritual, however, Pentheus must cross-dress and, when he is discovered as not being a "real" worshiper (i.e. not female or castrated under his skirts) he is torn to pieces.

Being one of the castrated sacred god-kings, Dionysus also wears red high-heeled "buskins" or half boots; the heels of sacred kings were never supposed to touch the ground, as they were associated with sacrificial hoofed animals, and thus they wore they "bull-footed" shoes, or heels, after their "rebirth" or castration. Yes, this is the first instance of actual high-heeled shoes.

Dionysus carried a staff with a pine cone on it, called a *thyrsus*, which represented his severed phallus. It was said to cause madness when one was touched with it. He wandered the world accompanied by a band of wild, drunken folk. Many were Maenads—wild women with wreaths of grapevines in their hair who kept up a constant roving orgy that often sucked in innocent passersby. Others were satyrs, goat-footed creatures with huge phalluses, and the castrated "womanly ones" like Dionysus.

Dionysus had two known lovers. One was a man he lived with as a "wife" for six months in repayment of a debt, and the other was Ariadne, the abandoned lover of Theseus, whom he married. Ariadne can be seen in the Cretan snake goddess, bare-breasted with snakes coiled around her arms. In later Hellenistic mythology, Ariadne is the daughter of King Minos of Crete, abandoned by her lover Theseus on the island of Naxos where she is rescued by Dionysus. In the older legends, however, Ariadne was a goddess in her own right, a goddess of the labyrinth (a metaphor for the underworld or unconscious). She had been promised to Dionysus in childhood. Theseus abandoned her, intimidated by her divine nature, and Dionysus arrived to keep the promise made when they were young. Together they created a cult of mystery and ecstasy, the initiatory rites of which can be seen in the Hall of the Mysteries in Pompeii.

The worship of Dionysus started in the Middle East and worked its way to Greece, which is why he appears in both the Greek and the Cybelline legends, but with different pieces in each. Only if one reads the story from both sets of legends can one fully understand his story. The myth of Dionysus is the tale of the shamanic god, the walker between worlds, the leaper into the void, into altered states. His worship was ecstatic; worshipers danced themselves into a frenzy, drank wine, imbibed a potion of milk and mushrooms, and had mad orgies.

It may seem strange to ordinary scholars to see an emasculated god at the head of an orgiastic cult (not to mention married), but transsexuals know better. Removal or rearrangement of the genitals does not have to mean sexlessness, nor does it impede the ability to have a relationship. Dionysus is a sacred king, a dying-and-reborn god (see Chapter 11, The Sacred Kings), yet, like many sacred kings, he traded manhood for life.

The early lives of transgendered people, before they get over their denial and deal with their issues, are often spread with chaos, violence, substance abuse, and outright insanity. Dionysus is the shamanic figure who walks the line between mysticism and insanity, between the "lesser madness" and the "greater madness". The lesser madness referred to specific times of letting go completely of reality and experiencing altered states; the greater madness was the more permanent—and more dangerous—state of continual denial (of the spiritual, of the mystical, of one's own nature). The idea, which is a good lesson for transgendered people today, is that periodically embracing ecstatic, transformative states keeps one, in the long run, sane.

Many of the transsexuals I've spoken to recounted decades of violence, drug abuse, and lack of emotional control; situations that were only solved by transitioning. There's a recurring death-and-rebirth metaphor that permeates our experiences, and that's no coincidence. Sex changes can be arguably the closest thing our culture has to a shamanic rebirth. In order to be a shaman, three things must happen. You must communicate with spirits. You must seek out mental states that allow you to experience altered perceptions that are different from those around you, in order to communicate and ally with those spirits ... and you have to die, and come back a new person.

Shamans in many cultures cross gender in order to gain power, and the transgendered in some cultures are automatically shamans. A shaman is a Walker Between Worlds, and those include the worlds of male and female as well as matter and spirit. Indeed, the crossing from the world of one gender to another seems to be treated almost like a dress rehearsal for moving from one plane of reality to another. Cross-gendered shamans are scattered from culture to culture, from Chukchi to Hopi to Zulu. The story by which an individual becomes a shaman usually involves a breakdown, a feeling of being "dismembered" and then put back together differently. A large part of the identity is usually destroyed, replaced by supernatural experience and the devotion of a spiritual "calling". Mircea Eliade, in his landmark book *Shamanism*, compares the startling resemblance of the shamanic experience across the world.

Madness is often an integral part of the shamanic death. In tribal cultures, the temporary insanity that permeates a new shaman's transition is par for the course, an expected thing. It is also considered normal that if the shaman is prevented from following the messages of their particular spirit guides, the madness will return; and therefore they ought rather to be left alone to do what they will, no matter how strange it may seem.

In Western culture, of course, temporary insanity is not seen as having any spiritual value; madness is something that must be cured and forgotten about as quickly as possible. This is in spite of the observation by many psychiatric researchers that a religious conversion experience is often indistinguishable from a psychotic break. Talk to some full-time transgender people about the year just prior to their transition, and you'll get remarkably similar stories. Loss of jobs, status, family, lovers, friends, and religion are familiar themes. All the energy of mind and spirit is focused on the impending change, often to the detriment of loved ones who need attention. The entire identity is broken down and replaced with a different one—a stigmatized one. The third gender person will always be painfully aware of just how different they are from the teeming masses.

So where is Dionysus in all this? He is just one of the classic examples of the undeniable link between gender crossing, the shamanic world, and altered states—which include both drugs and madness.

This leads us to yet another difficult knot in the thread of the third gender shaman—drug use. The Dionysian rites were characterized by mass consumption of wine and hallucinogenic mushrooms; Dionysus is first and foremost the god of wine and vine-culture. The high regard in which alcohol and hallucinogenic drugs were held in ancient times is somewhat different from our attitudes today. Still, the links must be examined and the depths plumbed, even in today's War On Drugs climate.

Other sacred kings are also associated with mind-altering substances. Shiva bears the sacred ganja or hemp, beer is sacred to the Teutonic sacrificial god Ing, and even the Aztec sacrificial god Patecatl is associated with *mezcal*. Mind-altering substances have been the shaman's tool for millennia. However, there are probably far more transgendered (and traditionally gendered) people who abuse these substances than use them respectfully for shamanic purposes. Substance abuse as self-medication has a long history among the battered lives of third gender folk in our culture.

Discussion questions

Have you ever died and been reborn? (In this life, that is; reincarnation is another subject.) If not, would you want to, or are you grateful that such a thing has never happened to you? If you think it would be a good thing, how would you want to be different afterwards? If you are in the middle of "labor" for such a rebirth, how does it feel? Do you think it only happens once in a lifetime, or can it happen periodically, several times?

What altered states have you ever been in? Include such things as substance use, singing or dancing, fever deliriums, meditations, etc. How were they similar or different? How could they have been abused? Were they? Where is the line between use and abuse of altered states? Come to a consensus on how to be responsible about using altered states. This may not be easy.

If you're transgendered, have you ever self-medicated in order to deal with the pain of your situation? Do you still do it? Are you tempted to? Discuss how this happens, and the particular needs that T.G. folk may have around keeping their lives addiction-free. (Note I said addiction-free, not substance-free. For some people the one is necessarily synonymous with the other. For others it is not. Of course, there is a lot of denial and argument around which path is right for which person, but this discussion is not meant to becomes bogged down in moral discussions of temperance, however entertaining they might be.)

Talk about how the term "shaman" has been clouded and misused in the modern Pagan/new age/spiritual community. (If you think it hasn't, discuss that.) Do your criteria for being a "shaman" differ from that of an earlier society? If so, why?

Do you cross gender in socially visible ways, such as cross-dressing or modifying your body? Does it change your perception or alter your state? If so, how? Are you permanently changed in some way by having done it?

Inner world activity #1

Are you an addictive personality? Part of addiction is the inability to place respect for the plant spirit ahead of your own need to self-medicate. You can't be spiritually responsible toward a plant substance if you are addicted to it. If you choose, for whatever reason, to consume a mind-altering substance (and if you choose to keep your body and mind clear of such things, that's fine too, see activity #3) during the period of one lunar month, perform a small ceremony to the plant spirit involved before each involvement. This includes cigarettes (the tobacco spirit), alcohol (the spirit of grape or grain, and don't forget the yeast spirits!) or anything else. As you perform this ceremony (which you can make up yourself) ask the plant spirit what it wants of you for an offering. Listen to see if anything pops into your mind. If going through this ritual every time you consume becomes annoying, ask yourself why this is so. Addiction involves taking the plant spirits for granted. Don't fall into this trap.

Inner world activity #2

Experiment with one or more of the legal, low-risk mind-altering substances on the following list. Evaluate and record your feelings and reactions. Ask yourself: Would you do it again? Could it possibly have addictive qualities? (None of these substances have the kind of physically addictive qualities that, say, a cigarette does, so what you're asking yourself about is psychological dependence.) Does the substance have any possibility of spiritual use for you? We suggest you encapsulate the experiment in a ritual where you ceremonially ask the spirits of the plant to be good to you, and then thank them afterwards.

(Raven's Note: When I originally write this part of the book many years ago, I did so because Dionysus made it clear that he wanted something positive about this to be in here. At the time, I didn't really understand how important it is to work with the spirits of the plants involved, especially when you're looking for an altered-state experience. A good relationship with the plant spirits will make the difference between a mediocre (or even a disastrous) experience, and a good one that teaches you something.

Since then, I've learned a thing or two or a hundred about plant spirits. There isn't room in this book to even touch on the huge scope of that subject here, but fortunately I've written about it in depth elsewhere. If this Inner World Activity strongly draws you, I suggest getting hold of the book Wightridden: Paths of Northern Tradition Shamanism *(Asphodel Press 2006) and reading the extensive section on dealing safely and respectfully with this sort of thing … because, believe me, respectfully is part of safely in these situations.)*

Suggested herbal substances

Galangal (*Kaempferia galanga*, mildly euphoric in small quantities, mildly hallucinogenic in large ones; make tea from the powder)

Passion Flower (*Passiflora incarnata*, we call it "passive flower" because it's such a nice relaxant)

Ephedra (*Ephedra sinensis*, Mormon tea, a caffeine-like stimulant, no longer legal to buy in the US, but it grows wild)

Damiana (*Turnera diffusa*, mildly euphoric, use in tea or tincture, or smoke it)

Valerian (*Valeriana officinalis*, use ground root in tea but don't boil it; it's supposed to smell like cow manure; much-used relaxant)

Lobelia (*Lobelia inflata*, use only a tiny pinch in herb tea or smoking blend, potent depressant)

Skullcap (*Scutellaria lateriflora*, use small amount like Lobelia, depressant)

Motherwort (*Leonurus cardiaca*, antidepressant, classically used for post-partum depression)

Bearberry (*Arctostaphylos uva-ursi*, smoke it for a mild hallucinogen; taken in tea it has no mind-altering effect and is a diuretic)

Lavender (*Lavandula officinalis*, can be smoked for a mild euphoric)

Some of the above herbs may be used in combination—combining Galangal with a small amount of ground nutmeg is useful, as is combining Valerian, Passion Flower and Skullcap for a nerve tea or tincture. Replace the Valerian with Damiana for a nerve-calming smoke. Lobelia can be used in a tea of peppermint and chamomile (which is itself a relaxant).

Inner world activity #3

If you choose, for whatever reason, not to use mind-altering substances— and for many people this may be a very useful decision—experiment with other ways of achieving altered states.

In some western magical traditions, there is reference to the "eightfold path" (not to be confused with the Buddhist eightfold path) of altered states, and ways of achieving them. They are: The path of meditation. The path of dramatic ritual. The path of sacred plants (substance use). The path of rhythm (drumming and ecstatic dance). The ascetic's path (fasting, sensory deprivation). The path of the flesh (sex magic). The ordeal path (creating an endorphin high through the use of carefully applied pain techniques or arduous exertion, from S/M to runner's high). The path of spirit-possession (lending one's body to a spirit or God).

(Raven's Note: Again, this is a section that I threw out casually in the first edition, not even knowing much about the Eightfold Path at the time. As I said in the new introduction, if I knew then what I know now ... I've since learned a great deal about all the arms of this path, including their speed bumps and difficulties. Again, if you're interested in this sort of thing, I strongly recommend the book Wightridden, *which I referenced above. It can help you decide what's for you and what's not, if anything, before you get into trouble.)*

Make a list of all the different mental states you can achieve deliberately by using these techniques. Which were possible for you, and which difficult? What uses could they have?

Inner world activity #4

If you've never cross-dressed, do it and go out to some social situation with a small group of understanding friends. Ask them to treat you as a member of the gender you are dressed as, for the moment. If you are a full-time transsexual, or if you cross-dress frequently, dress as someone you're not, a different sort of man or women than is usually comfortable for you. Take note of your feelings during this adventure. Is your perception changed? Is your state altered? Discuss, later, how you felt. A good thing to do might be for a whole group of people to experiment with this situation at once, and then discuss later how it felt.

Outer world activity #1

If you're in recovery from substance abuse and are involved with a 12-step program or other recovery programs, find out if there's a transgendered recovery group in your area. If there isn't, what would it take to start one? I know more than one transgendered person who is hiding in an AA group, afraid to come out to all the other people there. The issues of self-medicating for the pain of gender dysphoria or the social consequences of gender ambiguity need to be discussed in a safe place, without fear of misunderstanding.

Outer world activity #2

A transgendered person that I know once stopped in a subway station, seeing one of the ubiquitous homeless people wrapped in many layers and soliciting change. This person, however, seemed to be ambiguously gendered. When asked if s/he was male or female, s/he suspiciously replied, "Both!" "Me too!" replied the questioner. The question is, what to do about the percentage of bigendered homeless alcoholics? Transgendered people often have fewer resources and are in more danger than traditionally gendered people.

Talk to local shelters about the issue of homeless transgendered people. Many shelters (especially ones run by religious organizations) actually either turn them away or force them to room with persons of their birth gender, which in the case of male-to-females can be downright dangerous. They may have an assumption that all homeless transgendered people are prostitutes, or sexual perverts. Put together an education program and speak to any shelters that you can, making sure to coordinate lists of shelters, therapists, rehab programs and other resources that are transgender-friendly. Keep copies of this list on you and hand them out to any gender-ambiguous street people that you meet; it couldn't hurt.

It isn't unusual for transgendered people to become homeless after fleeing abusive lovers, but most shelters for battered women won't take them in, feeling that the genetic women would be uncomfortable. See what it would take to put together a battered people's shelter that would not discriminate by gender. In the immediate present, see if you can create a list of three-day "safe houses" for battered transpeople in transit, and make sure the shelter system has this list on hand.

Outer world activity #3

If you work in the mental health field in a capacity where you deal with mentally ill individuals, you need to know about gender identity disorders. Much of the psychiatric literature compiled about them is either out of date or researched using subjects who may not have been entirely truthful, as their right to medication may have been at stake. Talk to actual transgendered people who are not your clients in order to find out what this community needs. Some of us do slip into madness, the other side to Dionysus' realm—like the members of all communities—and you need to be cognizant of such things as hormone levels and how they react with medications.

You also need to be aware of the heinous practice of institutionalizing adolescents whose only abnormal behavior is a failure to conform to traditional gender norms, evidenced by cross-dressing or preferring activities traditionally reserved for the opposite gender. This practice still goes on today, with unscrupulous mental health facility administrators claiming to be able to cure gender-crossing behavior in adolescents with aversion therapy or drugs. In actuality, real cases of gender identity disorder are not "curable"; the transgendered community is frustratingly (in the minds of doctors) resistant to such things. Be aware that this happens and do what you can to help.

The Ritual: Bacchanalia

This ritual is a celebration of altered states, and as such must be handled carefully. Choose as your participants people who understand the sacred nature of altered states, and who are not just looking for an excuse to get plastered. People in recovery from drug or alcohol abuse need to be questioned closely; they can choose other, non-substance methods of achieving an altered state, or they can serve as Initiators.

There are many ways to walk between the worlds. Alcohol and drugs are, of course, one way; pain infliction to the point of endorphins is another, and ecstatic dancing is still another. Sexual arousal can be an altered state as well. Consider carefully which you prefer; if you really must ban all mind-altering substances you might prefer to concentrate on wild dancing, although this can be difficult for people with disabilities. If you're really worried about being able to create a Bacchanalia atmosphere and still keep everyone safe, don't do this ritual. Our choice was to choose our Maenads and Satyrs carefully, request that no one bring illicit substances, and allow everyone to choose their method. This ranged from dancing, swaying to drumbeats while staring at the campfire, our good Greek wine, to an herbal "flying ointment" that had been carefully tested and was not consumed internally.

You will need: A safe, private outdoor space in which to cavort. Lots of wine goblets. Good Greek wine in a vessel. A feast (see below for possible ideas). A campfire, if possible. A goat-shaped piñata of fabric or paper, filled with candy or other treats. Drummers, or maybe a boom box with recorded music. Maenads, satyrs, initiators, and two people designated to play Dionysus and Ariadne.

We made an ancient Greek feast of grapes, dates, figs, cooked barley and lentils with a leg of goat meat, salad greens with olive oil and barley-flour-and-honey cakes topped with almonds. At least one item of food has to be large and easily torn apart; we used the leg of goat, since no one was a vegetarian. An animal-shaped piece of bread would work fine. Scattered among the food were small "mushrooms", made of cupcake and painted red with white dots and stems, symbolizing Dionysus' sacred *Amanita*. We decorated the area with ribbons of purple and green, and grapevines. This ritual is best performed in the late summer, during the time of year when there are actual grapes and grapevines to be had.

With exception of Dionysus and Ariadne, all participants divide into three groups—Maenads, satyrs, and Initiators. Maenads are women (or not) wearing torn robes/skirts/scarves/togas and grapevines in their hair; satyrs have phalluses (can be flesh or not, most of our Satyrs just put strap-ons over their clothing or bare skin regardless of their own genitalia) and very little clothing. We managed to get hold of a few fawn skins for them to wear, which is traditional for both Satyrs and Maenads. Initiators wear long robes (or, if it's hot, belted tunics) and do not get into altered states. Only a few Initiators should be needed, but they and Ariadne form the "ground crew" for the rest of the Bacchanalia. We suggest that they be chosen for their steady, cool-headed natures and ability to cope with irrational people. Their job is to watch the borders for intruders, watch for fire safety around the bonfire, make sure no one hurts themselves or others, and see that people who accidentally hurt themselves are given first aid.

Dionysus wears a purple woman's *chiton* and a leopard skin, red high heels, a headdress with small bull's horns (can be simulated with paper mache) or a grapevine wreath, and carries a *thyrsus* (the stick with the pine cone glued to the end, streaming ribbons). Ariadne can wear full Cretan gear (laced bodice, bare breasts, and ruffled skirt) or Greek robes; she carries a serpent (can be fake) and a peeled flexible branch for a switch.

All gather in the woods or fields. A bonfire is built, and then the Initiators form arches by holding ribbons overhead, and everyone files through and forms a circle. Dionysus and Ariadne stand in the center, and when everyone is inside they walk around the circle from person to person. Dionysus holds the vessel of wine and Ariadne the switch. Dionysus asks everyone, "Drink or feel the lash?" If they agree to drink, they get a sip of wine; if not, Ariadne hits them (gently and playfully or hard; this is up to her judgment about the individual people and what they would or would not appreciate). The lash is not a punishment for not drinking; it symbolizes the sacred flogging as shown in the Villa of the Mysteries in Pompeii.

As each person drinks or is switched, they run back through the arches and to the campfire, where they dance. After the last Satyr or Maenad has run,

Dionysus follows them, and they run on a wild procession around the area, through woods and fields. This is less of a ceremony and more like a steeplechase. All end up back around the fire, where Dionysus kneels on the ground, holding the pinata goat. The revelers all seize the goat and tear it to pieces, seizing and eating the scattered treats, and Dionysus slips out from underneath and cries, "Let the madness begin!" Music is played and the Bacchanalia ensues.

Let everyone take the pace as they want it. This is not a structured ritual, since you can't structure such a thing. Let it go. It will peter out of its own accord eventually; this may take half an hour or half the night. If people dance themselves into exhaustion, let it happen. Anyone who needs food should go to the feast table. We provided no utensils and made everything edible with fingers (and provided no napkins either; that's what the Maenads' ripped robes were for!) so people could go back and forth from bonfire to table a dozen times. Anyone who presents themselves to Ariadne can get a switching or flogging, although she does not offer it except on request. The Initiators should be monitoring at all times, and if anyone seems to be having a problem, they should intervene.

At the end, make everyone lie face down on the ground. Here Ariadne paces around the circle, and everything goes quiet. "Take the memory with you," she says, "that you may know the greater madness from the lesser, and not be drawn into it."

Interview with Bella Kinney Kaldera (2001)

(Bella is a priest/ess of Dionysus, a galla *of Cybele, a counselor, artist, sociologist, and professional recycler. Oh yes, and a male-to-female transsexual on top of all that.)*

Could you describe yourself and your gender?

Bella: Firstly, I am both, mostly. I struggled for years with the question of identity and gender, peeling away the layers of who I was supposed to be (according to other individuals with their own agendas) imposed in my formative years so that I could finally begin to grow into a genuine person. In a manner of speaking, I had to eliminate all those people I wasn't before I could start to express who I was and be true to my own heart. I feel that I am both genders and always have been thus, but the trappings and socialization of male roles were imposed upon me against my will. As a result I drove my feminine animus deep into my subconscious mind, existing in a state of denial for many years. This state of mind was, however, unstable, and my feminine will eventually asserted herself after I had exhausted myself emotionally from maintaining that denial.

This reconnection didn't come overnight, but started slowly with my introduction to earth-centered spirituality, and culminated in a vision of Mother Cybele in 1987 on the Winter Solstice. She instructed me to "cease to desire, simply be", which gave me the empowerment to transition the next day to living full-time as a woman. I gradually came to the understanding that gender identity is a continuum, so my own presentation also need not be static; that, blessed with the attributes of both genders, I was wiser to accentuate the positive, whether that expression was masculine or feminine.

If my gender is trans, then my sexuality is bi. I find delight in my fellow humans, and I have enjoyed lovers of several genders, as many as I have had years on the planet. Steel requires forging in order to be useful, and my steel has been through such fires and endured such fierce pounding that I can claim to be of excellent temper.

And where are you now?

Bella: My current spiritual path is poly/pantheistic and eclectic; I do what works for me and I'm not concerned with dogma or lineage. My spiritual toolbox is stocked from years of comparative religion studies, and includes elements of Wicca, Buddhism, Native American spirituality, classical Greco-Romano-Nordic-Celtic Paganism and a fondness for Zen and Shinto. I have spent hours meditating in dojos and in forest glades; I have administered blessed sacraments from half a dozen creeds. As I am a citizen of the Earth, I listen for Her wisdom in all placed I might visit. Like Dionysus, I am an instrument of Her divine will, and I recognize that I have been given gifts, and as such I have a responsibility to act for the Goddess and to be an agent and a vessel for Her power and influence. She is changing the world and Her tools are people like myself.

How does your gender affect your path?

Bella: For us transgendered folk, the very question of Being is continually brought up. We must assert ourselves often against the most terrible opposition in order to simply claim our identities. As the God of the Old Testament says, "I am," we must also establish ourselves similarly or we will be disbelieved out of existence by those whose mores depend on dualistic thinking. Do I consider transpeople sacred people? Of course! The deity is indwelling within us all. Those of us who experience any form of rebirth have the option of redrawing the sum of their identities to include awareness of that spark of divine essence.

I am a semi-determinist in my conceptions regarding the whole free will issue. By this I mean that I feel that an individual has a particular set of challenges that he or she faces during each mortal incarnation. I fully accept the notion of reincarnation and I've recovered memories of several "past lives". I don't support the idea of "punishment" where an individual is reborn to some inferior station due to some transgression in a previous era, but I agree with the *Bardo Thodol* that individuals have the opportunity to choose rebirth according to their self-image and presence of mind at the very moment of death. I consider mortality and physical incarnation a privilege and a covenant with the divine indwelling, especially as I have "rebooted" my own transcendent life as a result of a personal vision. I think that this is the first lifetime that I have had the opportunity to experience life in both genders, and I'm grateful.

What do you think we have to offer the rest of the world?

Bella: Anyone who rebirths themselves or experiences a life-changing spiritual quest is forever impelled to tell again and again the story of their personal renewal. I know that I have been a positive influence on the transitions of several other transgendered individuals, and I am also aware that for many non-gender-challenged folks I have encountered, I was the first openly transgendered person they had met. I have a duty to educate others, since I'm a pioneer into forbidden territory and a survivor to boot, when so many of my sisters haven't made it. This sense of loss regarding those of us who have died from transphobic assassination makes me more strident and militant in my position on the front lines of the gender war. We represent mediation in the competition between the reproductive genders, and we can use our empathy to help to heal their wounds.

Chapter 5
Aphrodite Urania: Crossing the Boundaries

It's not enough to know
that you will walk with me
down the street and not
flinch from the stares.

It's not enough to know
that you do not feel shame
when they look at us and
(it's the playground all over again)
snicker behind their hands
or even not behind their hands at all.

It's not enough to know
that you don't look at my
hodgepodge body
with revulsion
missing what's not there
trying not to see what is
(like I often do)

It's not enough to know
you would defend me
to the death,
me and my right to exist
my right to a full cup of joy
instead of what tiny scraps I can glean

I need to be certain that you
see me and see magic
love me and love all of me
know me and know your future

to the very end
not in spite of
but because of
who I am.

      In ancient times, transgendered priestesses publicly served numerous Goddesses in Sumer, Egypt, Canaan, Greece, and elsewhere. From the earliest known writings of the western world, we learn that transgendered people are the blessed children of the goddess Inanna. she turns woman into man and man into woman. Throughout the ages we served in the temples and retinues of the Goddesses of Love, Fertility, Harvest, Hunt, War, Queens of Heaven and the Dark Night. In the service of all these Goddesses we gave our bodies as "qedeshim" (the transgendered version of the "qadishtu"), hierodules, sacred prostitutes. We served as a conduit through whom people could pay honor to the Goddess. We danced Her rites. We spread Her love and blessings.....The modern role of temple priestess involves a lot of educational work; people come seeking information on safer sex practices and for guidance in restoring a sacred element to the sexuality in their own relationships. This is the work of a sacred prostitute. This is a sacred role for transgendered people since the dawn of history. I have come home to my Goddess. I am proud to be a daughter of Aphrodite.

—Maureen, transgendered priestess of Aphrodite

The Myth

Aphrodite, the Greek goddess of love and beauty, might seem to be the most feminine of all the gods, without a single iota of gender-crossing behavior, but the truth is quite different. Stunningly beautiful, born from the severed genitals of Uranus flung into the ocean and the foam that rose from them, Aphrodite was unconquerable in love. She took it upon herself to sleep with all the deities, except for those sworn to virginity such as Artemis, Athena, and Hestia. Then, however, she ran into a problem. Hermes, the lithe, youthful messenger god, was not (at least at the moment) interested in women. So in order to interest him, Aphrodite grew a beard and partially transformed herself into a man. This apparently caught his eye, and the child they bore was called Hermaphroditus.

In the earlier myths, Hermaphroditus is born intersex. In later ones, he is born male and later "fuses" with a wandering nymph who wishes never to leave him. At any rate, this child of Bearded Aphrodite and Hermes, who in the alchemical tradition is a divine androgyne himself, gave hir name to an entire people.

The Bearded Aphrodite was worshipped on Cyprus, and caused later scholars of Greek mythology a great deal of confusion. How could this most feminine of creatures possibly have a male side? (It's a question that has been aimed at many a male-to-female transgendered person who has just come out as to their past.) Aphrodite Urania, as she is referred to, is by her title the daughter of Uranus, old sky-god of the Titans. He was murdered by his son Cronus, who cut off his genitals and threw them into the ocean. They disintegrated to foam, from which Aphrodite sprung fully formed and adult, ready to love.

This myth may have a particularly special meaning for male-to-female transsexuals, who may be able to relate to an adult female who arises spontaneously from severed male genitals. Aphrodite has many titles: Aphrodite Genetrix (dedicated to procreative sex), Aphrodite Porne (dedicated to erotic sex), Aphrodite Parakouptosa (dedicated to those who have killed themselves or others for love), and many others. Yet it is this title, Aphrodite the daughter of her father's severed organs, who is the guardian of "unacceptable" sex—homosexual sex, sex between different ages, classes and races—and shows a bearded face.

Aphrodite's priestesses were sacred prostitutes, and like the sacred prostitutes everywhere in ancient times, they numbered women, men and transgendered male-to-females among them. Aphrodite, of course, was invoked as the patron of sex workers everywhere. Sacred prostitute/priestesses were doing far more than merely turning tricks to support their temple. They were respected as doing a sacred duty and were considered to be embodying the goddess who bestows her favors upon her worshippers. The tradition of sacred priest/ess prostitutes seems to have come to Greece from Mesopotamia, where the *qadishtu* and *qadishem*, genetic female and transgendered priestesses regularly included sacred sex work in the temples of Inanna/Ishtar/Ashtoreth/Athirat/Tanith, the Great Mother of the successive waves of conquerors of Mesopotamia. Some *qadishem* were castrated; all were written as being feminine. Both types of temple prostitutes wore a multicolored costume reminiscent of the Biblical Joseph's many-colored coat; some retellings of that tale suggest that Joseph's father may have been encouraging him to become a prostitute, and he was "killed" by his brothers in order to preserve the family's honor.

Aphrodite shows up in the archetype of the *hetaera* (literally meaning "companion"), who was the high-class courtesan of ancient Greece, and Renaissance Italy. The *hetaerae* were beautiful, intelligent, well-educated women who were the intellectual as well as the sexual companions of rich, powerful men. One of them, Aspasia, was the companion of Pericles, the most influential man in Athens, and he sought her advice on much of what he did. Wives, at this time in ancient Greece, had more monetary security but far less freedom. They were kept cloistered and had few rights, and almost no political influence. This dichotomy between women who breed and provide security and women who are sex/companionship objects still pervades society today. Transgendered MTFs, not being able to provide children to a man, often end up in the latter category as exotic sex objects. Since they often have difficulty getting hired at other jobs—openly transgendered people are one of the most discriminated-against minorities on earth—many unskilled MTFs end up as sex workers as a last resort. They are then prey to violence, drug abuse, and many of the other banes of the sex industry. Some police departments may also develop prejudices against all transgendered people, associating them with sex workers since that's what they see the most.

Aphrodite Urania is more than just sex for pay, however; she is love, like all the other aspects of Aphrodite, but more specifically she is "unacceptable" love. She has always been the particular patron of homosexual love—which induced 19th century German writers to refer to gender-transgressing homosexuals as *Urnings*—but she is also the patron of love between those of different ages, classes, races, and outlooks. Whenever you fall in love with someone who is not what you expected, who makes you challenge your assumptions of who and what you are, you have entered Aphrodite Urania's realm.

Transgendered people, of course, frequently run into this problem from the other side. When someone who is heavily vested in their sexual and gender identity becomes attracted to one of us, they often find themselves falling into a mire of self-questioning. What would a relationship with this person make me? Gay? Straight? Bisexual? Male or female? A pervert? Their final reaction, unfortunately, can sometimes be hostile toward us as they struggle with their issues. In fact, repressed attraction can fuel the most deadly violence toward a third gender person.

Often we ourselves are confused about our relationships. If we are denying our transgendered nature, we may be attracted to people who embody or at least resemble who we secretly want to be, a kind of unconscious narcissism. Let them live it for us, we say to our secret selves. It may be important to us that they remain in this "role", and we may become upset if they change in any way, or we may find ourselves and realize that we are no longer a fit mate for them.

We may also worry about what sort of relationship will best validate the gender we wish to be seen as, and seek partners on that basis. The original wave of mental health helpers who began "certifying" transgendered people as "sane enough for surgery" believed very strongly that transsexuals should be heterosexual after transition, and it took the courageous efforts of many queer transfolk (such as the late Lou Sullivan) to change their minds. However, the idea that "normality" in gender means heterosexuality is still ingrained in the minds of many transfolk, who often become disoriented when Aphrodite Urania casts her mixed blessings on their lives. Others cling to the idea of being gay after transition, for reasons ranging from not wishing to be cast out of (or desperately wishing to join) the lesbian community, having had difficulties dating straight men, or preferring to chew off an arm rather than be a straight man. (Just some of the many reasons I've heard; most, of course, simply love members of their preferred gender.) Aphrodite Urania has tricks in store for all these folks. Never assume that you know just who you'll love next, she says. Never assume anything.

The one biggest taboo for us, it seems, is our ability to date each other within our community. Although the number of transgendered people who are in relationship with—or are brave enough to claim they prefer—other transgendered people is rising (including so-called "reverse couples" or "cross couples", consisting of a MTF and a FTM) we are still the only minority who is openly discouraged from dating our own kind. The idea makes one wonder about standards of "normalcy" and what relationships are perceived as "validating" or otherwise.

Elementally speaking, Aphrodite Urania is the god/dess of the northwest, poised between the watery sea of emotion and the earthy body. Although water and earth together make most people think of mud, they are the first two things necessary for fertility. She is swamp, clay, sandy shore, henna that dyes skin and hair, heart and body at one, love and sex no longer split apart. Aphrodite Urania sends us a message: that no matter how bad things get for us, no matter how difficult and confusing it can be to navigate the relationship swamp with a double set of motors (often pulling in different directions), our destiny as crossers of boundaries and builders of bridges is an inevitable task— and, eventually, after the work is done, an inevitable joy.

Discussion questions

What would your sexual preference be if you were with a traditionally masculine man? A traditionally feminine woman? A feminine man? A masculine woman? A man with a vagina? A woman with a penis? A hermaphrodite?

What sort of person would it be most difficult for you to be in love with? Are your reasons social or personal? Would you try it anyway? What ideas or parts of your identity would you be willing to give up in order to be lovers with someone? What wouldn't you be willing to give up? What have you learned about love and gender from your past lovers?

Inner world activity

Create, in your own mind, the imaginary lover who it would be most socially difficult for you to be with. Create a picture of them and name them. Talk to them. Ask them for advice on things. Fantasize and make love to them.

Outer world activity #1

Contribute to COYOTE (Call Off Your Old Tired Ethics, 1626 N. Wilcox Ave. #580, Hollywood, CA 90028 http://www.coyotela.org), the primary lobby for legalizing prostitution and making the lives of sex workers everywhere. Write letters to newspapers, senators, congresspeople, etc. urging decriminalization of prostitution. No one should have to go to jail for any kind of consenting-adult sexual arrangement. Another good organization approved of by Aphrodite is the International Sex Worker Foundation for Art, Culture, and Education at http://www.iswface.org.

Outer world activity #2

A high percentage of transgendered femmes are sex workers, largely because it's so hard to get hired to do anything else when you're visibly transgendered. Many of them suffer from drug addictions, or are working the streets in order to buy their hormones. Take a transgendered working girl to lunch. (Don't put any other demands on her.) Try to start a support group that is for street queens and eventually works towards getting them off the streets. Talk to the local free health clinics and ask them what services they can offer to various types of transgendered people, including but not limited to sex workers. If they need educating and suggestions, give it to them. If you're transgendered and have the aptitude, volunteer as a part-time counselor.

Outer world activity #3

Many police officers automatically assume that all transgendered people are sex workers, and that the ones who are sex workers are doing it out of sexual perversion. Get a group of transgendered people together (don't do it alone; this is one exercise I'd suggest requires strength in numbers) and get your local police department to let you speak to them in a transgender education seminar.

They need to be taught about how to handle transgendered people, from sex workers to the person stopped on the highway for a broken taillight whose license gender does not match their looks. Explain, for example, that transfolk on hormones who have been arrested or must stay overnight in jail need their confiscated medication or their health may suffer. Explain the inevitable nature of transsexuality and that many are unhirable; the streets are the only option they may be able to come up with. If there's a group like the one in activity #2, ask the policemen to carry its literature and pass it out to likely candidates. If there's an accepting clinic that can help them be at less risk for venereal diseases, make sure that the literature lists it, and any transgender-friendly addiction-recovery groups. Until prostitution is legal, we must try in small ways to make our modern-day *qadishem* a little safer

The Ritual: Crossing Boundaries

This ritual is meant to celebrate love in its many unexpected forms. Although no one is actually going to be making love in this ritual (although I suppose you could do it that way), be sure not to invite anyone who is so terribly invested in their sexual identities that they have no room for playfulness.

You will need only a pile of costume pieces. These can be hats, jewelry, scarves, ties, skirts or pants (make things loose with drawstrings so as to fit a number of people), wreaths, strap-on genitalia, etc. Encourage people to bring more of such things; the only requirement is that they be easy-on-and-off, and fit a variety of bodies. You will also need a number of blindfolds, and a source of music to dance to.

When everyone arrives, Aphrodite Urania stands in the middle of the room, dressed in long flowing robes of blue-green, aqua, sea colors. She has a beard (which doesn't have to be real) and eye makeup, and should wear pearls if possible. She greets everyone and can either repeat her speech in the Hermaphrodeity Ritual, or make something else up of her own.

Everyone goes through the costumes and puts on various paraphernalia. The idea is not to create a whole outfit, but to have several symbolic items that appeal to you. Then Aphrodite Urania goes around the circle and blindfolds each person, saying, "Love is blind!"

The participants mill around the room, blindfolded, and Aphrodite Urania grabs them in random pairs and slaps their hands together. Anyone she joins must hold hands until everyone is joined in random pairs, and then everyone can remove the blindfolds.

"Love crosses all boundaries," she says. "You never know whose eyes you will be looking into next, nor who you will become when you are with them." Then she instructs each pair to switch costume paraphernalia, helping each other to don the other person's things. (Nobody gets to complain or switch partners!) Then the music is started.

Each random pair gets a couple of minutes to dance with each other in the center of the circle, taking turns. Although no one necessarily has to touch anyone else, the dance should be done as flirtatiously as possible.

When everyone has had their turn, the circle should be opened with a group hug.

Interview with Arthur Scott and Dawn Koro (2001)

(Arthur Scott and Dawn Koro are what is colloquially known as a "cross couple" or "reverse couple"; a female-to-male transsexual involved with a male-to-female transsexual. Such pairings were rare until recently, as therapists felt that dating a "normal" person was a surer sign of "success" in one's new role, but Dawn and Arthur aren't the sort to follow anyone's lead but their own.)

How do you define yourselves and your genders?

Dawn: Me and my many genders? I'm a chick with a dick. Oh, I suppose you want a serious answer. OK, I was raised as a man, I live as a woman, my documentation is as a woman. I present myself as an ordinary woman in my work situation. Everywhere else I tell people I'm a transsexual person, and my friends know about my surgery, which is an orchiectomy (removal of the testes).

Arthur: Let's see: I grew up identifying as a boy, but puberty hit and things started sprouting, and everybody told me different. I proceeded to ignore them, and to lead as masculine a life as I could. When I hit high school I used to pray to have a sex change, because I really knew that this was wrong. My female body felt incorrect; it wasn't in line with how I felt inside or how I wanted people to see me, and I finally did change over. I've been on testosterone for three years, and I've had chest surgery.

My identity at the same time is still kind of fluid; I'll look in the mirror and still not quite know if I'm looking like a really butch woman or a transman or just a straight-out man. I can see it's my face, but I don't always know what gender to put on it ... and I don't care, really. Dawn gets a lot more exercise than I do when I get ma'amed, which happens occasionally since I probably wear far too much jewelry for an ordinary guy, and I refuse to give it up. But I could care less what they call me.

Dawn: I did my transition in '91, I've lived as a woman for seven years now, and I'm feeling increasingly comfortable with a sense of androgyny. Sometimes when Arthur and I are making love, I fantasize about being a boy, or a girl, or something else.

Which brings us to the next question: How do you characterize your relationship?

Dawn: Queer couple, straight privilege! I think of him as a transguy—in my mind, a step above ordinary guys. For me, that's the absolute ideal, the best of both worlds.

Arthur: It's always been a real turn-on for me to not be quite able to tell someone's exact gender, and have that not matter.

Dawn: I find that increasingly true for me, too, to be attracted to androgynous people. So we're really a very good match. I'd only ever known two other cross couples before; I assumed that all transguys, because they pass so well, would obviously only want genetic men or women, and why would they settle for me?

Arthur: Hey, there's absolutely nothing about settling here! No way. Absolutely the best of both worlds. I've had discussion about being a transperson in relationship with other people, and the general consensus seems to be that being somebody's best of both worlds only works if it's mutual. You can't be in a relationship where you are the fantasy item and they are not, even if you love them with all your heart.

Tell me where you both are in terms of your spirituality, and where it fits in with your gender issues.

Dawn: I guess I'd like to turn that around. My gender issues can really only be understood in spiritual terms. When I first came back from four days at Fantasia Fair, four days of being a woman continuously, I had this profound sense that the only word that could be used to describe my experience was spiritual. It was making contact with and honoring and nurturing the deepest, most mysterious part of myself; the part that would always be there but could never be understood in rational terms, and would never go away, would just be there like the air I breathe. And I'd better learn darn well to pay attention to this part of myself, and help to foster its growth. And if that's not spiritual, I don't know what is!

Arthur: I was raised Jewish and went to a very strict Jewish high school. I came out of that and went straight from Lubavitch Judaism to exploration. I was a deacon in the MCC church for a while. I've explored several faiths, and for the last 13 years I've been practicing Buddhism.

In March of '98 I started moving forward with my transition, but there was this little voice in the back of my head saying "Wait a minute!" When I was a child, I'd chosen to believe in reincarnation, because I remembered very clearly choosing where to be born, and I remember myself in that prebirth moment as male. And one of the questions I'd been tormenting myself with was, "What horrible thing did I do to women that caused me to choose this life of suffering, and what karmic stuff am I going to call down on myself by mutilating yet another female body!"

Then I was sitting with friends and chanting one of the Buddhist prayers that talks about eradicating or expiating one's negative karma from past lives, and fulfilling one's wishes in this life, and in the future. I was sitting there chanting, and I suddenly realized, "Hey! I'm free! I'm done! I've expiated my karma and I can go be the guy I should have been!" And I don't know what the lesson was that I was supposed to have learned from spending 36 years in a female body, but whatever it was, I'm sure I've learned it!

Dawn: I sought a spiritual path for a long time. I was raised Christian Scientist, but as soon as I went to college I let go of that and became agnostic. I hung out with the Unitarians, and then I got married to a woman who was very much into mystic spirituality, past life regression and all that, and I was the "ground" for her while she floated off and did her thing; I was the dutiful spouse who followed her path, but I couldn't find where that plugged into me. When I met Arthur, I again tried to be the dutiful spouse and tried to plug into his variety of Buddhism, but found that it just didn't work for me either.

To me, spirituality can't be abstract. It's got to be grounded in the physical world, and in relationships with other people, and be something I can do on a daily basis that concerns my whole self, and especially my physical self, not just my head. I guess I think of religion these days like I think of theater. You don't ask if theater is true or not; you ask, does it move you? Is it something that leaves you feeling more profoundly touched than when you came in? Does it work?

It's also become more and more clear to me that sexuality is sacred. There's nothing that establishes a higher energy or a connection between people that is so close to the infinite, and the sexuality I've experienced with Arthur is so much richer than anything I've experienced before; it's how we celebrate who we are.

So what do you, as transgendered people in relationship, exploring all these things that many people don't get to explore, think that you have to teach or to say to everybody else?

Dawn: That your sexuality, however you experience it, is only a very, very small portion of what is potentially there. As the assumptions drop one by one in terms of roles and such, the possibilities expand geometrically.

Arthur: That exploration is OK, and it's OK to play with a role in order to discover the power it has for you. And it's OK to come out of that role if you decide that this power is not for you. As Gary Trudeau says, "A complex man is an army on the move." The more complex you become, the more whole you are, as you better understand more and different parts of yourself.

Dawn: That physical intimacy doesn't necessarily mean heterosexual intercourse leading to orgasm. We, as transgendered people in relationship, know that there's lots of different ways of being close and sexual with each other, and that you're limited only by your imagination. Even the physical restraints of your body are just another challenge for your imagination.

Interview with Daniel Kirk (2008)

(Daniel Kirk is a FTM radical sacred whore who plies his trade quietly among transgendered clients who need sexual healing.)

Tell us about your gender identity.

Daniel: I love gender. Being male comes more naturally to me, but sometimes I think that if I'd been born male I might have transitioned to female. It isn't so much that I want to be one or the other, but that I want to be both. I want to understand both. For a while I wasn't sure if I really wanted to transition, because I never wanted to be entirely male. There are great things about being a woman, and great things about being a man. Hard things too. I think what finally decided it for me was that the struggles involved in living as a woman brought me further from myself and isolated me, but the struggles of being a man brought me deeper into myself and connected me. I do miss the physical beauty of the female body and feminine presentation, but that has taught me about the beauty of masculinity. I'd played with gender roles in the bedroom, in nightclubs, and in the SM/fetish scene for years before transitioning, but finally living in the "real world" as a man taught me things about maleness that I never could have learned in play. Gender isn't just an internal process. It is a public performance. It is both how you see yourself and how others see you.

What does sacred sexuality mean for transgendered people? How is it different?

Daniel: It depends on what is meant by "sacred sexuality". All sex is sacred. All things are sacred. In that sense, sacred sexuality can be a matter of recognizing and emphasizing the inherent sacredness of one's sexual expression, whatever that is. But a more specific use of the term "sacred sexuality" is when sexual expression is approached as a venue for spiritual growth and transformation. At its highest expression, it is when sex becomes an act of worship. Most people have a hard time understanding what that means because they don't really understand worship. They think it is going to church or saying prayers. They've never experienced religious worship as true communion with God, so even if they found that communion in sexual ecstasy they wouldn't understand it.

Most people never explore any aspect of their sexuality in depth, so they never come close to this kind of experience. Transgendered people are automatically faced with hard choices about sexuality. We can't help but face them. Sex confronts us with deep issues about our bodies and identities. Non-trans people might face these issues too, but few of them are confronted with them so early and so frequently. To have any kind of healthy sexual expression, trans people need to directly confront issues that most people can avoid their whole lives. We either succeed or fail. We can't have a lukewarm mediocre sexuality. It is either painful or transcendent. Often both. Sometimes simultaneously. Most non-trans people have the option of complacency. They might take the hard road of sexual self-exploration, but they don't have to. Transgendered people aren't given that choice.

But self-exploration is just the first step in sacred sexuality. It is a prerequisite. If don't have a reasonably healthy way of expressing your sexuality, you'll just get mired in your own shit. The very act of having sex at all presents a great challenge to many trans people (and many non-trans people). To take it to the next level you need to be able to be fully present during sex, focused on the experience, not on your issues. There is a great book—*Tantra For Erotic Empowerment* by Mark Michaels and Patricia Johnson—that guides the reader through the foundational self-exploration needed to approach sex as a sacred activity.

Tell us about your spiritual path. What does being a sacred whore mean to you?

Daniel: It means providing spiritually meaningful sexual experiences as a professional service. Like "sacred sex", at its most basic, being a sacred whore can mean being any type of sex worker who recognizes the sacredness in their work. I use the word "whore" because I refuse to be ashamed of what I do. Calling this work sacred isn't an attempt to redeem an otherwise profane act. It is recognizing the inherent sacredness and inherent potential for sacred expression in it. To the pure, all things are pure.

There are a lot of trans folks, mostly MTF, involved in sex work. In a different world, this might be a good thing, but in this world it is not. In this world, people don't choose to become prostitutes because they feel called to serve others by manifesting Divine Love through the body. No. Some are coerced or even forced into it, but more often it is just the last resort of someone who doesn't know what else to do. It is dangerous work. Prostitutes are not respected or treated fairly. The sacredness of our work is utterly denied, and we are treated as barely human. We die young, of disease and overdoes and suicide and violence, often with no one to mourn us. This is a terrible thing.

As a sacred whore, my work is more often about healing than recreation. Even the folks who come for recreation often wind up experiencing some type of healing. That isn't because sexual healing is more sacred—the recreational sex is transcendent and celebratory and a true act of worship. It is just that so many transgendered people are in need of healing. So many have been sexually abused. So many have hated themselves for their sexual desires. So many hate their own bodies. So many have spent years trying to have sex as someone they are not. So many cannot find a lover who respects and values them. Just being touched in a loving way can be a profoundly healing experience for many transgendered people.

What is it important for transgendered people to know about their sexuality?

Daniel: It's as sacred as the rest of you. You are God, You are Goddess. You are Both and Neither. You are a living embodiment of the sacred.

Chapter 6
Athena: Dealing With The Patriarchy

You were so seductive, Athena,
seductive as you can only be to an adolescent
others may have embraced Aphrodite or
Dionysus or Hera but I
the child whose home
erupted in daily violence
found your armor so bright and safe
your promises so grand...

I outgrew you, though,
when I left home and more earthly
pleasures called,
bowed out of the ranks of glory
went AWOL from the epic—
I, a hero? Never,
the best I'd ever do would be
security and a love-warmed bed
and be grateful.

But now you call me again,
because the world is racked and rent and
it needs saving
even if there are no more heroes,
only weak fools like me who
break too easily under your demands.

And yet, perhaps, lady in armor,
father's daughter, favored son,
in spite of my protestations to the contrary
there are still some lessons
you have yet to teach...

The Myth

Athena was born from her father's head. Her mother, Metis, was Zeus' first wife, but she was prophesied to bear either a daughter of great wisdom or a son who would unseat his father. Not wanting to take the chance of a son, Zeus tricked the pregnant Metis into turning into a fly and ate her. The child, however, gravitated to his head where she threatened to burst out, so Hephaestus clove open his father's head with an axe and Athena sprang forth, fully armed, with a sword in her hand.

She was the goddess of battles, but not of war (that was Ares' domain). Athena's job was strategy, not fighting; she was the general rather than the foot soldier. In peacetime, she was the patron of handcrafts and statesmanship. Always, she was serene and thoughtful, rarely flying off the handle like her divine relatives.

Athena requested that her father grant her eternal virginity, like her sister Artemis and her aunt Hestia. In ancient times, virginity did not necessarily entail physical celibacy, but only the forswearing of being partnered with anyone. To be "virgin" was to be single, to put one's own needs and desires first. However, Athena handled her "virginity" differently from Artemis or Hestia. Artemis shunned all men except for a few trusted hunters, and lived in the wilderness with bands of women. Hestia was a recluse, living a monastic life. Athena, however, showed neither fear of men nor of the worldly life; dressing in male clothing and wearing armor, she preferred the company of men to that of women and made herself the patron of heroes such as Odysseus, Perseus, and Jason.

Athena was the speaker for the patriarchy, the tradition that stated that the father was more important than the mother; that male (of the time) ideals should take precedence over traditional female ones. In the *Orestiad* by Aeschuylus, she tells us:

> There is no mother anywhere who gave me birth
> and, but for marriage, I am always for the male
> with all my heart, and strongly on my father's side.

Athena was Zeus' darling; of all the children he bore, she was the eldest and his right hand. Indeed, she seemed to be the one he was grooming to rule, daughter or no; perhaps he thought to stymie the forces of the matriarchy by making as his heir a woman who was strongly loyal to him and to his ideals.

"Truly you do trouble me, Athena!" Merlin Stone cries in her book *Ancient Mirrors of Womanhood*. And it is true that Athena is troublesome to feminists, and woman-identified women everywhere with her insistence on blind loyalty to the father and the father's rules. Intellectual antifeminists have been referred to as living examples of the Athena archetype. To those who are rediscovering the old heritage of earth and water, flesh and feeling, Athena seems too airy, too intellectual, living in her head amid theories and not touching the ground. Yet Athena is, in her own way, transgendered; her cross-dressing and masculine behavior gives her a potent power in mythology (and in our minds). In the Orphic hymn to her she is referred to as "male and female, dragon of many shapes". She is also a shapechanger; in the Odyssey, for example, she appears as various birds and old men.

The price she pays for being not only allowed to act transgendered but being praised for it is to put all her magic and resources squarely at the disposal of her father, and what he stands for. She takes this choice even though it requires eternal virginity to be seen as "one of the boys" yet not a competitor, and she does not seem to think the price is unfair. It might not be a choice that every one of us might take, yet who will be the one to stand in Athena's shoes and judge?

Athena was originally a Libyan goddess, and she is identified with the Libyan (and later Egyptian) goddess Neith, a warrior, archer, and weaver who is sometimes shown with an oversized artificial phallus. Neith may have been the proto-Athena, brought to Greece with the Achaean conquest. However, Athena is much more than just a warrior and bureaucrat; she is also the patroness of artisans and creative work, all those who work with hands and heart. She is a weaver, and although she can be merciless with those who are too arrogant about their work (such as the tale of Arachne shows) she is linked to the giving of soul, of spirit, to otherwise inanimate objects of art. Athena values civilization and the commitment to the cultural arts that this implies; she knows full well that cities are not built on war alone, or even primarily, in spite of her armored figure. As Athena Ergane, she is the worker, the maker; creation rather than procreation.

She is also associated with the serpent, that symbol found in the company of so many other androgynous deities—Shiva, the mysteries of Dionysus and Ariadne, Lilith's association with the Serpent in Eden. Athena's Medusa head, worn on her shield, may be the symbol of an ancient Libyan priesthood overthrown by invaders. Her other symbol is the owl, which she shares with Lilith.

You can find Athena in the gender community as well, without looking very hard; she can be seen in both female-to-males and male-to-females. Women who show masculine behaviors at a young age may or may not be accepted by other women, starting with their mothers, who may attempt to enforce feminine behavior in their "little girl". School, and the derision of more stereotypically feminine girls, may drive them even further away from female-oriented space.

As adults, they may find themselves in a double bind, regardless of whether they are attracted to men or women. In traditional society, masculine women are seen as wannabes; if they prefer men, they are stereotyped as pathetic, wistful tomboys who need to be trained to be "real" women, and if they come out as butch lesbians they will be seen by men as competitors for femmes, and shunned if not attacked. One wonders if Athena's sexlessness is a kind of "harmless" camouflage, allowing her to be respected for her work while not being threatening to male sexual egos.

On the other hand, many masculine women are not welcome into female society either, and this is not just a reference to suburban coffee klatches. Many butch lesbians in the women's community, especially in the '70's and '80's, were regularly shunned and criticized by other, more women-identified women. Their behavior was considered "male-identified" and therefore unacceptable, and their sexual style was thought to resemble "the way men have sex" (although in truth, the untouchable "stone" butch resembles Athena's impenetrable virginity far more closely than any male archetype), leading them often to reconsider their involvement in the women's community altogether.

It isn't too hard to see Athena turning to the male world largely because she knows that women will not understand her. "Mommy will never like me for who I am," she says, "but at least I know how to play Daddy's game." This can result in the classic "patriarchy supporter" who is often a high-ranking, hard-driven executive, or if there is genuine gender dysphoria, the sort of female-to-male transsexual who may despise femininity and cling to traditional masculine norms.

I've noticed that Athena-type butches who transition to male tend to end up as Ares or Apollo men, the working-class dude or the suited executive. If they identify as gay men, they may tend towards conservative "sweater gay" life, preferably with a long-term partner who is much like themselves. In contrast, Artemis-type butches who had more of a political and personal investment in feminism and women's values (and may have found the lesbian community much more painful to give up) find themselves in a difficult place when their inner natures drive them to sex reassignment. Their internal male models tend to be more like scholarly Hermes or intense, alternative-sexualitied Dionysus. (Ironically, both the children born from Zeus' body, Athena and Dionysus, eldest and youngest, are gender-crossers, but Athena is the groomed heir and right-hand sidekick while Dionysus is the son born to sacrifice in order for his father to keep his throne.)

Athena also appears among male-to-female transgendered folk as well; just like Aphrodite who arises full-grown from severed male genitals, Athena leaps full-grown from a man's head—or a "man's" mind. Athena-type MTFs often take one of two paths: either they separate male and female roles rigidly and split themselves down the middle while doing it, or they appear as somewhat asexual androgynous-female career women, much like the pre-transition Athena FTM.

Athena should not be dismissed with such alacrity, however; as transgendered people we are subject to a bewildering amount of hostile bureaucracy, including doctors, surgeons, lawyers, and the people at the DMV. Merely acquiring a passport becomes a long and painfully complicated process when applied to us. The rules and regulations of patriarchy cannot always be sidestepped, and it's often a good thing to have a friend to walk one through it. Athena is that friend, and if you treat her with respect for her choices—which are hers alone, and which she takes responsibility for—she will be a good companion to your quest.

Discussion questions

Do you see a difference between "female" and "male" ways of thinking? If so, is it inborn or cultural? Is it affected by hormones? Do you value one over the other?

Is there anything in traditional culture that you find valuable and might think twice about throwing away? How do you get along with your father, or male mentors? What does it take to get men to appreciate a transgendered person? How about women? When does a masculine woman start to be a man? Where does the line get drawn, and why do we need to draw it?

How have you handled bureaucracies and annoying regulations in the past? Do you think you handled them well, or are there ways you could improve?

Inner world activity #1

Alone, think like a strategist. What do you have to do in order to get what you want? What is holding you back, and what can you afford to lose? Make a list of everything you are not getting, and how you would have to change in order to succeed in your goals.

Inner world activity #2

If you're transgendered, think about what effect being that way has had on your creativity. How is creativity different once you've accepted this about yourself? If you're not transgendered, imagine how your creative work would be different if you were of a different gender. (If you're not sure, you might try asking someone of that gender that you respect.) Try it that way for a change.

Outer world activity #1

In a group, think like a strategist. What can your group do as a whole to change the way bureaucracies think about transgendered people? You might suggest calling hospitals, AIDS testing centers, suicide hotlines, shelters, fire paramedics, the police—any arm of the system that might need to provide emergency services to a needy and possibly misunderstood third gender individual—and offer to speak about how to treat us. Come across as helpful, not holier-than-thou. If possible, work with a group that already does such things through the gay or feminist communities. Volunteer for speakers' bureaus.

Outer world activity #2

Pray to Athena for strength and coolness of head. Then look at your driver's license. Does it have little boxes where "M" or "F" is marked off? Call your State Department of Motor Vehicles. Some of them have contingencies for people of indeterminate gender; they can get a special piece of paper signed by a DMV higher-up stating that gender is not necessary on a license. If they don't have one of these contingencies, see if you can get them to implement it. You will probably need the help of two or three therapists who work with gender people and are willing to testify that having a gender on a license can be counterproductive for transsexuals in transition or people who find it necessary to live intersex. If they do have such a paper, get it and copy it and distribute it. The next time you get your license renewed, take a copy and get the gender removed from your license. *Do this even if you are single-gendered and straight.* Encourage your friends to do the same, especially if they're single-gendered and straight. The name of the game is solidarity. The ultimate goal, of course, is to get gender removed from licenses altogether.

The Ritual: Mentor

Light candles of white or light blue. On a white cloth, lay out all the items of clothing or otherwise that make you feel protected and strong—your armor. Place also on the altar some representation of your most creative work. (If you don't have any creative work, maybe you need to talk to Athena about that.)

The following prayer is taken partly from the Homeric Hymn to Athena and partly from the Orphic Hymn to Athena. It's a good thing learn and say when you need to be clear-headed.

> I begin to sing of Pallas Athena, the glorious goddess, bright-eyed, inventive, unbending of heart, pure virgin, savior of cities, courageous Tritogeneia. Hail Athena, male and female, begetter of war, counselor, dragon of many shapes.

After invoking her with the prayer, explain your needs as you would to a counselor. Athena does not make things happen for you; she is not a deity of wish-fulfillment. She helps you facilitate your own solutions. Over the next few days, listen carefully in your own mind for the solution that will come. If the solution is already obvious to you and you are asking her for courage, ask her to bless your "armor" as you go forth to battle. Remember to wear some of these items as you face your fears.

Interview with Ted Heck (2001)

(Raven's Note: When I first interviewed Libby Heck, she was a pre-transition FTM active with the Society of Friends. A couple of years later, I ran into Ted Heck at a conference where he was helping with staff duties. I was happy to see that he had transitioned and was doing well, and I apologized that this book had already come out, and that I was not able to publish his words under his real name. I have since remedied this situation.)

How would you describe yourself and your spiritual path?

Ted: I'm a 32-year-old transgendered (female to male) person who is pre-everything (hormones, operations, etc). I intend to begin transitioning in about a year. In urban areas, most people can tell I am still female-bodied, and assume I am a rather masculine-looking dyke, which is how I have identified since I was 16. I tend to be attracted to very masculine women. In fact, my ex just transitioned to male this year. And I'm still attracted to him, damn it. It bites because he's in a relationship, and probably not interested anyway.

I consider myself very lucky to have been raised as a member of the Religious Society of Friends (a.k.a. Quakers). Friends, as we call ourselves, have a very non-judgmental attitude toward all people. We believe, first and foremost, that there is "that of God" in every single person, regardless of outward factors such as race, belief system, nationality, etc. This core belief is the reason that Friends have a strong tradition in the struggle for civil rights, prison reform, labor organizing, and anti-war movements. In the last fifteen years or so, Friends have moved firmly into the position that gay and lesbian people are very value members of their meetings (meetings being the equivalent to churches, synagogues, etc.) and have chosen to fully support same-sex marriages of any kind. While I don't think there is any formal decision or position about how transgendered individuals fit into friends' society, it is difficult for me to believe that it would even matter. I know that before I realized I was going to transition, if I had heard about a transsexual Quaker, I would have thought it unusual, but it would not have crossed my mind to not be supportive of him/her.

How do you see your transgendered identity in terms of your spiritual practice?

Ted: First, I should say that I believe that all people are sacred, and that Friends as a whole, as well as myself, believe that no person is more sacred than any other. But I would also say that my gender status puts me in a unique situation, which may be valuable in ways that are different from most people.

I most definitely see my status of being nontraditionally gendered as a gift in many ways. I also see it as a very unique journey that I've been given the option of following. There aren't many people who get to follow this path. a lot of times, I feel alone and angry about being stuck with the way I am. I don't fit in most places, and it's scary and lonely. But I also have a perspective on the world that most people don't have, and I've been through things that most people can't really imagine. In this way, it's a gift because I can reach out to people, make connections that others can't see, or wouldn't think of. I can be a bridge between male and female, and often even between other types of people who are different from each other because I have an unusual understanding of what it means to see different perspectives.

Another way in which it is a gift is that I am most definitely stronger because I've had to struggle. I've been put to the test by other kids when I was young, by people I've never met being rude or even threatening to me simply because of my appearance, and by people who I worked with treating me differently because they found my gender expression threatening. I have listened to horror stories of people I knew, or knew of, being beaten and worse by others because they were like me. Some people are terribly damaged by these kinds of experiences; for some reason, I have become stronger through it. And there is no way I can not consider this a gift which was given to me for a purpose. I strongly believe that a large part of my personal spirituality is tied into helping to create a world in which more people are given the opportunity to be themselves in an authentic way.

What do nontraditionally gendered people bring to spirituality that might be of use to others?

Ted: A unique perspective on the world and on the people in it. A challenge to those who will take it, to examine how one's beliefs and assumptions about gender color his or her attitudes about the world, about interactions between people, and about the nature of the Powers That Be (God or whatever you want to call it). I think most people don't consider these things. And I think it only right and good that my presence causes people to question themselves and their world. When I find that I have somehow opened someone's eyes and allowed them to be more accepting and loving toward their fellow human beings, then I have given my best. That's what I live for.

Interview with Marina Payne (2008)

(Raven's Note: When I wrote the first edition of Hermaphrodeities, *a few of the friends who kindly looked the manuscript over commented with surprise on the fact that not all of the interviews were with individuals who had come to a solid, finished place with either their gender or their spiritual path. Leaving aside the fact that both are often an ongoing journey, and if you think you've learned everything about either, you're actually stuck in a cul-de-sac and are ignoring the path, I think it's important for people to hear the words of folks who may not be "there yet". It shows that the process is as important as the goal, and as rewarding. It also makes us think about our assumptions as to where "there" is, a point that we would all do better to consider. Thus there are interviews with transgendered people like Marina Payne, who shares her ongoing spiritual journey with us.)*

Tell us about your gender identity.

Marina: Hm. Well, I would have to say I am somewhere in the "Not Female" range. Currently I am examining and meditating on where I fit on the continuum, and I am not at this time considering most kinds of medical alteration. I have considered using herbal augmentation for encouraging hormonal shifts, but have not tried anything yet. Since 2005 I have consciously identified at various points as FTM, male, androgynous, genderqueer, and genderfluid. I do want to continue my social and wardrobe transitions in a more masculine direction for a while longer, and see where that takes me. I have been increasingly comfortable identifying as male the more I am aware of the nature of my gender.

The reason I identify as such is hard to define, as it's more about what either "feels correct" or "feels erroneous". If I was to try to put these perceptions of self into words it would have to be that I am, at least in some ways, more comfortable with the social assumptions that go with male pronouns, and that many of my behaviors and presentations are unconsciously more commonly male. (I have had others bring this last bit to my attention.) I am becoming comfortable in an aware male-identified mind now; it feels more natural, and I feel a calm that never surfaced when I was trying to be female. I don't like any box society offers, but I am much closer to a man in how I currently feel comfortable perceiving myself than as a woman.

Tell us about your spiritual path, and how you got there.

Marina: The religious/spiritual path I have found that makes sense to me is a blend of Druidic, Buddhist, Shinto, and magickal arts. I have woven in some aspects of other paths as well, but what I keep returning to in depth are these. I am a Polytheist and Animist.

How did I get here? I am half Japanese, and half a European-ancestry blend. I was raised attending Jodoshinsu memorials for my grandfather, and the energy of the rituals and everything about what I knew of the path called me home. I only recently found a need to peruse this path deeper, possibly even into the priesthood, depending on some other directions my life may take. That is how I recently returned to Buddhism.

I was settled into a large part of my spirituality when I became aware of my trans nature. It was during the time I was acclimating to this new dynamic that I rediscovered what was to be another large part of my Spiritual Path. In the process of discovering myself, I was forced to reexamine my practices, values and beliefs. Finding out that while I looked female, I was *not*, explained a fair amount as to why I had always been terrified of "all-female spaces", including a women's circle at a Pagan gathering I attended. When I gave it a shot, I ended up feeling physically ill during the sharing and "being deeply female". Later, this and other moments would make much more sense.

In my first year of awareness of being transgendered, I returned to much of the root teachings of my chosen traditions, and read what I could, asked questions of the leaders, really started to pry in ways I had not for some time. It was during this time that I became both much more attuned to Buddhist teachings, and committed to going deeper in Druidic teachings. If nothing else, I also figured that deepening my religious connection would help me with the rest of my trans exploration.

Going back to the topic of gendered spaces ... I had grown up between the Episcopal Church and the Jodoshinsu Buddhist tradition. Both religious groups had men's study groups and women's study groups, and those divisions always seemed odd to me. Now I understand that I would likely fit in neither identity, and even if I did, since surgical or other medical change is not in my foreseeable future, I would likely never be accepted anyway into all-male circles. I tried hard to consider going to some woman-only retreats my then-sweetie was hosting. She led the women's circle where I fell apart. I wanted so badly to be part of her world, but I also felt a much deeper connection with the teachings of the men's event, which resonated on a much more primal level.

In regard to Deities I worship and honor personally, I have found that many of them, including Shiva, Dionysus, Athena, Artemis and others have androgynous traits. I have only recently realized how much this relates to some of my personal experience, and it is something I am looking at further. My experience with relationships with highly feminine divinities has been rough at times, sometimes due to misunderstanding, sometimes due to insecurity and dysphoria, or feeling that I was not female enough, or other doubts. For example, not only did I not feel Wicca was the right religion for me, I have a hard time relating to many Wiccan practitioners due to the highly gendered nature of much of their religion. Interacting with the forms of Pagan religion that are somewhat monotheistic and hold The Goddess above others also makes me uncomfortable. The hardest thing is constantly feeling excluded. Now I am used to this, as only a fraction of my experience this lifetime fits with any given community, but from a spiritual community mindset it hurts differently.

The rest of my spiritual journey is a bit more of an independent study. Since finding the Order of Bards, Ovates and Druids, I have felt as strong a pull to that path as well. For over fifteen years now, I have read what I could about Druidry of several kinds. At the same time I learned about various parts of Native American and neo-shamanic teachings, and have learned much from my animal and plant allies. More recently, I have discovered Hellenic and other Reconstructionist groups, and am learning more about these ways. It is very exciting as the Hellenic ways have been of interest to me for some time now. These paths speak to me almost on a cellular level, and I have found that what I know of them honors all life as equal, cats, ants and humans all being equally sacred, and that is something important for me in them.

What's most important for transgendered people to know and remember?

Marina: If I had to pick one thing for transgendered people to remember, it is that we have the honor in leading societies on journeys not many take. Many of us have the opportunity to live deeply, and examine ourselves and how we interact with that self and others. Another very important part of this journey is that we should remember that there can be as many gender identities as there are individuals ... there are so many ways to explore Being. Not everyone is traveling from Point A to Point B, then stops. For some it is mutable, by choice or not; for others, there are not predefined points on any spectrum. All identities are equally valid, and if we are to grow as a transgender community we need to learn to respect all of the shades within it.

Interlude II:
How to Change Your Boring Maypole Ritual

When the Platypus Clan, a group of androgynes at a Pagan gathering, went to the Maypole ritual the next day, we felt a bit left out. The men all went out to the woods to cut a pole and carry it in, and the women all dug the hole. Then, when the pole was brought in, the cries went back and forth—"Bigger hole!" "Shorter pole!" Needless to say, the bunch of us sitting on the hill and watching this two-gender heterosexual ritual felt a bit antsy. After a while we started yelling, "Tastes great! Less filling!" at them.

When we went to another Pagan gathering, we decided things would be different. We started setting the tone for the weekend as three-gender (at least) space by offering up a geodesic dome built by one of our MTFs as official third gender space. Our posted policy was inclusive rather than exclusive, saying, "You don't have to be like us to hang out here; you just have to like us." Then we followed this up by doing a lot of work shifts, preferably as an openly third gender group. (We ended up running the entire meal plan.) Finally, we offered to run the Maypole ritual—and they let us!

We kept some things the same, but added one important fillip. When the men came in with the pole, we stopped them a few feet away. Then we spoke to the group, saying: "Long has the war between men and women been fought, and many are the casualties. We who are of both genders offer our minds and our bodies as a bridge to bring women and men together. With this act of magic we bring healing to the world."

Then we made a human chain with our bodies and brought the group of men to the group of women, bringing them together so that they could place the pole in the hole. Instead of raucous, the ceremony was suddenly hushed, and the pole was set in place in complete silence. Everyone stood looking at the Maypole and each other for a few moments, and then the cheer went up.

After this, we went our ways and eventually formed our own Pagan groups. However, we brought this particular division of Maypole ceremonies with us to our various new forums. When some of us got involved in the early forming of the First Kingdom Church of Asphodel, this is how we ran the Maypole ritual on Asphodel's first big Beltane weekend ... and it's been how it's done ever since. For us, more than a decade later, it is now tradition. We couldn't imagine having a Maypole and doing it any differently. As a tradition, this is an easy, fun, and validating way to make ourselves known in the community ... and to provide a place for traditionally-gendered folks who are exploring the idea of being ritually third gender, if only for a day.

When you hear of a Maypole ritual, go and get in the middle. Speak for us and the powers that be will hear. We will never have a place in the community if we do not make it ourselves.

Chapter 7
Baphomet: Sacred Perversion

> Tell me who's your bogeyman,
> That's who I will be,
> You don't have to like me for who I am,
> But we'll see what you're made of
> By what you make of me.
> 　　　　*–Ani DiFranco*

Hymn to Baphomet

I am Baphomet
Rex Mundi
Lord of Perversion
Child of Earth
Sacred Abomination
Secret warrior
Survivor of the great purge
Baptized in wisdom
Wounded in the service of Earth from which I sprang
and to which I was not allowed to fall.
I am the sacrifice that Death refused
I am the one who must live on wounded
When the gods were driven from the circle of Midgard
When the Sidhe closed their doors and withdrew
When the warriors of old fell and were slain
I hid and survived alone.

I am Baphomet
Secret warrior
I am no soldier, girt with sword and shield
for all those were slain by the White Spears
But I am born of this world, this earth,
the realm of flesh and shit and humus

my hooves are rooted in this place
and I chose to stay and fight
a one-deity war against the invaders.

I am the peasant who mines the bridge
I am the hunchbacked servant who puts ergot in the bread
I am the witch filling an ox heart with thorns
I am the fair girl who sees the cruel lord
knows he must die for her people to be free
knows her slim hands and warm cunt are no match
goes apart to a lonely place
feeds herself with poison, day by day,
year by year until her fluids reek of it
then goes to his bed and slays him with her love
Will she be welcomed back to the village afterwards?

I am Baphomet
Lord of Perversions
What they throw away I save
What they devalue I hold holy
What they tread underfoot I raise up
What they cast off as ugly decorates my holy raiment
What they fear becomes my weapon
I am both man and woman
I am filled with lust for both man and woman
I am only as cruel as your own repressed desires
and only as hard on you as you are on yourself
I will prey on your mind, legions of sterility!
Here I stand with horns and hooves and hair
and I cannot be made pure and heavenly.
Here I stand with goat's beard and woman's breasts
and I cannot be made simply man or woman
Here I stand with hard cock and wet cunt
and I cannot be made into a safely sexless androgyne

Here I stand with whips in my hand
—those whom I love I chastise with many rods—
and I cannot be made to kneel and serve
Here I stand, uprightwing boys—
are you ready for me?
Pray to me for the perversion of your enemies
for I shall turn them upside down
and dangle them in the filth of their own making.

I am Baphomet
Child of Earth
Your body is my chalice, let me drink of you.
I hold nothing more valuable
than flesh and shit and humus
I hold nothing holier
than earthly desires.
When the Mother was silenced
I alone heard her cries
When the Great God Pan was declared dead
I alone lived on
When the Most Sacred and Holy Mystery
was stripped and driven through the marketplace
I alone was secret and apart
And when the earth was poisoned and tainted
So was I.
I am innocence destroyed
I am the memory that can never be banished
that which will never quite be made clean again
but cannot be made to die
And this, too, is sacred.

I am Baphomet
Sacred Abomination
Lover of the Whore of Babalon

Among the straight I am the queer
Among the queer I am the freak
I am Lord of the disenfranchised, the shabby, the outcast
I am leader of the desperate
I am friend of those who cannot fit in.
I am Giver of Assurance
I am Giver of Ecstasy
I am strength through stealth.
I am the one who stole the white one's finest warrior monks
and turned them to my worship
and if that weapon broke in my hand
At least it was lost to him.

I am Baphomet
Rex Mundi
Crowned King of this world by my own hands
because there was no one left to crown me
Crowned King of the Age of Darkest Repression
because there was no one left to take it on
Crowned King of the tainted world of filth
because I was the only one left who valued it.
I have stayed with this world through all its pain and torment
I have suffered with this world
I have changed with this world
I have lived in human time
day by day, year by year,
I have learned my enemy's ways
and I can help you through his maze.
I am he who manipulates their hierarchy and laughs to himself
and I am also he who takes a shit on the boss's desk.
I am the underground force
that is always with you.
My wild woods were cut down
and I learned to move through steel and concrete.

My roots were soiled
and I survived.
I was cut off from the life force
and I did not die
and I did not forget.

And on that day that I work for
and fear
And on that day when the doors open
and the old gods reclaim once again their land
their earth from which we all sprang
will they recognize their child?
Will my scars be honored
or feared?
Will I be revered
or asked to step aside?

I am Baphomet
Baphe Metis
Baptized in wisdom
I have much to teach.
All lonely places are sacred to me.
Whenever it comes to pass that you look about you
and find all your kin and kind are destroyed
and yet you will not give up
Then I am with you.
And whenever it comes to pass that you look about you
at those who are supposed to be your kin
and they are deciding you do not fit in enough
for them to risk themselves for you
Then I am with you.
Let my wisdom be the staff in your hand.
I am Baphomet
And you have much to learn.

The Myth

Baphomet is a mysterious figure, and perhaps that is appropriate. Although revered by many mystics and ceremonial magicians, everyone seems to have a different idea of who he is. The Knights Templar were burned for worshipping this hermaphroditic phallic god. In the desert near their Spanish castle, strange figures are carved into the rock that have three faces in one, symbolizing past, present, and future. Local legend casts them as yet another symbol for Baphomet's all-encompassing power. The traditional figure of Baphomet, however, is of a goat-footed, goat-horned, winged hermaphrodite, much like an androgyne Pan. Medieval woodcut Tarot decks showed Baphomet as the Devil card, in all his bisexual glory, since transgression of gender symbolized evil in those days.

This form of Baphomet's is rather suspicious in some pictures, especially the presence of breasts and the large, outsize phallus, often a different color than Baphomet's body. In Thomas Wright's *The Worship of the Generative Powers in the Middle Ages in Western Europe*, written in 1866, drawings are shown of the carvings on several coffers and bowls associated with clandestine worship of Baphomet. On one such carving, a statue of Baphomet is kissed by worshippers. On another, a robed and crowned figure holding two twisted serpents (reminiscent of Ariadne) stands with robe open to display hir body. The body is female, with breasts and vulva, but the face is heavily bearded. Is this one of Baphomet's priest/esses, or is it another form of Baphomet himself?

Baphomet's form may be related to the legend of the Jack-A-Roe, a figure who appears in several folk songs as a woman who cross-dresses, often to be a soldier. The original Jack-A-Roe figure goes back much farther, to a tale of medieval German and English witch covens who worshipped the Goddess and the Horned God —Pan, Cernunnos, or Herne. These parts were played by actual coven members, the real faces of whom were often known only to a few in the coven for reasons of security. Apparently it was of the utmost importance that the "Man in Black", or the avatar of the Horned One, who witch-hunters assumed was the devil, never be found out to be a human being. According to legend, one way a coven got around this was to have the Horned God played by a woman wearing a horned mask and an artificial phallus, which she presumably used to have intercourse with the coven, providing them with a taste of sexual ecstasy. She was referred to in some English legends as the Jack-A-Roe, and the hermaphroditic Devil card may still bear her visage.

The name Baphomet may come from the Greek Baphe Metis, meaning "baptized in wisdom", showing the Gnostic roots of the vanished Baphomet cult which may be an offshoot of the Orphic mysteries; or it may stem from the medieval Arabic *abu-fihamet*, with the similar meaning "father of wisdom". However, unlike other androgynous deities whose worship is documented, most of what is accepted as Baphomet's rites are fairly contemporary, created inspirationally by individuals and groups who seem to see the enigmatic roots of this deity as an opportunity for new revelation.

As explained before, this book does not attempt to separate ancient and therefore "legitimate" myths from "illegitimate" ones borne of personal revelation, since I believe that any myth and symbol that is associated with a transgendered deity or archetype has something to tell us, if only about the society we transgendered people have to survive in, or the value in which we are held in varying cultures. Why has this half-animal hermaphrodite figure become a muse for so many in the modern magical community? What can we learn from the new myths that have sprung up around Baphomet, Rex Mundi?

First is the aforementioned title, Rex Mundi—king of the world, referring to the fact that Baphomet is powerful only on this material plane of earth. Some people who work intensely with Baphomet claim that his title of Rex Mundi, and his connection with this world, is even more deep than this. They claim that, unlike other deities who spend most of their time in other realms and only occasionally ritually "possess" a willing human body, Baphomet is always present here in this world in some body, living in our time and space ... and that in order to "carry" his presence, the body must be somewhere between male and female.

Baphomet is half animal, like Lilith, Pan, and may other deities whose shapeshifting appearance links them with the natural world. Shapeshifters in general will tell you that once you've shifted something as basic as gender, imagining one's self crossing the lines of race and species is not nearly as difficult, so it's not surprising that so many deities who cross one, cross another as well. As a primal androgyne, He is reminiscent of Zurvan, the ancient Persian deity of Infinite Time who is pictured as intersex and bore of hirself the twins

Ahura Mazda and Ahriman. More specifically, Baphomet is half goat, a creature that is associated with hardiness, survival in wastelands, and strong sexuality.

Like Lilith, Baphomet is a highly sexual deity, an avatar of sacred sexuality. Indeed sex magic is one of the traditional ways of invoking and appeasing him—but Baphomet puts a strange twist on it. Baphomet is known also as the Lord of Perversions. This can be seen as society's horror of transgendered figures, especially those who are openly sexual. It can also be used to point out another uncomfortable fact, one that many in the gender community would rather not look at, and that is the real and unbanishable connection between genderfuck and kinky sex.

There is certainly such a connection for fetishistic transvestites (people whose gender identities are squarely that of their birth gender, but who find that dressing and acting like the opposite gender is erotically stimulating), and a huge amount of literature and visual porn has grown up to satisfy their needs. In the various SM/fetish communities, there are also quite a few who wouldn't exactly call themselves transvestites, but who enjoy "genderplay" as a fun sexual activity. Examples are the proliferation of "daddy-boy" relationships among butch dykes, which mimic similar relationships in the gay male leather community, right down to the uniforms, mannerisms, and sometimes at least during sex play, the pronouns.

Demographically, the percentage of people in the gender community who experiment with unusual sexual practices (such as consensual SM, fetish play, and other sexual theatre), is higher than anyone wants to admit. I was interviewing a noted psychiatrist who handles many gender people, and he commented on the sizeable number of transgendered patients who practice SM (sadomasochism) or have multiple fetishes.

There may, of course, be purely social reasons for this. The SM/fetish community, such as it is, can be very tolerant of anyone of any gender expression due to the number of people experimenting with genderfuck on their own. There is also the fact that SM can be a way for people uncomfortable with genital contact to get hours of erotic activity without the expectation that genitals will be involved. Another explanation might be that when your feelings about your genitalia and your social gender—which is supposed to determine your sexual role—are mixed and ambiguous, it might not be so hard for your sexual "template", as it were, to miss the traditional heterosexual or even homosexual target, and instead settle on something nonstandard, and possibly not even focused on other human beings. Or it might—who knows?—be another biological sexual preference.

However it comes about, Baphomet the sexual pervert is part of hirstory whether we like it or not. One of the attributes of the Lord of Perversion is the ability to use that which is shocking and disgusting to the repressed masses as a tool of magic. Where there's fear, there's power, says Baphomet. Where the thing is that you were taught you shouldn't do (often for no good reason), there lies that which will set you free.

The ancient Tantric sages, recruiting for their religion which competed with the newer Brahmanic Hinduism, created a "love-feast" which included meat, fish, and wine for the (heretofore vegetarian) initiates. Later, in the inner circles, "meat" was shown to be symbolic of fellatio, "fish" for cunnilingus, and "wine" for various body fluids; the "love-feast" of the inner circles was ritual sex. The first "blasphemy" was designed to shake the complacency of the initiates so that they would better be able to question their beliefs, and it prepared them for the second one. Similarly, unconventional sexual techniques frequently open people up to the possibility of experimenting with gender roles.

Gender bending is, in many ways, the ultimate sin in this culture. Even many gays and lesbians leap to assure the masses that they are just completely normal men or women who happen to be attracted to other perfectly normal men or women. Gender is rigidly legislated in our culture, and so is the distribution of power. Gender bending turns sex role rigidity on its head, and SM does the same for power relationships with its implications that power can be given, taken or swapped at will.

SM as a form of pain infliction can also be yet another way to achieve a shamanic altered state. Certainly the *gallae* of ancient Europe and the Near East used ritual flagellation to the point of maximum endorphin release to create an alteration of consciousness (see the chapter on The Gallae of Cybele). At the Villa of the Mysteries in Pompeii, where the initiatory rites of Dionysus and Ariadne are illustrated, flogging with a switch is part of the ceremony. Baphomet is sometimes shown with a handful of birch switches for flagellation of the worshipers, reminiscent of this tradition.

Baphomet is sometimes associated with a female (or femme) lover/consort who is supposedly the archetypal Whore of Babylon, and she is often referred to as Babalon (Aleister Crowley changed the spelling for his own aesthetic/numerological reasons) symbolizing the power of sacred sexuality that was demonized by later religions. As a sacred whore and Baphomet's consort, she is the special protector of those who make their living from selling "perversion" in particular, such as professional dominatrixes, transgendered sex workers, etc.

Baphomet and Babalon are both characterized by an utter and complete lack of shame and an abundant amount of self-confidence in themselves, their effectiveness, and their sexuality. As Rex Mundi, Baphomet is invoked in order to gain enough "chutzpah", if you will, to get one through a trial ahead. Because he is androgynous and comfortable with that, he can be invoked to give a temporary relief from pervasive body discomfort. However, he is impatient with those who refuse to take action to deal with their problems, and may find ways to "push" someone into actions, possibly through dire circumstances. Invoke at your own risk, but the rewards can be great.

Discussion questions

What do you find sexual about social gender roles? (Certainly they are sexualized in mainstream culture; how much of that works for you?) Do you take on a particular role during sex? Do you experiment, switch back and forth, write your own script? Have you ever found cross-dressing erotic? If you have started out as a transvestite and then fully transitioned from one social gender to another, do you still find it erotic? At what point did it stop? Do you find it erotic in others?

Do you ever play with gender during sex? If not, why not? What would happen if you did? Do you play with power during sex? Do you see the sexual role of one gender as having more power than the other? What would happen if you were to switch that image in your mind during sex play?

Have you ever gone into an altered state due to deliberate pain infliction or endorphins? (Runner's high counts!) What did it feel like? Why do you think that it is downplayed as a legitimate altered state?

Do you have any fetishes? (Think about parts of bodies or clothing or genders or even personality traits that make people more attractive to you.) Discuss the other definition of "fetish", the one that refers to magical objects. What is the connection between these two terms? Can the first kind of "fetish" be used as the second kind?

Inner world activity #1

Think about the sort of person you are most scared of having sex with, that it would be most unacceptable to find oneself lusting after. Set up a sexual situation (it can be role-playing with a partner or simply masturbatory fantasy) in which you are that person, having sex with yourself, or someone else if you desire. Don't imagine yourself as being you in relation to them; be them in your mind. The more frightening the monster, the better. Afterwards, think about it felt to be that person. Write it down or talk about it.

Inner world activity #2

If you have a fetish, experiment with incorporating it into a ritual. Suspend your disbelief and find something sacred about it, something magical that it symbolizes for you. For example, I think of my leather fetish as a shamanic commodity, and my leathers as "organic armor". When I don them before sex, I am doing a ritual to armor myself in such a way that I will be protected yet still receptive enough to be open to my partner. It doesn't matter how bizarre or culturally stereotypical your fetish is; it can symbolize something magical to you. Do a private ritual in which you acknowledge your fetish as the "power medicine" that it is.

Outer world activity #1

Is there erotica on the market that represents you and your desires? If not, why not? Try making it yourself—write it or film it—or writing to makers of pornographic materials and telling them what you'd like to see. The face of erotica is driven by consumer demand. The only way to crowd out bad porn (and by bad porn I mean poorly made, boring stuff with a stereotypically limited range of subjects and activities) is to make better porn and flood the market with it. There are a lot of folks out there who would buy it if it was available. If nothing out there resembles you, do something about it, even if only to let the publishers hear that. If there is something out there that you like, buy it—and write to the manufacturer or publisher telling them to make more of it! Your pocketbook, however meager, is the best way you have of controlling the variety of erotica on the market.

Outer world activity #2

If you do have a particular fetish, you're probably not alone. Get together with other people who are like-minded and talk about it. Share with them the discussion questions and the activities. No one should be ashamed when it's better to be empowered. One of the wonderful things about the Internet is that no matter how bizarre your fetish, there is someone out there who has made a website celebrating it. Find them, and become empowered. No one should be ashamed of their sexual desires, even if those desires cannot be realized.

Outer world activity #3

Rent pornography with transgendered people in it. What does it say about our sexuality? You'll notice that female-to-males are noticeably absent from porn. Why do you think that is? What would you like to see with regards to erotica with our people in it, both MTF and FTM? Write or film some. If you not only don't recognize your fetishes (as in activity #1) in erotica, but you don't even recognize yourself in it, it's as if society is saying that you aren't desirable, and something needs to be done. Rent video equipment and film erotica with as many transgendered people as you can convince to help, seen the way they want to be seen. If something like this comes on the market (and maybe after this book is published, it will) buy it and tell your friends to buy it.

The Ritual: All Acts Of Love And Pleasure

This ritual was developed at an SM play party. It is a larger, "group affiliation" version of the private fetish ritual. It may take a long time, and everyone needs to be thoroughly briefed well ahead of time in order to make it work properly. We did not demand that everyone who participated take a turn in the center of the circle, as there is a perfectly acceptable role for people who want to applaud, cheer, drum, shake rattles, or whatever.

You Will Need: A safe, secure space where no intruders can interrupt and that is comfortable for everyone to have a good deal of room in. (Some people's fetishes take up space.) Items for the four directions of the room. These can come from your imagination. We placed a whip and a lacy fan in the East, a candle and a pair of high heels in the South, a vibrating "yoni" and a glass cup filled with lube in the West, and a collection of dildoes wreathed with leaves in the North. Everyone should take part in decorating these altars, contributing whatever it is they feel might be appropriate. One bowl of M&Ms or other small candies is also needed.

The rest is provided by the people in the ritual. Ask everyone to think of some activity that turns them on and that they don't feel is exactly socially acceptable. they can bring props to demonstrate activities, or just speak about them.

Four people are chosen to delineate the circle by acknowledging the four directions, and create sacred space. Then the priest/esses step up. In our ritual, Baphomet was invoked my a butch dyke leather top who wore a horned mask, a large phallus on a furred, tailed harness, and fur leggings that ended in leather "hooves", and carrying a riding crop. Although the individual who invokes Baphomet does not need to have such an elaborate costume, they should at least have breasts and double genitalia (none of which need to be made of flesh), and a commanding, confident attitude is a plus. The other priest/ess played Babalon, the Sacred Whore. Babalon should present as "femme" and wear red; anything else is up to the priest/ess performing the role. The pair do represent a kind of "butch-femme" paradigm, but the actual sexes of the individuals can be whatever they like within those borders. Our Babalon was a pre-op MTF who wore scarlet belly dancing gear.

Baphomet recites the "Hymn to Baphomet" at the beginning of this chapter. Then Babalon says the following:

The body's truth lies in the rivers of energy
that rise up from our roots,
and this (takes hold of genitals) is our roots.
We know our own truth from these messages,
for they are truly come from the God/desses of love
using our own flesh to speak to us.
And anything that causes the rivers of energy
to rise with joy and ecstasy
is sacred, no matter what it is,
no matter what anyone may say.
For all acts of love and pleasure
are Our rituals.

One at a time, each person gets up and has the center of the circle to themselves. When we did this, some people spoke about their fetishes (often telling salacious stories or reading hot poetry), some read aloud erotica, some showed off their fetish gear in a fashion show, and some performed theirs on the spot, alone or with help. The most important part of this ritual, however, is this: After presenting their sacred perversion, each should then speak about what it has taught them about themselves and the world. For example, cross-dressers might speak about what playing with gender has done for the way they see men and women, SM players might recount what they have learned about power and altered states, etc.

The tone of this ritual must be completely nonjudgmental. Even if someone talks about a fetish that they cannot perform because it might be harmful or unsafe to themselves or someone else, and therefore it must be kept in fantasy only, their courage and self-discipline must be applauded and appreciated. Lots of clapping, cheering, drumming, and music playing during performances is encouraged. Those who take part should be made to feel proud of themselves, not shameful in any way. Do not challenge or question anyone's preferences and what they have or have not learned.

As the final part of the ritual, each person goes up to the bowl of M&Ms, which should be in front of wherever Baphomet and Babalon are enthroned. Each person selects a piece of candy and names it with a judgmental attitude that they are better off without, e.g. "I thought that (whatever) was terrible and that the people who did it were all sick, but I see now that this isn't the case at all," or "I've been ashamed of myself for liking (whatever), but now I refuse to carry that shame any longer." They then present the candy as an offering to Baphomet and Babalon, who eat it and promise to excrete the "bad attitude" transformed into something else.

Sacred space is opened, and all feast, make merry, continue to celebrate their perversions, or whatever.

Interview with Drew Campbell (2001)

(Drew Campbell is a FTM leatherman who is the author of Miss Abernathy's Concise Slave Training Manual, *and co-editor, with Patrick Califia, of* Bitch Goddess.*)*

How do you describe yourself and your gender identity?

Drew: I'm a female-to-male transsexual. Surprisingly, perhaps, that's easier for me to articulate than the rest of the factors that make up my identity and self-understanding: queer; Anglo-Irish ethnic heritage; upper-middle class background; Pagan; Ph.D. in German literature; married to a woman; monogamous; professional writer and editor; pervert (BDSM/leather); fat; polyglot; New Yorker living in San Francisco...

Describe your current spiritual path, and how you got there.

Drew: It's a very long story. I was raised as a Protestant Christian, first in the Congregational Church and then in the Episcopal Church. I grew up in an area of Long Island where Protestants were a tiny minority—everyone around me was either Jewish or Catholic—so my religious identity was very vague. I was confirmed in the Episcopal Church as a teen and, as a result of the unsatisfying answers that I received to my burning theological questions, I immediately stopped attending.

Slightly before this time, at age 13, I had a very intense spiritual experience—a vision—in which a Goddess appeared to me and claimed me for her own. This statement probably sounds a little crazy to people who haven't experienced this sort of thing firsthand, but I was left with no doubt about the reality and importance of this Goddess, whom I later learned to call Brighid. She has been my Mentor and Matron ever since.

For about 15 years, from my mid-teens until two years ago, I was on an active search for a viable spiritual path. I studied a lot about Paganism, learned Irish, visited sacred sites in Eire. I investigated Buddhism. I gave Christianity a second and then a third look, and even began the process of becoming an Oblate (a religious who doesn't live in community) in an Episcopal contemplative religious order. I studied Judaism intensely for a while, learning Hebrew and studying Talmud. All the while I maintained Pagan spiritual practices—kitchen witchery, if you will—and a private devotion to Brighid and the other Gods and Goddesses whom I honor.

Two years ago I went through an intense spiritual crisis, in which I felt I was being asked to make a commitment to my Gods. This is not the sort of thing one can ignore—the Gods can be very impatient and very demanding. At this point I maintain a dual Pagan path: I honor the Irish Gods as well as the Greek pantheon. I also honor my blood ancestors and the spirits of the land on which I live.

How do your sexual (SM, fetish, etc.) practices fit into your spirituality? How do you use them as spiritual tools?

Drew: I view submission to a human being as a way of expressing devotion to the Gods. When I top—which I do almost exclusively now—I try to embody that divine energy for my bottom. In the past, when I played primarily as a submissive and masochist, I tended to choose partners who understood the spiritual dimensions of dominance and were able to manifest that for and with me.

I've written a lot about this process in *Miss Abernathy's Concise Slave Training Manual* and in my essay in *Bitch Goddess*. I feel very strongly that, while as a culture we desperately need to bring the sacred back into the material world, this kind of spiritual work should not be undertaken lightly. I've seen and personally experienced so much psychic damage done by people—both tops and bottoms—trying to use S/M as a substitute for therapy, that I've become very cautious. I wouldn't work with anyone who hasn't already done extensive psychic archeology in formal psychotherapy and (if they were topping) didn't have verifiable professional training in spiritual counseling and some pretty rigorous ethical standards.

I also use sadism (and in the past, have used masochism) as a way of accessing deep emotions, particularly anger. Anger is such a taboo, especially for people socialized as women, that it's often impossible to get to it without touching the instinctive level—the fight/flight mechanism, for example. By planting us back in our bodies, S/M makes it possible to experience these feelings directly and intensely.

How did your sexual practices affect your process of gender transition?

Drew: S/M was the key that helped me unlock my gender difficulties. I'm not a textbook transsexual, in that I wasn't aware at an early age that my ongoing psychic discomfort was directly related to my gender. My problems started at puberty, so for many years I assumed I was dealing with some combination of internalized homophobia and body-size issues. But no amount of therapeutic attention to those issues helped.

I began cross-dressing and developing a male persona in scene. As I said above, the sheer physicality of S/M play was a way to get back into the reality of my body—and it was a very uncomfortable reality. The acknowledgement that I was in constant psychic pain was enough to make me seek out new ways to alleviate that pain. The ways I'd developed as a child—not being in my body, mostly, or deadening the pain with food, drugs, or alcohol—simply wouldn't work anymore.

The first FTMs I met were perverts—friends of a friend. At first I was very skittish around them, in the way people can be when they are desperately trying to avoid facing some large and frightening truth about themselves. These people were mirrors for me. They showed me a part of myself I'd been studiously ignoring for years. The simple fact that they had transitioned and were still alive—and gainfully employed, in satisfying relationships, and otherwise "normal"—was a revelation.

Transition has changed my S/M play considerably. I've found I no longer need masochism; I'm in my body all the time now. Much of my submission had been linked to age play (with me as a teenage boy), and transition helped me grow beyond the stage of arrested adolescence that I had lingered in for so long. I think I had avoided growing up in some ways because I couldn't grow into what I intuitively knew I was ... a man. Once that became a possibility, I was able to let go of the need to stay young and dependent. Also, as my sexual response has changed with my changing body, I have found different activities more or less enjoyable than before.

Is there a particular ritual or ritual form that has been especially healing or useful to you as a gender perv?

Drew: I think we, as a community, need more rites of passage, particularly ones that acknowledge sexuality. One of my friends, right after he started passing as a man, went off to a back room and had his first sexual experience with another man. There were no negative repercussions, thankfully, but the experience was not very safe and it certainly wasn't fulfilling for my friend on any emotional level. There has to be a better way to come out as a gay transman than to emulate all the most superficial aspects of gay culture.

Honestly, the most healing thing for me, ritually, was my wedding. I wrote the ceremony myself to express both my wife's beliefs (she's Christian) and my own. We had family members from both sides and close friends in attendance—votes of confidence from all around. At dawn on the morning of the wedding, which was held in our garden at home, I went out and prepared the space with libations and invocations of my Gods. The ritual asked for the blessings of our blood and spiritual ancestors and called Land, Sea, and Sky as witnesses to our vows. We swore according to an old Irish formula, updated—"I swear by that which my people hold sacred." As a ritual, it worked: "the veil opened," as a friend later said. Not only did it make public our commitment to each other, but it was another step for me as a man. I'm no longer a bachelor, but a paterfamilias, a householder.

What do you feel that we as transgender folk—especially "unusual" ones—have to offer everyone else?

Drew: If we do nothing more than allow people to look beyond binary thinking, we will have made an enormous contribution to the evolution of the species. I think we all underestimate the complexity of human beings (including ourselves) most of the time, just as people try to boil the Gods down to a clearly defined set of attributes or actions and then get confused when They act "out of character." If I have one message for the rest of the world, it's that "nothing is that simple."

Interview with Lee Elder (2009)

(Lee Elder is a devotee of Baphomet, among other Gods, and an FTM tantrika.)

Describe your gender identity and how that relates to your spiritual path.

Lee: I was born female, and am medically transitioning to male. I've always felt like I am a little bit of everything, and am fluid on the gender spectrum. People read me differently, and I respond to any pronoun and do not usually bother correcting people because it doesn't matter much to me. If someone asks what I prefer, I do say that I prefer male pronouns, though all pronouns feel strange to me. For a long time I didn't know if I was going to transition, because I don't fit in the male box a whole lot better than I did the female box in terms of what is socially expected. I eventually decided that getting my body closer to the middle would be more personally comfortable than not, and would be a better housing fit for the shape of the parts of me that are not made of meat.

After discovering that I am unusual in my gender identity and expression even in FTM circles, I have determined that I am thoroughly *ergi*, third gender. This means that my presence often causes people to become uncomfortable and confused, and sometimes triggering their own latent gender issues. Being *ergi* can either be something you try to hide, or it becomes a way of being. If you don't try to hide it, there's just no getting around the fact that you're going to be walking around with your gender oddity hanging out (not usually literally of course) and people are going to see it and you will have to deal with their constant reactions. It takes a good amount of flair and/or calm to cope with this daily, so it really does affect your method of being in the world.

So my identity does not so much relate to my spiritual path as it has become my spiritual path. Along with this function comes a responsibility to tend to whatever I stir up along the way, as it is not a path of causing chaos but of encouraging natural change. Being myself authentically in the world is what I feel I am supposed to be doing, and learning to do that without fear is my ultimate goal/assignment/ curse/privilege. I often think of it in relation to the Sanskrit word *sadhana*, which describes any kind of ongoing work that is undertaken as a spiritual endeavor as continually mindfully as possible. Or rather, I *try* to think of it like that, though more often it feels like surfing due to the unpredictability and inevitability of wipeouts and occasional dreams involving sharks.

Describe the work you've been doing with sacred sexuality, and how that relates to trans people.

Lee: I began with learning about Tantra and Kundalini yoga from a female perspective, and shortly realized that the bulk of the information available out there is for heterosexual binary-gendered couples only. I knew that couldn't possibly be all that there is to the subject, as I was finding ways of doing things on my own. I was for the most part unpartnered during that exploratory period, and was beginning to figure out that I had a "psychic cock" that I could work with, and eventually taught myself how to astrally shapeshift from one end of the gender spectrum to the other and then to the middle. Figuring out the middle has been the most difficult and interesting part, and is very much ongoing. As my physical body responded to the testosterone therapy, it got a little easier to find middle, but more difficult to find female.

In talking to other trans-spectrum folks both casually and in workshops I've given, it is clear that everyone is so beautifully different from one to the next that writing a detailed how-to on sacred sex for trans people would be an impossibility. One specific method will not work for everyone, so self-knowledge and exploration must be the focus of any trans specific sacred sexuality discussion, along with a bare-bones outline of how that specific exploration could be undertaken. That's the work that I am currently doing.

Anything to say about transgendered people and alternative sexual practices?

Lee: When you yourself are alternative, the alternative becomes your usual, so the word "alternative" tends to lose its meaning a bit! There is a popular idea that trans people are more likely to have unusual sexual practices, and this is likely true largely because the configurations of trans bodies often call for creativity in terms of positioning, elective equipment and prosthetics. Also, if your body doesn't appear or feel the way you think it should, you may not like being touched in ways that people who are comfortable in their skin usually touch each other. You may find that an alternate pleasurable sensation can become erotic, and that may be a substitute for or a component of sexual stimulation that works for you. On the other hand, there are plenty of trans folks who do not feel uncomfortable in their skins, especially after transitioning, and there are plenty of folks who never feel the need to explore anything alternative despite having an atypical body or identity.

What's the most important thing that you would tell transfolk about themselves, their bodies, their sexuality, and how to survive spiritually between those ambivalences?

Lee: The hard-line divide between male and female, man and woman is socially constructed and accepted by most people as indelible. Nature shows a different picture, as does history across cultures. I feel that the most important thing for a trans-spectrum person to know is that they do not have to allow themselves to be cut in half by that line if it falls on top of them. You can bend that line wherever you want to. You can bend it with your mind or your body. However you were made, yes, that was for a reason, even if you want to change. Evolution is just as Divine as creation ever was.

Chapter 8
The Kurgarra and Galatur: Into the Darkness

me and Hel

Death sits in your kitchen chair
across the table wrapped in darkness.
You cannot see under Her
robes to the bones and the screaming and
it is just as well. Her finger flicks in derision.
I have not come for your body.
You relax, a mistake. *I have*
come for your soul.
Much worse. You tremble. *Write,*
She says, pointing to paper
and pencil. *Write all the things*
about which you are ambivalent.
The things you love and hate both. Those which
snap you by reflex into old patterns. Write.

You write, you
weep. Like a mother wondering
which of her delinquent sons
will go to jail forever. Lover, child,
career, friends, causes.
Pieces of flesh. You
set down the pencil. *One,*
She says. *You may keep one*
as a keepsake. All others must go.

It is the bones and the screaming
now, inside you. You consider
offering Her your body, instead.
Would you die for these ambivalences?

Which of your fingers will you cut off,
which of your children will you present
with a sacred case of survivor guilt?
You wish to Hel it was
Her consort sitting there; He might
urge this on you, scowl and
stand tapping His foot, for years, even,
but He would not grab you by the scruff and
pull you through the gate
ready or not here we come. He is the
Voice that Urges, She is the Force
That Compels. She has no patience.
You will not be permitted
the luxury of confusion and fretting.
One, She says. *All others must
Go.* And when they go, they will be
Gone. This is the Real Thing.
There is no Do Over, no Only Joking.

You are allowed three seconds
then you must drop the weight.
For the gate through which you must
pass is no great portal
it is as tight as the neck of Her womb and
there is no room for heavy luggage.
You must be ready to fly. *For you see,*
She says, and it is the last
explanation you will get,
all else must be taken on faith,
*Someday you will stumble onto the rocky road
that is your true path
and the fall would have killed you
if you hadn't been traveling light.*

The Myth

The myth that I usually use to illustrate this step on the path of the transgendered mysteries is not one where we play the main role; in fact, we are only a tiny cameo in it ... but it's a telling cameo. The myth is the story of the Descent of Inanna, as recounted in the *Enuma Elish* from ancient Sumeria.

In this tale, Inanna the Queen of Heaven—beautiful, intelligent, powerful, high-ranking, goddess of fertility, sexuality, wealth, resources, and magic, with an adoring, handsome husband Dumuzi—decides that there is more to her life than this. She "hears the call of the world below" and decides to venture into the darkness of the Underworld, the realm of her sister Ereshkigal ... even though no man nor woman can pass the gates of the Underworld alive. She tells her faithful handmaiden Ninshubur to go for help if she has not returned in three days, and descends into the darkness. There she is stripped of all her rank, magic, riches, memories, and at the end, even her name. Ereshkigal wrathfully "fixes her with the eye of death" and hangs her corpse on a hook above her throne.

Ninshubur flies to the gods of the Sun and Moon, but they have no power over the Underworld and refuse to help. She then turns to Enki, the god of invention. He also has no power to pass the gates of the Underworld, but he knows who does. From his spit and the dirt under his fingernails, he creates two creatures neither fully male nor fully female, referred to in the story as the *kurgarra* and *galatur*. The gates of the Underworld open for them without demonic interference, and they pass them "like flies" and come before Ereshkigal's throne.

The Queen of the Dead, in this story, is weeping in pain. Her job is to rebirth all the dead souls through her own womb, and she is in pain, and no one in the upper realm cares. The *kurgarra* and *galatur* do not argue with her, or persuade, or remonstrate, or even beg for Inanna. Instead, they weep for Ereshkigal and give her their sympathy at her plight. She is so touched by this that she offers them anything ... and they ask for the corpse on her wall.

So it is that Inanna comes up from the Underworld flanked by two third-gender creatures (and a horde of demons, for Ereshkigal is not done with her yet) who have saved her life. There is more to the story, involving Ninshubur,

Dumuzi and his sister Geshtinanna, but as our two figures of interest drop out at this point, I will let interested parties look it up themselves.

What we know about those two words—*kurgarra* and *galatur*— from other surviving stelae of the period is that those terms were used to refer to bigendered priest/esses who worked in temples. Supposedly they wore costumes divided down the middle vertically, masculine on one side and feminine on the other, rather like the Hindu *Ardhanarisvara*; we also know that the formerly male wore them right-to-left in one direction, and the formerly female wore them reversed. What we don't know, as it did not survive in the archaeology, is which way the uniforms went for whom, or for that matter which was the *kurgarra* and which the *galatur*. However, the fact that these sacred roles have a "creation myth" (as it were) and a spiritual purpose is telling.

It's just a tiny cameo in a bigger story. Hardly anything, really ... but the figures of the *kurgarra* and *galatur* haunted me. No man nor woman could pass the gates of the Underworld alive ... but they could. Why? What was it about their nature—and, logically, mine—that allowed for such a thing?

The question remained a mystery to me for some years, lingering in the back of my mind. The key to it came, ironically, in a book about male mysteries that a friend urged me to read. In his book *Iron John,* Robert Bly posits three archetypal life sequences that are represented by the colors of red, white, and black; the Hindu *Gunas* that are associated with sacredness in many cultures. Traditional Neo-Pagans will recognize the white-red-black sequence, the woman's life pattern, as the Goddess's sacred colors: white for the maiden, passionate red for the woman who comes into the fullness of her sexuality as lover and/or mother, and black for the wise crone. Bly focuses on the men's sequence, which he sees as red-white-black. Hotblooded, warlike young men full of new hormones start as red, and then they move into white as they learn about rules and discipline, and end as black when they become wise sages.

The third path, however, which Bly refers to only casually as an "alchemical" path traveled only by "magicians" and higher seekers, struck something deep inside me as I read about it. The more I read, the more I understood and recognized that this is our pattern, our sequence, our path. The alchemical pattern starts with black, instead of ending there; the "black beast" of unaltered coal, unsmelted metal, unrefined earth. Many of us who have lived with nonstandard gender will recognize immediately the concept of starting in blackness; when other children are discovering their innocent sexuality and tentative joy in their new bodily urges, we are realizing, with varying degrees of horror and anguish, that something is terribly, terribly wrong with us. This feeling can be as nonspecific as a vague sense of being indefinably but definitely "alien", "outsider", different in some heinous way that will cause our immediate expulsion or persecution if it were to be discovered. It can be as specific as the frighteningly irrational body "wrongness" that can cause physical mutilation of or total emotional separation from the hated "wrong" flesh. Some of those who are intersexuals have the added issue of actual nonconsensual mutilation, violation, and family shame heaped upon them. Histories of depression, repression, alcohol and drug abuse, denial, frantic overcompensation, broken relationships, madness, and despair litter our "hirstories" like the flotsam of a legion of wrecked ships. We begin our lives in the dark.

Elsewhere in his book, Bly speaks of the *katabasis*, or bottom point in the trip through one's personal underworld; the point that my high school poetry teacher referred to as, "when the Valium runs out". We two-souled people are born teetering on the edge of that pit; the *katabasis* is only a few steps down for us. Sooner or later, we will end up there.

Its proximity, however, can also be a guarantee that we can get our *katabasis* time over and done with sooner, and go on to better things. I remember a time when I was living in a tiny cabin beside the Quabbin wildlife sanctuary, unemployed, broke, sick and in withdrawal from the female hormones I'd been administered for years that the doctors had finally insisted I stop taking. My mental state fluctuated; there were times when I was not particularly sane as my abnormal endocrine system sawed back and forth and tried to balance itself. Worse, I was aware of those times of psychosis, as one would be aware of a bad acid trip that refused to stop, and I felt hamstrung, as if body and mind had both betrayed me. One night I cried out to my Deeper Power one of the three big questions of my life before my transition—"Why is it important for me to have this experience? Why do I have to be here?"

The answer came, simply, like a quiet bolt of lightning: It's necessary for your life's destiny that you have the experience, not only of being in this terrible place, but of coming back from it. "Oh," I thought, feeling foolish. "That means I will come back from it. That makes a difference." The second stage of the pattern is white, like the first light of dawn that appears over the horizon, breaking the unrelieved blackness of the night. It is the joy that we feel when we discover that we are not alone, that we have come out the other side, that the changes we have made are, indeed, beginning to free us from despair. "I didn't actually have any moments of complete, unmitigated joy until after transition," was another comment I heard often.

For the first time in our lives, we dance in the light that others may have taken for granted. We also do foolish things, because after being in the dark for so long, we may be blinded by our own joy and do stuff that is, in retrospect, pretty stupid. We may act stereotypically—MTFs may giggle too much and dress like their mothers or like '40's movie stars; FTMs may go through aggressive, pushy, loud-mouthed stages and order their partners about or worry that they aren't "man" enough without the right amount of muscle. We may have fantastic, silly inappropriate fantasies, like the MTF I knew how wanted nothing more than to marry a rich (and preferably very tall) man who would support her so she would never have to work again.

We may also come up with idealistic theories that shore up our own personal grievances and discount the experiences of others, or we draw great, sweeping generalizations about who is or is not part of our communities, or try to force our way in where we are not wanted in our newly acquired enthusiasm for living. The white light distorts things, in its own bigger-than-life way, as much as the darkness does.

The final stage is that of the color red, and it is likened to the blossoming of a rose, or to the sacred red dragon. In each of these sequences, red is the color of fleshly longings and bodily functions, and the time when one comes to terms with them, and to an understanding of their sacredness. Men face the issue first, with youthful potency, and women in their second stage with the issues of whether or not to bear children. Statistics show that libido is highest in men of around 19 and women of around 35. For those of us with body dysphoria issues, however, we may not come to a time of feeling joy in the body until much later. Since so many of our issues are with our anatomy and what has been or needs to be done with it, we can be cut off from that earthly joy for most of our lives, or at least most of our lives before transition. The stage of red is one of power; of confidence not founded on the rigid denial of the black stage or the dependence on external perceptions of the white one, but the power of hard-won experience and comfort with oneself. During the red stage, we loosen up, because we can afford to be generous. We care less about what doctors, friends, and society thinks of us and our choices, and we get on with our lives, which have deepened into color for the first time.

This, then, is the quiet gift of the *kurgarra* and *galatur*. Once you've been down into that pit, been disenfranchised, been cut off from the life force and returned, it can create compassion for those who go down and get stuck. It is given to us to quietly help the trapped Inannas of the world, and to still have compassion as well for Ereshkigal. We understand mourning for what is lost but not regretting its necessity, and we also understand that castigating one's darknesses never helps. We can pass the gates of the Underworld and look at the corpses trapped on the wall, and say to them, "What force needs to be propitiated before you can leave here? For whom must you weep, and mean it? For what must you promise to care, and mean it? What bargain must you make with the darkness, what sacrifice is worth an end to this pain, that you must give your word for and then keep?" For the bargain you make to get out of the Underworld is a deal made with Death, and you don't break a deal with Death. Not if you value your quality of Life, that is.

Our compassion can come from more places than just having been in the Pit. "I'm just like everyone else, only more so," one transgendered seeker pointed out, meaning that s/he could identify both with men, women, and those in between—and beyond that, the desperate search for identity that led through so many forms of gender also created an understanding of and empathy for many different sorts of people. By the time we find out who we are, we've been so many people that we can connect with a pretty big percentage of the crowd, at least in some ways. That's a gift that we may not recognize until it bumps us in the nose. Having numerous abandoned lives and roles looks like failure to us, a pile of disasters. It's not until later that we realize that it's an asset. It may be a long time before we realize that it was training.

As an example, I've tried just about every sexual preference that exists. I first attempted heterosexuality from the female side, then I tried out lesbianism (up to and including a tiny foray into feminist separatist space), and then settled back into female bisexuality, then moved to the butch side of butch-femme lesbianism again, then transitioned and tried out the heterosexual male game, then tried out the gay male scene passing as a man. I've also been in relationships with other transpeople—the bizarre and beautiful dynamic of a reverse couple, poised somewhere between straight and queer with all the joys and difficulties of both; the deep intimacy and (sometimes) terrible envy of a same-sex trans couple. It's not that I was successful at all of them (actually, I only managed long-term success with the last two) but I know the games, the rules (fair and unfair), the lure, the desire, the expectations, and the common disasters. No matter what the sexual preferences of the couple (or triple) who lands on my doorstep with their troubles, I can say, *Yes, I see why this is sacred and desirable, and I also see why it's falling apart. What are you willing to sacrifice to make it work?*

We are, in our own way, living and walking examples that someone can make what seems like a terrible sacrifice and find more peace, not less, through that giving up. That's a hard thing for most people, the giving up. Not that it's all that easy for us, but we are driven to it in a way that others are not, and that is a kind of privilege. It's the map to the Underworld, where we can be guides. We always have been, as this ancient story of our spiritual Ancestors proves.

Discussion questions

What stage are you in, in your life? (Some people will experience more than one of the three stage-combinations at the same time, and this should also be acknowledged. Have them discuss how the two combine and conflict.) Are you still in the black? Have you passed to the red, or the white? Divide people up into their stages, and have them talk to each other about where they are at together. Then let them come together and hear from each other how they navigated through each stage.

How can you use your experiences to help those who are stuck, and can't get themselves out? Do some people just need to be stuck for a while? Where's the line between lending a helping hand and trying to be a messiah who rescues people unhealthily? When does compassion get taken advantage of? Discuss the joys and pitfalls of lending aid to each other, and to the world.

Inner world activity

Once a month, preferably on the dark moon, create a safe space and face one fear. If it's a fear pertaining to other people, enlist safe friends to help with it. (If you have no safe friends, maybe it's time to get over fears about making them! You have a lot of work to do.) It's best to start small, though; don't necessarily leap straight into the biggest fear of your life right away. Start with a tiny phobia or neurosis. It's best to build up mastery experiences of success with small fears. If you fail, remind yourself that the moon will be dark again next month, and the month after that, and the month after that. There is no deadline, only the need for sincere effort.

Outer world activity #1

Do something for a transgendered person who has been swallowed by the darkness and cannot yet escape, through depression or madness or some other terrible shadow over them. I'm not talking about trying to fix them here, I'm talking about spending a day or two helping them to get done some simple things that need doing. Do their dishes. Fix them food. Buy them a small thing that they've been needing. Help them get through paperwork or make scary appointments. Take them to scary appointments and be supportive. Take them out if they need distracting. Don't try to tell them what to do; just find out if there are little things that need doing, and help there. There are many small things that you can do for someone who is in a dark and difficult place. It may not save them, but then again it might just give them that tiny spark of light whose memory they will rely on to give them strength to get through.

Outer world activity #2

Get together a support group for transfolk with mental illnesses. If this is not something that you can relate to personally, find someone who can facilitate such a thing, and help them find a safe place to hold it, and perhaps mental health professionals who are willing to be resources in a pinch. This is not a group therapy sort of thing. It's a support group for people who want to get through their problems, but are having trouble with motivation, courage, or just knowing where to go next. The group should do a lot of bookending (having a support person call you just before and just after a rough activity that you're procrastinating about), and helping each other to face difficult structures, bureaucracies, etc. Just being the person to create the space, bring sandwiches, and then step aside is an immense service to the Universe.

Ritual #1: Psychopomp's Prayer

(There are a lot of rituals out there in the world for someone who is going through an underworld period ... and yet there still aren't enough, because such rituals are usually so personal that they must be created personally for each person. On the other hand, I've never seen anything for the loved one who is going through their own problems but whom you cannot directly help. In cases like that, asking for greater help is often necessary. This ritual is specifically for third gender people who are going through a period of depression, sorrow, or bad times.)

You will need four black candles for this rite, placed at the four directions around you so that you must turn to light them one at a time.

(Light the candle in the North, and say:)
O Guardians of the Gateway to the Darkness,
One who is in my thoughts has taken your road
And passed into the realm of dust and shadow.
Kurgarra, galatur,
Sister-brother, brother-sister,
Sprung from Earth, be solid as Earth,
Walk with them through the dark gates,
Let their feet never stumble,
Give them guidance when they fall from the path
And light one spark to see the road ahead.

(Light the candle in the west, and say:)
Gods of the Darkness, hold this one gently
And let their trials and troubles be only
What they need, and no more, and let them survive.
Kurgarra, galatur,
Sister-brother, brother-sister,
Sprung from Earth, be solid as Earth,
Weep for them at the dark throne as I weep,
Show all the Gods below that they are cared for
And deserve release once they have done their work.
(If one can shed tears for them, this would be a good thing.)

(Light the candle in the south, and say:)
Gods of the Darkness, pass this one through your fires
And keep them hung like a corpse
Only for a short time; let the sacred hands
On which I call take them down and lay them out.
Kurgarra, galatur,
Sister-brother, brother-sister,
Sprung from Earth, be solid as Earth,
Let the food of life pass their lips!
Let the water of life pass their lips!
Let them be made whole again.

(Light the candle in the east, and say:)
Guardians of the Gateway to the Darkness,
Release this one in good time,
Keep them no longer than is necessary.
Kurgarra, galatur,
Sister-brother, brother-sister,
Sprung from Earth, be solid as Earth,
Walk with them through the opening gates,
Let their feet never stumble,
And may each portal split asunder
And bring them once again into the light.
(Let each candle burn down until it goes out.)

Ritual #2: Blinding Light Prayer

(Sometimes people get through the darkness and get stuck in the light, where they do foolish things they will regret later, out of overenthusiasm. During this period, it's even more unlikely that they will listen to you say anything to them, so this prayer ritual is for those who need to be gently pushed out of this stage.)

You will need four white candles, set up in each of the four directions, as per the ritual above.

(Light the candle in the east and say:)
O Powers of the Sunrise,
I honor the light that has dawned
In the life of the one I think of,
But all suns burn the eyes of mortals.
Let them not be so filled with their own vision
That there is no room in their sight for the feelings of others.
Kurgarra, Galatur,
Sister-brother, brother-sister,
Children of Invention, look ahead into the future
And warn them against the pitfalls
They will not look down to see.

(Light the candle in the south and say:)
O Powers of the Noonday Sun,
I honor the blazing heat that warms
The life of the one I think of,
But all suns burn the skins of mortals.
Let their souls be not so filled with fanaticism
That there is no room to appreciate the paths of others.
Kurgarra, Galatur,
Sister-brother, brother-sister,
Children of Invention, look ahead into the future
And warn them against the pitfalls
They will not look down to see.

(Light the candle in the west and say:)
O Powers of the Sunset,
I honor the rosy light that blesses
The world of the one I think of,
But all suns fade and die in time.
Let them not waste time chasing what cannot be had
And forget what is already waiting for them.
Kurgarra, Galatur,
Sister-brother, brother-sister,
Children of Invention, look ahead into the future
And warn them against the pitfalls
They will not look down to see.

(Light the candle in the north and say:)
O Powers of the Full Moon,
I honor the light that shines with fey glamour
Over the dance of the one I think of,
But all moons can lead to lunacy.
Let them not squander hopes, love, and riches
On glamour that will never be real.
Kurgarra, Galatur,
Sister-brother, brother-sister,
Children of Invention, look ahead into the future
And warn them against the pitfalls
They will not look down to see.
(Let the candles burn down until they go out.)

Ritual #3: Prayer for Blossoming

(This prayer is for one's self, asking the Powers That Be to help your life blossom into color. It is not to be done until you are sure that you have survived both the preceding stages, and made the mistakes that go with them. If you are not yet ready, it won't work.)

You will need four red candles, set in the four directions as per the rituals above.

(Light the candle in the west and say:)
Flame of the heart, burn warm within my breast
And grant me wholeness in all my emotions.
Kurgarra, galatur,
Sister-brother, brother-sister,
I have knelt with you on the cold stones,
I have wept tears of compassion for Death,
And I deserve Love in all its forms.

(Light the candle in the north and say:)
Flame of the body, burn warm within my skin
And grant me wholeness in my relationship with my flesh.
Kurgarra, galatur,
Sister-brother, brother-sister,
I have built this self with dust and spit and time,
I have rebirthed myself from the trodden earth,
And I deserve Pleasure in all its forms.

(Light the candle in the east and say:)
Flame of the mind, burn warm within my thoughts
And grant that I may always see clearly.
Kurgarra, galatur,
Sister-brother, brother-sister,
I have been a light in the darkness of others,
I have held my torch that they might see,
And I deserve Clarity in all its forms.

(Light the candle in the south and say:)
Flame of the spirit, burn warm within my soul
And hold me to my true purpose in this lifetime.
Kurgarra, galatur,
Sister-brother, brother-sister,
I have gone down in the darkness and arisen,
I have danced in light and emerged from blindness,
And I deserve Joy in all its forms.
(Leave the candles to burn down until they go out.)

Interview with Vickie Boisseau (2008)

(Vickie Boisseau is a transgendered intersexual who can be found in many places spiritually, including both Christian and Pagan groups at the same time. Like all of us, she creates bridges rather than furthers chasms in understanding.)

Tell us about your gender identity, and your story.

Vickie: I came into this world on the 26th of October, and from what I now know, no one knew what to make of me. For the first three days of my life, I was female. What happened after that is a complete mystery, as nobody is willing to talk about it. After two days it was in some way decided that I was not actually female, but male with ambiguous genitalia. This fact has been covered up by the entire family since that time, never to be spoken about. The lies and deception that have occurred throughout my life have taken their toll on me, making me very insecure and unwilling to trust people, even those close to me.

My years in school were a minefield of secrecy; it must have been explained to the teachers by my parents that I was very different to other boys, since I suffered the humiliation of only being allowed to go to the lavatory after every other child in the class had gone. In the 6th grade I started to grow breasts, and from that point on I was not allowed to take gym. My mother sent a letter from my doctor to excuse me from gym because I had "testicular feminization". I found that I could not always avoid such situations and so devised a method of strapping that would hide my embarrassment, which worked as long as I was not to take my shirt off. Even then nobody in the family would talk to me about what I was going through, and how deep the family secret really was. I cannot remember the exact amount of surgery that I underwent to correct my AIS-L2, but I know that it was enough to require me to repeat the first grade, and keep me out of school long enough to be behind all the other children of my age, something that has stayed with me until this day.

If I thought that junior high was tough, then I had even more yet to come. My time in high school was fraught with problems; I learned at a very early age to cover up my secret in order to survive the ravages of my next 4 years. I developed a reputation for being the weird guy; this was my way of not allowing anyone to get to close to me in case they found out about me. My first real girlfriend broke our relationship off after 6 months when I didn't ask her to take it to the next level, because I was afraid of what she would have said after she saw my genitals. So I continued on my lonely journey through life, never able to confide in anyone in the fear that I would be seen to be a freak. On the odd occasion when I did feel that someone was getting close, I would detach myself from them just to be sure that I did not give anything away.

I was married in 1989 to a woman who loved me for what I am and not what I should have been. I fell in love with her the moment I saw her; she helped me through the most difficult years of my life and stood by me regardless of what I had been through. She wiped away my tears and stayed with me through two nervous breakdowns and one suicide attempt. I sometimes feel that I was preventing her from leading a normal life and that my presence denied her things she would be entitled to if I were "normal".

The greatest joy in my life was when I married in 1989; this was for me the ultimate compliment, and proved that I could be loved for who I was. My wife was fully aware of my condition as I had never held anything back from her. She was the first person who ever got really close to me emotionally, but even then my insecurity was still there and I knew that I would lose her one day, either to someone else or because of all my problems.

After about 13 years of marriage I finally had to talk to someone, and finally I started to come out to my friends as a more feminine person. They were OK with it, but my wife didn't like it; she thought it would make people see her as a lesbian. Finally, she decided that she wanted a divorce so that she could find someone else. I never thought I would get through, but I did. I was devastated that my marriage had failed, I didn't know how I would cope without my wife by my side, but I could understand that she could not take any more and needed to be free from me and all my problems.

During my quest for a diagnosis and the truth, I was being treated by an endocrinologist who suggested that we test the entire family for traces of the gene. This was to prove impossible as the family had been told to never reveal the truth. I just wonder how many more relatives I have with the same condition, and how many of them would welcome a shoulder to cry on, instead of all the secrecy and shame that the family have placed on our predicament. I have reached a point in my life where I feel capable of helping others with AIS or similar problems. I hope to be able to use some of my experiences, good and bad, to help others move on in life.

What is your spiritual path like today?

Vickie: In trying to find my spiritual path, I have gained knowledge from many religions and attempted to find commonalities among them. I find valuable the Pagan and Native American way of following and honoring the cycles of nature. Today I mostly follow a path of non-denominational Christianity, which I consider to be one of the better examples for me on how to live one's life, if one leaves aside the Christian-right "family values" types and embraces the genuine message of Jesus to love our neighbors and our enemies as our selves.

I consider myself a non-denominational Christian eunuch. I find a special home in two places in the Scriptures of the Christian faith. In the Hebrew Testament in the Book of Isaiah, chapter 56, the prophet quotes God as follows:

> ... do not let the eunuch say, "I am just a dry tree." For thus says the Lord; To the eunuchs who keep my sabbaths, who choose the things that please me and hold fast my covenant, I will give my house and within my walls, a monument and a name better than sons and daughters; I will give them an everlasting name that shall not be cut off.

And in the gospel of Matthew 19:12, Jesus says:

> For there are eunuchs who have been so from birth, and there are eunuchs who have been made eunuchs by others, and there are eunuchs who have made themselves eunuchs for the sake of the kingdom of heaven. Let anyone accept this who can.

For I am such a eunuch born of my mother's womb, so when I was growing up Roman Catholic they taught me that people like me, and gays and lesbians, are an abomination before God. But then I read these passages in the Bible and discovered that people like me are not only acceptable before the Creator, but even honored. My present church is the way church should be, loving and accepting of all people who walk through the door, whether GBLTI or of any nationality or human condition. All are welcome and loved for who they are. In fact, I am not only a member, but also I have been ordained as an Elder in the church. My leadership role is an important part of my realization that I am not only accepted, but also an essential part in the life of the church.

What do transgendered people have to teach the world?

Vickie: We need to remember that we are not here by accident, but by design. The medical people think we are here as a condition to be corrected, and some people think we are not part of the Creator's good creation. We are, however, as the Creator created us to be: both male and female, made in the image of the Creator and deeply honored by the Creator.

I believe that we have been put here by the Creator to be mediators between the genders, and that we have an important role to play as those who understand both genders. The Native Americans revered us for our skill in being able to go deeper in our understanding of both genders than those who are singly male or female, which enables us to bring about reconciliation and tolerance of differences. We can better see both sides of the coin to see both sides of a given situation and help show the other side to those who only see one side. We may also have been put here as an object lesson to help people learn about and except the differences found in people.

Chapter 9
Obatala: Healing the Wounds

> One who has a man's wings
> and a woman's also
> Is in himself a womb of the world,
> And being a womb of the world,
> continuously, endlessly
> gives birth....
>
> *—Lao Tzu*

The Myth

Obatala, the African Yoruba *orisha* or deity of healing and compassion, is seen as both male and female in one being, a sacred father-mother. He is seen as the creator of the human race; in some tales he fertilizes hirself, in others he divides into a heterosexual couple in order to birth/sire humanity, and in at least one tale he molds humanity out of clay and breathes life into them.

This tale has a slightly different ending. Obatala molded one batch of people every night, breathed life into them, and in the morning they awoke and went on their way. However, one night Obatala got drunk, and the people s/he created were twisted and deformed. The next morning, he was horrified at what he had done, and he swore that he would never again touch the stuff. That is why, although each of the orishas have a special liquor that they prefer as an offering, Obatala will only accept pure white coconut milk to drink. He is also the patron of all those born with birth defects, and those who work with the elderly and handicapped.

"Pure white king, pure white queen," sings the hymn to Obatala, who is lawgiver, judge, and peacemaker, the orisha of the white cloth. His judgment is clean, fair, and compassionate. He symbolizes the highest possible ethical standards, and is the clearest and most objective judge. He is known as Oxala in Brazil and Blanc-Dani in Haiti, and is pictured as an elderly African androgyne with white hair, clad all in flowing white. Followers of Obatala have the duties of peacemaking, as well as laying out the dead and preparing them for burial.

Legends say that Obatala himself was sacrificed in order to feed humanity. During a terrible drought, he mixed the sweat from his body with ground rocks to create fertile soil. When even this was not enough, he was sacrificed and cut into eight pieces, which were scattered about the country. A great agricultural civilization grew up around each of these severed pieces, with Ile-Ife being centered around Obatala's head.

Obatala is the third gender deity most directly concerned with nurturing. Amid the battled of matriarchy and patriarchy to determine whether humanity was spawned, like real humans, from a female deity, or like the Judeo-Christian belief, from a male womb, Obatala simply and evenhandedly solves the problem. Both a mother and a father to his people, Obatala is the epitome of unconditional love, and yet is also a fair and impartial judge, the keeper of the law. Unlike other deities who may be childish or irrational because they embody just those human qualities, Obatala embodies that combination of compassion and objectivity that many counselors, parents, and other nurturers strive for yet rarely achieve.

Parental duties in our culture are just as split as nearly every other trait. Mothers are supposed to be all-giving, all-nurturing, yet at the same time so emotionally tied to their young as to be unable to separate themselves. Fathers are allowed to set limits on their emotional involvement with their children, as long as they are willing to sacrifice themselves for the child's simple survival. This position gives them the appearance of more objectivity, and thus the job of lawgiver falls to them. Of course, it's never only that simple.

Obatala sidesteps the question of what the differing duties of a mother and a father are by simply being both, by keeping a balance between giving and lawgiving, by being the best of both. It's said that the hardest job in the world is that of parent, and that mother is simply the job of parent with the additional faculty of being a female role model, while father is parent with male role model added. If this is so, then Obatala is a parent in the purest sense, combining the best traits of male and female nurturing and showing, in the end, how to be human.

There is also a touching meaning in Obatala's particular care of those with birth defects. There is growing acceptance among the medical community with regard to classifying transsexualism as a birth defect, caused by inappropriate hormonal "programming" during fetal development, much as intersex conditions are now seen. (There is also a verbal backlash among segments of the transgender and queer communities that resent the implications of the term "birth defect", and the ensuing idea of "correction" by well-meaning but parochial medical personnel, an issue that the intersex community already struggles with.) Beyond any medical truth, however, many of us who do choose to change our bodies have had mysterious feelings from a very early age that something was "not right" with us, that we were not like other people in some way, that we had not been "made right". Obatala's compassion and caring for our situation is a source of strength we can turn to for nourishment. We are his "special" children, under his protection.

It is said, also, that Obatala appears to you as the sex you need nurturing from, and this will be different for each person. (Obatala does seem to come across as more male than female by an overwhelming majority of people in many different countries (which is why his pronoun is usually male), which may say something very strongly about the lack of decent "fathering" and nurturing male role models.) In mediation, many of us third gender people learn to do this, putting forth supportive female and male "faces" by turns so as to let everyone there know that we understand them. Eventually, we learn to put forth faces that reflect understanding of whatever polarity is causing conflict, and so bring it to a compromise. Our experiences as living compromises ourselves helps up to bring each side to the center.

Obatala is also concerned with healing, and the huge amount of trauma apparent in our community shows how much we need this. In my state, as many as one-quarter of post-transition transsexuals are on some kind of fixed-income disability. Gender dysphoria often comes hand-in-hand with psychological syndromes such as post-traumatic stress disorder, dissociative disorders, depression, and anxiety. (Anecdotally, there also seem to be a surprisingly percentage of gender dysphoric people with high-functioning autistic-spectrum disorders, especially among young people.) Even assuming for a situation with good parental and family support; even assuming that we were able to hide enough of our gender-transgressive behavior to avoid harassment, queer-bashing, and assault; even supposing that we were able to cover up

enough to stay employed and not end up homeless or on the streets; there is
still a great deal of intrinsic trauma and discomfort in having such an
ambivalent relationship with our own bodies and social roles. If we were raised
in families where such things were viewed as negative or evil, it may have taken
years to discard the crippling, ground-in guilt and shame. We need the strong,
soft, objective care that a father-mother figure gives us; a figure that does not
require us to side with Mommy or Daddy, or with the male or female sides of
ourselves.

Another issue that we need to come to terms with is the healing of our
own bodies, especially that of transsexuals who are dependent on hormones and
surgeries to gain and maintain the shape that will save their sanity. There are
few studies and little information on the side effects of long-term hormone
usage, except for its negative effect on the liver in some cases. There is little
information on how surgeries last long-term, and how to take care of our
morphed bodies properly. Part of this, of course, is that we are generally willing
to take the risks anyway, for our own sanity. When other doctors complain to
my naturopath about her willingness to treat transsexuals even when their
hormones create additional physical problems, or interfere somewhat with other
treatments, she reminds them that untreated transsexualism has a strikingly
high fatality rate. We don't have the luxury of time-tested, secure treatments;
we can take what's given or get nothing.

It's an ambivalent and difficult situation; I am reminded of the surgeon
who castigated the roomful of FTMs who didn't want to get phalloplasties
because they were waiting for the iffy surgery to improve. The surgeon pointed
out that the only way that such surgeries improve is with continual practice on
the bodies of "sacrificial" subjects; that MTF surgery got to the point that it is
now because generations of MTFs were willing to put up with substandard
vaginas, and now their sisters have a better deal thanks to them. His words
appalled everyone in the room, including myself, and the fact that there might
be a grain of truth in them was even more appalling. Still, if we had a less
freakish class in society, would surgeons find a way to get better without
sacrificial bodies? Not being a surgeon, I can't say.

Being "medically managed individuals" means that we are dependent on doctors to continually help us in maintaining our sense of connection with our bodies, and this can be difficult. No one is writing the *Our Bodies, Ourselves* for transsexuals, and I don't see very many transsexuals going into medical school for the purpose of treating their brothers and sisters and creating a fully trans-immersive clinic. Health care can be spotty, depending on where you live. We are also dependent on the products of large, corrupt pharmaceutical companies to survive. These are hard things that can weigh us down. How does one create sacredness in the midst of medicalization?

Sometimes, all it takes is mindfulness. One FTM came to me with his first vial of testosterone, wanting a ritual for the first shot. We were both aware of the origins of that drug—slaughterhouse byproducts from possibly ill-treated animals—and we were also aware of the general track record of the pharmaceutical company that produced it. On the other hand, we both wanted and needed it. I drove the hormones into his body with an injunction that his flesh would transmute the burden of that associated wrongdoing because his life was lived with values that opposed its makers. He would take this spiritually tainted substance into himself, and use it to fuel a new life that would add itself to the side of values that were not materialistic and cruel. In this way, step by mindful step, we can subvert, reclaim, redeem all poisons. This, in itself, is an act of healing not only of the world but of the self as well.

Discussion questions

Is your nurturing style more "male" or more "female"? Who made the decision to assign those labels to those particular styles, and why? Is there a biological basis, or is it completely social? How did your own parents influence your nurturing style—for better or for worse? Did you learn how to nurture from them, or from somewhere else? What do you think it would have been like, having a parent who was a blend of both mother and father in one being? If you are transgendered and have children, are you this parent for them? If not, what could you do to achieve this position? How do your male and female sides handle nurturing differently? How about conflict? Has being third gender allowed you to understand a wider range of people, and if so, how?

Inner world activity #1

Honor your inner nurturer—and yourself—by setting aside one day to nurture no one but yourself, and your male and female sides. Ask each of them: What is it you need in order to be nourished? How can you nurture the other, and me as a whole? Do those things, without guilt or hurrying.

Inner world activity #2

Obatala is also known as a fair and just lawgiver. Think about the behavioral "rules" you have absorbed from your upbringing and your past decisions. Are they fair to your male and female sides? Is someone being shortchanged? If so, they deserve a chance to plead their cases. Lay a white cloth on the floor, big enough to sit on. This is the seat of the lawgiver. Sit before it, and let the part of yourself that feels it is being discriminated against by gender speak its piece. Then move to the lawgiver's seat and sit silently for a long time. Breathe deeply and center yourself, and then speak to that part of you from an objective but compassionate viewpoint. If you find you cannot reach this viewpoint, adjourn "court" and spend time over the next week sitting on the white cloth, striving for such a voice. In order for your internal lawgiver to be respected, s/he must make rules worthy of respect and arising from justice and mercy, not fear or contempt.

Outer world activity #1

If you think you have the temperament for it, take training in mediation and nonviolence training. Go to any event or gathering as an openly transgendered person and offer your services free as a mediator and peacemaker.

Outer world activity #2

If you're transgendered, start a Circle of Healing for other transfolk. It doesn't have to be anything elaborate, just a place where people can get together and talk about the pain and anguish they've gone through. Make a rule about being as nonjudgmental as possible; try to keep advice-giving to a minimum. Instead, acknowledge each person as having been heard and make them feel valued and safe.

The Ritual: White Bath

This is not a traditional Yoruba ritual; I suggest that if you are interested, you should contact a local priest of Voudoun, Santeria, Umbanda or Candomble. Anyone, however, can talk to the *orishas*.

Perform this ritual on a Sunday, Obatala's day. You will need to set up an altar, preferably in the highest point in the house. It can be small, if necessary. Lay down a white cloth and a small figure of an elephant. Give Obatala a cup of coconut milk, and feed him some pears, snails, or black-eyed peas. Light coconut incense.

Greet Obatala thus: *Maferefun Baba-Iya!* Ask Obatala to help you with whatever unrest is in your life, and to bring you peace.

Go run a bath of hot water, and pour a few cups of coconut milk into it. Lie down and relax until you are completely at peace. Obatala will take care of things.

Interview with Dani Everton (2008)

(Dani Sousa-Everton is a massage therapist in Massachusetts.)

Tell us about your gender identity. Where are you on the spectrum?

Dani: I'm female bodied, but I was pretty much born with a male brain. I'm effeminate, and I think if you took the physical sex out of the equation, I may have had a (stereo)typical gay boy's life of playing house and also playing kickball. I think if there was a number line with male being 0 and female being 10, I'd be about 3.7. I prefer male pronouns, even though I wear panties and the occasional makeup when I'm performing. (By performing, I mean fire dancing, or doing a body-mod photo shoot with my friends who need to fill up portfolios.)

Tell us about your spiritual path, and how you got there.

Dani: I was raised Christian, but I think it was far different than the typical description. I think my mother really is a Christian, or at least what other Christians should aspire to be. She taught me about love, that God/Jesus loved *everyone*. For years I didn't know that she helped the poor, and when she told me, I asked, "Why didn't you tell me sooner? I always thought you just worked on Sundays!" She told me, "You don't brag about what you do." Because of this, Mom and the family jumped from church to church. There was a lot of petty drama wherever we went. Mom was either too foreign or too feminist for their liking. We stopped going to church, but we never stopped believing.

Mom also raised me rather mystical. It might have been the fact she came from Sao Miguel in the Azores, and there were a lot of traditional folk beliefs and *brujas*. My baby blanket was actually made by a *bruja*, which is kind of cool now that I think of it. Things like believing in the evil eye or Tarot were common. You'd go to mass and then to the fortune teller afterwards. I leaned more towards mysticism, I think, because I was readily accepted there as an "other". While my mother loves me to death and deals well with me being transgendered, other places couldn't.

I found Wicca really early on, at about 12. I remember reading Starhawk from the library, and feeling so left out because I didn't feel I was female. I wondered if I could even practice Wicca, which has such an emphasis on the feminine, even though I was rejecting that. Pagan women online would tell me, "Oh you got your period! That's so lovely, a gift from the Goddess!" and I'd literally cringe. After years of soul searching, coming to terms that I do in fact feel male in my mind, I ended up being an eclectic pagan with a bit of old Portuguese mysticism thrown in. I feel devoted to service, and mostly a healer path. I was always told I had "Jesus hands" when massaging my older relatives' hands, and they'd give me a dollar (I was five, I thought a dollar was super). When I had the opportunity to become a massage therapist, I was overjoyed. I knew this was what I wanted to do. I later found out how spiritual healing can be.

How does your transgender experience affect your spiritual path? Do you see it as an integral part?

Dani: My first Reiki treatment was phenomenal. The teacher guided me through a meditation, and it was the most profound spiritual event ever. I was crying, not sobbing, just a slow river. In the meditation, I was led to a garden. I was crossing a bridge over a small pond, and I saw something come from the water onto the bridge. It was me. I mean, it didn't look like me—he was obviously taller, much more square-framed, longer hair, more of my Dad's chin, and a willowy body ... but it was like my brain was finally looking in a mirror for the first time. I spoke with Myself (for the sake of reference, this spiritual Me will have capitals), and I could faintly hear my Reiki Master's voice in the background saying "...ask a question." I blurted out, "When can I become a man?"

Myself kind of looked perplexed. "There's no *becoming*. You are." I could hear the subtle wispy voice of my Reiki Master again, "...receive a gift," and I was confused now. Myself seemed to know what to do, and embraced me. My nose came to his chin, and I am about 5'7", so he was tall. I stood stark still. "That'll be your gift, the healing touch," he said. I felt something go through me, and beyond me. I knew about gender variant people being healers in tribal societies, and I felt like the universal thread that connected that ability was coming through me. I feel like I can pass that along now too.

After I was slowly led out of the meditation, there was a lump in my throat and things felt clear. I had always figured that there was a "before" and "after" thing with my gender—that the only way to be male was to "become" male. But, clearly, I had always been male, with a different-flavored coating.

I firmly believe that my spiritual path is to help people through touch. I work with a variety of clients: rape survivors, children (some with anxiety attacks), injured people, my family, animals, and myself. I give great gratitude to the Higher Spirits (as I call Them), and no longer go on about how life is unfair when I talk to them about my female body. I see Their purpose, and the ability for healing in this mismatched body which I can put to good use. Because of this, there is no distinction between being transgender and being spiritual for me. They go hand in hand.

What do we have to teach the rest of the world about spirituality?

Dani: To put it bluntly, "Hey look at all the things we can do, motherfuckers." To put it in better words, I think we can make a positive voice for ourselves. We can become great people. I think we're reclaiming the roles that were held thousands of years ago when we were respected individuals. However, there are still those who are too "afflicted by the madness" to see this. We'll get there, eventually, and maybe my (future) adopted children can see them openly. Maybe they'll even do protests about gender specific bathrooms in kindergarten. Maybe my children will someday show a new generation about patriarchy, sexism, and transphobia. It'll happen.

Interview with Joshua Tenpenny (2008)

(Joshua Tenpenny is an FTM massage therapist, Asian bodyworker, and Shiatsu practitioner. He is the developer of the Body Congruence theory and bodywork.)

Tell us about your gender identity.

Joshua: I'm a post-transition FTM. I don't have a solidly male gender identity, but I am comfortable presenting entirely as male. Being trans, or even being male, isn't a huge part of my identity at this point in my life.

Tell us about your spiritual path of healing.

Joshua: My background was in computer engineering, but at some point I decided that I couldn't work with machines for the rest of my life. I've always found it very natural to communicate with people through touch, which led me to my career as a bodyworker. This happened shortly after transition, and I found it ironic that I was moving from being one of the few women in a male-dominated field to being one of the few men in a female-dominated field. And unlike engineering, my gender often becomes a subject of conversation with colleagues and clients. People respond very differently to the idea of being touched by a man rather than a woman.

During the course of my training, I did bodywork on a wide variety of energy-aware people, and I saw how their psychological and spiritual experiences were reflected in their energetic responses to touch. Many of the people that I worked on were transgendered or had other issues around body and identity. Through this process, I developed the theory of Body Congruence, as a way to help their physical body work in harmony with their energy.

While the physical aspects of bodywork came to me quite easily, I didn't have the same knack for energy work. Because of this, I have a very physical approach to energetic healing. I primarily work with the physical body to affect the energy, rather than the other way around. Learning Asian techniques which use the body's energy channels has provided me with a detailed and systematic way to work energetically, without requiring a strong intuitive energetic connection. My body has always been my most effective tool for healing.

How does your work relate to transgendered people in general?

Joshua: As a bodyworker, I recognize how important it is for people to develop a healthy relationship with their bodies, and how difficult this can be when there has been incongruence between a person's sense of identity and their physical expression of gender. Bodywork can help connect a person to their body and develop a healthy relationship, but individuals with unique forms of gender expression often have concerns about being touched and how their bodies are perceived by others. I try to create a supportive environment where individuals can receive bodywork without concerns about having to explain or hide binders, body hair, prosthetics, or other aspects of their gender expression. To get the most benefit from any form of bodywork, it is vital that the individual be comfortable with their provider and knows that the provider is comfortable with them.

What's the most important thing you can tell transgendered people about their bodies and their health?

Joshua: You have a body. That isn't such a bad thing! Learning to love, accept, and respect your body can be one of the biggest challenges a transgendered person faces in their personal development. Even if you do not like your body, even if it causes you great pain, it is yours and you must take care of it. In some ways it is like raising a difficult child. You can't just say, "I hate this child, I want a different one," and expect to get anywhere with that. Punishing or neglecting your body isn't going to make it change. Love your body, and take good care of it.

Chapter 10
Sacred Kings: Sacrifice and Transition

One of the moments that was pivotal to my decision to transition happened several years ago when I was in a meeting, wearing a dress, with long hair, and trying to pass as feminine. The meeting was about the inclusion of gay and lesbian people in a Christian ecumenical organization, and one of the participants was a Lakota Sioux woman. She was talking to the mostly straight people in the room about her tribe's beliefs in two-spirited people, about how they were sacred because they embodied the male and the female. She said all of this while looking directly at me, and I was very unnerved, particularly that someone could see through all my female disguises. I went up to her afterwards to talk, but before I could get a word out, she said, "This is your path and you will have to walk it," and walked away. It really made me take notice, and I began to face up to what she'd said, spiritually, from that point.

–Justin Tanis, FTM clergy
Metropolitan Community Church

The Myth

Before I transitioned, my lover carefully crafted me my first strap-on harness and picked out an expensive prosthesis to use in it. At first I was afraid to use it, afraid I'd like it too much, but eventually I became (as I'd feared) very attached to it. Then disaster struck. I'd always been an ambivalent housekeeper at best, and one day the whole thing got lost in the rubble of my messy room. I tore apart the house, my panic rising when my search seemed increasingly futile. I can only describe the emotion that I felt as that of castration. I'd lost my cock! Whatever would I do! Luckily I had an option not open to most traditional sacred kings; I went downtown to the sex store and bought another one for $8.95. Ah, if all spiritual crises could be solved so easily.

Later, as my hormone problems grew and I had no luck finding doctors who would take on an intersexual who wanted testosterone, my menstrual periods grew to a terrible, debilitating flood each month. My regular doctor was alarmed by the fact that there wasn't enough blood in the whites of my eyes. I referred to my menstruation as my "Attis time", because during its flood I was painfully aware of my lack of male genitalia, and I couldn't use my harness. "If your genitals cramped painfully and gushed blood once a month on top of being the wrong ones," I challenged a MTF friend once, "you'd have cut them off a long time ago!"

The myth of the sacred king—Ing, Tammuz, Dumuzi, Dionysus, Attis, Frey, Christ, and others too numerous to mention—is one of the defining archetypes of Western culture. In ancient times, the fertility of the land depended upon the ceremonial ruler's ability to magically become one with the land and its people, either in soul or in body. Kingship was originally as much a ritual as a ceremonial duty; the king was high priest and sacred phallus as well as ruler and war leader. In some cases, he was required to marry (at least ceremonially) a priestess representing the Earth and its fertility. In most cases, especially in the early days, he was also sacrificed when he grew old, or a famine struck, or some other situation needed a messenger to heaven.

Somewhere along the line, kings who didn't want to give up their actual power created the custom of the "sacred king", the stand-in for the ruler whose presence separated the physical and spiritual aspects of kingship into two different men. The "sacred king" was crowned, robed, and allowed to act as though he were king in every way except that of political power, for a period ranging from one day to seven years, depending on the specific culture. then, at the end of his term, he would be ceremonially castrated, in order to give his sacred blood and phallic energy back to the Earth, and sometimes—but not always—killed.

In many legends and accounts, the sacred king doesn't die, or doesn't quite die. He is, however, changed. Attis remains in a state of perfect preservation, forever somnolent like Sleeping Beauty. In some ancient Norse lands, the sacrificial representatives of the Norse grain god Ing/Frey, if they lived, were allowed to live on as women, forming the core of secret magical groups of "unmanly men" who wore women's clothing and were accepted into society this way. Odin (whose twelfth title is *Jalkr*, "Eunuch"), spent a year living in women's clothing under the eye of the goddess Freya in order to learn the *seidhr* or women's mysteries. The Greek deity Dionysus is castrated in the temple of Cybele in order to be purified, and after that wears woman's clothing and carries his disembodied phallus on a stick, the pine-cone-topped *thyrsus*. Ritual castration—making dangling genitalia into a bleeding hole—seemed to be a primitive way to ritually make a man into a woman, and thus give him the Goddess's magical powers.

Part of the experience of changing one's gender role full-time in this society is the sense of sacrifice we encounter—of normalcy, of acceptance, and sometimes of our friends, family, spouses, jobs, homes, children and other things most people take for granted. "I had to give up everything I had," one transsexual said to me, "in order to gain everything I ever wanted." As discussed previously, there is a sense of death, of one's life being torn apart and restarted, often painfully; of laying down the old life in exchange for an uncertain future. We die, socially and psychologically, and in other ways. Then we come back in a different form. Yet another transsexual's comment was: "It's like being reincarnated ... only you get to come into it as an adult and keep all your memories."

Transition, for us, is a time of rebirth, and not in a painless manner, but one more likely resembling an actual birth: crushing pain, fear, struggle, prolonged agony, and a release that is mingled joy and relief. It is one of the hardest things that anyone can do, even if one is reasonably sure that one will not be homeless, jobless, and alone in short order, something that cannot always be assured. We sacrifice ourselves, our identities, our lives, much like the sacred kings of ancient times. Like them, we may also go under the knife.

Male-to-female transsexuals will see immediate parallels with their own experiences in the king-to-woman paradigm, but what is not so obvious is that female-to-male transsexuals live the sacred king archetype in reverse, turning the traditional sequence of man-to-castrated-and-bleeding-man-to-woman around to become woman-to-castrated-and-bleeding-man-to-whole-man at last. Who is more like Ing, or Attis—the MTF on her way out of surgery, or the FTM who is painfully aware of his lack of a penis? There is a point on common to both sides, and it is one of pain and loss, after which new life begins.

As we've noted in the chapter on going into the Underworld, transition is that point just before the blackness yields to the white—often the worst and darkest moment of all. It's common, wry knowledge among transsexuals that the year just before transition is the worst one of all. It's not just the one where all the external bad things happen, it's also the one where you behave the worst. People's partners nod knowingly when it's brought up—"Good God, yes, he (she) was terrible during that time. I almost left, but fortunately he (she) finally got through transition and ceased to be a jerk."

Still, the external factors do make a difference. The final pre-transition year isn't just the worst because it's the year that you finally get sick of living like this and decide to do something about it. I've seen people calmly and levelly decide to transition in a few years, create a life that can sustain the change, and figure that they'll sail through it ... and then, suddenly, a year from their projected date, everything falls down. Obstacles come out of nowhere and hit them. Other people in their lives have breakdowns. Their company folds and they get a pink slip. It's not, as some have worried, the Universe telling them not to take this path. It would have happened anyway. It's a kind of cosmic housecleaning, getting all the disasters out of the way, clearing out the deadweight from the life about to be transformed—or at least marking out what's deadweight to be cleared, and you're supposed to see the signs and do it yourself.

Declaring your intention to the Universe to undergo this kind of great, transformative life change stimulates the Universe to do whatever is necessary to make sure that it is truly a great transformative life change, not a casual makeover that one can slip through with hardly a wrinkle. That's as it should be. The few who don't go through this ordeal, who have somehow managed to stack the deck so that they slip by the Universe's intentions ... they're the ones that I fear for even more, because it will catch up to them. When you know you're going to have to change, it's easier to get used to the idea of Change. When you've gotten to what looked like the Promised Land and you think everything's going to be all right now, getting hit with the avalanche at that point is much more disheartening.

Transition usually ends up being about a lot more than getting the letter on your driver's license changed, coming out to your friends, and buying a new wardrobe. It also involves adjusting to a whole new set of societal perceptions, which we may or may not entirely enjoy. We discover, sometimes to our chagrin, that the work of making choices isn't over; it has merely shifted to a new set. Do I come out or stay in the closet? Do I disclose my condition to that cute thing at the bar now or after the first kiss? Do I stand up to that dude making the sexist or homophobic comments, or keep my mouth shut and my eye unblackened? Do I stand up and tell my story, or stay quiet and pretend to be normal? Is that mannerism, that activity, that career choice, that shirt too feminine or masculine? Will I have to give up things I like in order to fit in with my chosen gender group? Do I care about what they think? Should I?

"I'm realizing that my clothing choices are terribly limited; that they have to be if I want to put across a male exterior," says a FTM from Michigan. "It's not easy to find something that's acceptable for me. I'm bored with most male clothing. This cramps my style."

"I really had no idea that I'd be so discriminated against," says a MTF transsexual from North Carolina. "I'm lucky in that I pass well, but even then I'm less likely to get a job in my field than a male candidate is. They say they're not sexist, but they lie. And I had no idea how terrified I'd be walking the streets—no matter how I'm read I'm someone it's OK to attack. And the guys in my office make sexual comments, and when I think it's directed at me I can't handle it, I flush and want to die."

"When I was a dyke," says a young FTM at a gender conference, "I'd get in people's faces about bad behavior and they'd yell at me, but that's all. Now I look like a guy, and I got in some drunk's face about harassing my friend, and he punched me! I honestly didn't realize that would happen."

It isn't fair, and it isn't right, and we'd all like to change it someday, but we have to live in it now. Rigid sex roles, enforced with strict painful techniques up to and including violence, are alive and well and show no signs of spontaneously croaking any time soon. Both male and female roles have parts that are excruciating and suffocating, varying with region, class, and ethnic background. For many transsexuals, the new roles may seem vindicating, exciting, especially in the beginning. It may take time for it to dawn on them what a difficult time both men and women have in our society. Violating the rules brings punishment, subtle or overt, and following them slavishly dulls the spirit.

Finding worms in the golden apple sought for so long may be one of the causes of post-surgical suicide.

Some transsexuals, especially younger ones, are wary of—or downright hostile to—traditional roles, and want to express a countercultural, rebellious or unique flavor of manhood or womanhood. For them, stepping out of one tight box and into another is no bargain. For these folk, reluctance to take on the social unfairness of the role that is forced on their chosen gender forms part of their reason for delaying or rejecting a gender change. They may need to come to terms with how to handle the social aspect first, before taking on the physical changes.

For myself, I hated the idea of wearing drab colors and acting tough or reserved, of not making eye contact, of embracing the idea of confrontational violence. Of pro football and ties and short hair. I felt that I couldn't possibly be a "real" transsexual, since a "real" man would long for and embrace all these things. Right? It kept me holding on to an increasingly uncomfortable feminized body past my thirtieth birthday. I didn't want to be a man like any of the men I'd grown up with. The idea revolted me. I wanted to wear lace and brocade and yes, occasionally skirts. I wanted to make eye contact and extravagant gestures. I knew there were guys who were like that, although at that time I didn't know any. I also knew that they were likely to get beat up a lot.

I saw a talk show on FTMs about the time I started wrestling with the issue; I tuned in excitedly and saw a row of neatly dressed guys in conservative suits, sitting with rigidly male body language and talking in monotones. At one point a female audience member stood and pointed out that they all claimed to be happier now that they'd changed, but they didn't look all that happy. "Of course I'm happy," said one of them in a deadpan voice, never cracking a smile. I cringed.

I'd like to believe, decades after the fact, that these guys were suffering from the twin demons of cultural overcompensation and stage fright; that they did, indeed, giggle occasionally, but I could be wrong. I did eventually meet men who were like me, or like who I wanted to be; most were gay or bisexual, and they did worry about being beaten up, but it didn't stop them. They did what they wanted, and fought the battle against male cultural training on a daily basis. They were role models. *I could be a man like that,* I thought. *I can do this.* (And I did, and to date I have not been beaten up. Knock on wood.)

Discussion Questions

What does this transition symbolize to you? What do you expect to get from it? (Be honest.) What traits are you taking from your upbringing that are useful and that might give you an advantage over "genetic" men and women? What traits do you feel that you need to purge, and why? Are the reasons ones of social camouflage? Being liked? Bad habits that create obstacles? How do you intend to go about changing things?

What sort of a man or woman do you intend to be? Who are your role models? How do you feel about how men and women are "expected" to be? Do you intend to be a rebel? Do you feel guilty about that? Why? Do you intend to be fairly average or stereotypical? Do you feel guilty about that? Why?

What have you sacrificed to get where you are? What will this transition force you to sacrifice further? Do you think you are ready? Does this feel like a rebirth? If so, what part of you is dying?

How do you feel about your genitals? Don't just answer in simple terms, such as "good" or "bad"—talk about it in detail. Will the fact that you will never have functioning gonads make a difference to your manhood or womanhood? If so, why? If not, why not? What psychological crutches do you use to get around the problem of mismatched anatomy?

Inner world activity

Go through your desk drawers and start giving things away. As you decide what to give away and what to keep, ask yourself why each thing is no longer appropriate. If it was meant for someone that you were only trying to be, it need to go to a better home. However, don't purge everything. I suggest keeping some things for the sake of honoring the memory of the survivor that you were. Then either have a party, or make your giveaway part of the ritual below. Explain to each person you gift what the item meant to you, and why you feel that it is an appropriate gift for them.

Outer world activity

Even if you're not transgendered, go to your boss or work staff or place of volunteer work or any other place or organization you spend a lot of time with. Ask about the issue of transgendered people and how they would be treated if they were to transition on the job. Discuss how it would be better to have a supportive, inclusive policy in place before any are actually hired, so as to head off future problems. The policy should address issues of workplace bathrooms and staff education. Offer to find some transgendered people to come in and speak. (There are plenty of groups who would offer to help.) If you are rebuffed, try to get someone else in the company or organization to bring up the issue, and then someone else, and someone else. About the sixth or eighth time that someone brings it up, it might get taken seriously.

The Ritual: Transition

Transition is the second great turning point in the path of gender change, after the initial coming-to-terms with the issue. For some, transition is just the next in a series of steps that may end in surgery; for others, who choose not to alter themselves further, it is the final moment of truth. In any case, it is the death-and-rebirth moment, the Phoenix rising from the flames, the leap off the cliff. It is terrifying and paralyzing, and it should be. It is also exhilarating, and it should be. Transfolk may commemorate this moment in many different ways, as unique as each of them, but there is usually a sense of "crossing", of rites of passage as profound as the puberty rites our culture should have and doesn't.

The transition ritual that follows has been adapted for use by a variety of people, all of whom added their own unique twists to it. One FTM who wanted to leave the women's community with a positive experience on both sides had a suit of ceremonial armor made, and brought a sword. The women who had been invited to form the first circle dressed him in armor and buckled on his sword, as women had once done for knights who were their champions. They asked him not to forget everything he had learned by living in their "queendom", and asked him to be their champion in the "kingdom" he was headed for. He pledged to remember, and to defend whenever possible, and they sent him on his way.

Another MTF asked all the heterosexual men in the first circle to tell her that she was beautiful in their eyes, and accepted kisses from several, feeling that what she wanted most to hear from them was that they no longer saw her as one of them but as something more desirable. Yet another, transitioning from a gay man to a lesbian relationship, had a special finish with both her lovers, current and former. The gay man she had amicably separated from made love to her one last time in an upstairs bedroom, and then escorted her into the first circle. After the last circle, which contained her new female lover, she retired to a different bedroom and celebrated her new partnership as a woman.

I would like to stress one very important thing before we go on, for the sake of everyone out there who is thinking, "But I'm not sure I was a (fill in the blank) before, and I'm not sure I'm going to end up completely a (fill in the blank) after this change." This ritual of transition does not have to mean that you are changing an internal identity from solidly male to solidly female, although if that's what it does mean to you, that's fine too. What this ritual is about it the social change from one role to another, something that will probably be fraught with difficulties but hopefully will be worth the trouble.

Just as standing up in front of a lot of people and pledging to each other does not legitimize, guarantee or solidify a couple's love, living as male or female in this society does not have to mean that you actually believe you are one or the other, although you might and that's OK. That wedding ceremony is done for the sake of the couple's relationship with the larger community that they live in, who they want to acknowledge and congratulate their love. We need to be acknowledged and congratulated when we make such a large step with our public identities, when we sacrifice the might-have-been for the what-will-be.

First, you'll need a place to hold it that has at least three separate areas, close enough to walk to but far enough apart so that any chanting, singing, or other noise done in one group won't bother the other ones. Everyone invited should divide up into three groups—male, female, and third gender. How you want to go about defining each one is your prerogative, but we strongly suggest that you let each person define themselves and choose their own group.

Choosing friends to take part in this should be done carefully; they should all be at least supportive of the initiate, and willing to see you through this change with good grace and goodwill. The facilitator and leader of the third group—the chosen gender—should be chosen with special care. If you don't have any close friends of your chosen gender, maybe you should think about why that is before going through with this transition. It's a lonely place to dislike everyone of the sex you're going to be living in.

The initiate starts with the group they are leaving, wearing what they can of the clothes they used to wear. This part is a giveaway; the initiate gives away as gifts to the people in the circle as many items as they think are appropriate and that they no longer need. The friends in this group remind the initiate to remember them, and what was learned from them, and to take the best with them. Then the initiate moves into the second group, which is the third gender people, who smudge, christen, or otherwise purify them, while helping them to change clothes and assuring them that no matter where they go, they will always be welcome in that circle.

Then the initiate goes on to the third group, their chosen gender. It's important that the initiate know little or nothing of what is about to happen there—ideally, the leader of this third group should have been chosen some time before and have worked out whatever sort of welcoming ritual they come up with. If there are specific needs—for instance, if they expect the initiate to do a four-mile forced march with bad knees—this should be figured out in advance, but as much mystery as possible should be maintained. We all go into the unknown with no map except our own inner will and the compass of others' experiences.

Afterwards, everyone meets at the center point and a circle is formed; everyone gives the initiate their blessing and well-wishes, and speaks whatever words they want to. We never asked anyone to bring gifts for the initiate, but they always do anyway.

Interviews: Two Transition Rituals (2001)

Maureen's Story

(Maureen is a male-to-female transgendered Pagan and minister with the Church of the Sacred Earth.)

I grew up with a transgendered identity that I did not know how to deal with. The name my mother gave me at birth is Maureen. It took my family about a week to convince her that she did not have another daughter; that her child in fact had a penis and should be given a boy's name. That's when my name was changed to Brian.

At least from the age of five, if not earlier, I had constant dreams of being changed into a girl. This different identity was something I was very much aware of, but also embarrassed that other people might find out about it. As a teenager in the '70's, the only visible role model available was the drag bars, and they seemed a rather unhealthy environment and I stayed away from them. But there was always the yearning to find some way to express this different identity.

In the '80's, I did find a strong spiritual life in Paganism, for several years doing solitary rituals marking the changes of the seasons and later joining with groups of other Pagans to do rituals. Over time, this led to a personal ritual path of shamanism, and eventually becoming a minister of the Church of the Sacred Earth. The process of becoming a shaman is one that involves strong transformative and healing rituals. Being a minister involves helping people with rites of passage. Eventually the light dawned; I could use these ritual skills to create a rite of passage to reclaim my name. I still had no role models to follow, but I now knew how to use ritual to journey into the unknown realms of the spirit and there find the center.

In the early '90's, I asked a group of friends to help me create and do the ritual. This rite of passage marked a change not only for myself, but also for my identity in the community, so it was important that members of the community participate. We rented a retreat center in a very rustic setting for a weekend night. There is a place at the site called the "monk's hole" that may have once been a root cellar, dug down beneath the roots of a very large old tree. It is a very calm place, and now used for meditation. In the evening, we started a fire in the woodstove in the cabin, and shared a meal. Then we all did an opening circle together to mark the cared space and the cared time and to focus our intent. The women went off to the monk's hole to specifically consecrate that space and prepare it for this ritual. Meanwhile, the men helped prepare me to be sent off.

When the women signaled that they were ready, the men led me down a long winding path through the woods to the monk's hole. As a final ritual and practical act of being in the men's world, I peed in the bushes. They said a final blessing and words on the mystery of being male, handed me over to the women, and then returned to the cabin. The women gave their blessings and final instructions for the vision quest to come, stripped off my male clothing and then helped me naked down into the monk's hole. They made sure I had what was needed to be reasonably comfortable in the hole—my drum, some water, and some blankets if needed, as it was a very clear and chill November night. Then they too returned to the cabin.

I remained alone in the dark beneath the tree, meditating, drumming, chanting, dancing, finding that place in the center, finding that stillness in the dark earth where the seed waits to grow, finding the darkness in the womb from where new life is born. Some long time after the sun rose again, I heard the procession of the women returning. they helped me from the hole, dressed me now in women's clothing, and led me back to the cabin. The men were not there, but outside by a fire. Inside, the women spoke some words in the mystery of being female, then pierced my ears and gave me back my name Maureen. We went outside to join the men, and there we all gave recognition to my new role in the community. I was still part of the men's circle having a penis and having been raised male, but not completely of it by being named differently at birth and having chosen to leave the full company of that circle. I was now part of the women's circle having reclaimed my name and having chosen to join their social roles, but not completely of it since I do not have a vagina and was not raised female in our society. And I am also partly outside of both these circles having experienced the life of being different genders. We all shared food again, closed the ritual, and cleaned the cabin to depart.

Since then, my identity has continued to change and grow as I use the name Maureen in more and more circles of my life and as I continue to work on physically transforming my body. With every change, I am more centered in who I am.

Henry's Tale

Henry's tale isn't told by Henry himself, but is illustrated, with his permission, by two of his friends. I was one of them. Another was our friend Julian, who wrote the following letter to Henry Samuel Rubin, on the occasion of his transition ritual. The three of us were what is referred to in the transgender community as "litter-mates", meaning individuals who come to their decisions to transition around the same time and support each other as they go through it together. We all came out of the same female-to-male support group, which was where Henry told us about his experience at Walden Pond.

He'd been obsessing over his decision as to whether to go ahead and change. I remember him saying to me, "If I do it, I'm nuts, and if I don't do it, I'll go nuts!" Pondering this, he took a long walk along the large frozen pond. Deciding that the ice was firm enough to hold him, he decided to walk across it, but the whole way over he was plagued by the thought that he might fall in. Despite his fears he pressed on, determined to make it all the way across on the ice. At one point he became genuinely worried and turned to go back, only to find that he'd come so far that it would be easier to keep going than to return. Then he saw the fresh footprints of someone else's boots, and realized that he was not the first one to come this way, and if the ice could hold his fellow-traveler, it could hold him as well.

He made his decision on that night, seeing the same parallel in his gender issues. If others could do it and still be alive and vital, so could he, and anyway he'd gone so far it would be impossible to turn back and be the same person that he'd been before. A year later we gathered at the edge of Walden Pond, and Henry went from group to group, giving away his female items, being smudged by the third gender people, and going on to the men's group. Afterwards, when he donned a prayer shawl and was presented with a wine-cup for his new "Bar Mitzvah", Julian read him the following letter.

To Henry from Julian:

When you first told me your plan to commemorate your transition into manhood, I thought immediately of another similar ritual; the Bar Mitzvah, the occasion on which the celebrant proclaims himself a man before his community and before God. And since you are Jewish, I almost asked you if you had been Bar Mitzvahed. But of course you hadn't. So I asked you the second question that came to mind; "Did you have a Bat Mitzvah?" You said just, "Yes," and I didn't ask any more questions.

But I wanted to. I wanted to ask you, when on that day you stood before your family and friends in your best dress, probably new, if you said out loud, "Today I Am A Woman." And I wanted to ask you, how did you feel? Did you feel proud? Did you feel humiliated? Ashamed? Sad? Angry? Did you feel like a fraud? Did you feel anything? Or were you already so good at wrapping yourself in oblivion that you didn't know what you felt? Or maybe you felt nothing at all.

And I wondered where, on that day, was the man, Henry Samuel Rubin, that we are here today to celebrate. Was he inside you, as he always had been, curled tightly in upon himself, but alert, cunning, watching and waiting, even perhaps already "slouching toward Bethlehem to be born?" Or was he then someone yet to be called into existence by a sheer Nietzchean will to power? Someone still to be given shape and form out of the inchoate energy of the universe? Someone conceived in your own imagination, eventually to burst from your skull, just as Athena burst fully formed out of the head of Zeus? Athena, who, appearing as a man, guided Odysseus safely home. Athena, goddess of wisdom who, motherless, absolved the matricidal Orestes, honoring Agamemnon the father over Clytemnestra the mother.

Either way I am honored to be here to celebrate this public affirmation of your journey into manhood. For I too have chosen a similar path, and I know that this choice means risking everything I have acquired and everything I have become for what I might be. It is fueled by hope, hope that someday in the near future I might look in the mirror without flinching, hope that I will run my hand over my chest, and instead of alarm, disgust, hopelessness—or nothing—feel instead beneath my fingertips my own life force inside the body that I finally inhabit.

Part of the reason that I can allow myself to hope, past when hope seemed pointless, frustrating, dangerous even, is you. Because if you could risk the safety of a liveable, if mediocre, existence on the possibility of a passionate, but uncertain real life, then maybe so could I. For this, my most heartfelt thanks.

I commend your courage and integrity, and with my love, friendship, and faith, I offer you, my brother, congratulations.

Chapter 11
The Gallae of Cybele: Strength in Numbers

I do not come to you
save that I confess to being
half man and half
woman. I have seen the ivy cling
to a piece of crumbled
wall so that you cannot tell
by which either
stands: this is to say
if she to whom I cling
is loosened both
of us go down.

–William Carlos Williams

The Myth

There are two endings to the story of Agdistis. One states that s/he dies screaming when Dionysus cuts off hir parts, and a pomegranate tree grows from hir blood. The other story tells a different tale; according to this version, Agdistis does not die, but lives on with hir woman's parts, having the affair with Attis and then causing the madness at the wedding.

Attis does not die, for both Cybele and Agdistis repent and pray for his life. It is partly granted; he lies undecomposing and sleeping for eternity. Every year, two days before the Sanguinaria (see below) a young pine tree, representing Attis, is cut, swathed in linen, and carried in a procession.

The gallae, or male-to-female transsexual priest/esses of Cybele seem to have begun in Phrygia, and were documented there 2300 years ago. When the religion of Cybele was imported into Rome for political reasons (the Romans wanted to pretend that they were descended form the Trojans and thus thought that importing an eastern religion would enhance their credibility) the gallae came with them, scandalizing the conservative Romans. They immediately passed a law stating that the gallae could not hold citizenship, and that any Roman who went through the ritual castration and became a galla would lose their citizenship as well. Although they had temples, called *metro'on*, gallae were frequently "on tour" most of the time, wandering from place to place and telling fortunes and blessing homes for their living.

According to Apuleius and many other contemporary writers, a procession of gallae was a sight to be seen. A shrine containing a statue of Cybele was borne strapped to the back of a donkey, adorned with flowers. The gallae followed, dressed in bright-colored women's *chitons* and *stolae*, heavily made up, bedecked with jewelry and golden hairnets over their bleached and curled locks. Archigallae wore a tall mitred cap that was copied by the early Catholic Church; the Pope essentially wears the same headdress today! Roman writers bemoaned the fact that the long, curly hairstyle of the gallae was at one point catching on among the young male populace at large, as was eyeliner. Many of these priest/esses carried antique (for that era) swords and battleaxes, or played the sacred drums and cymbals. Others carried whips of wool and leather with the pastern bones of sheep braided in, and they would dance ecstatically and whip themselves into a frenzy of endorphins until, in this altered state, they could be approached for spiritual advice and prophecy.

Once a year, on the Day of Blood (the Sanguinaria, March 25), the ritual of self-castration was performed. It was done in public, on the steps of the temple, and in front of the entire populace who would cheer and urge them on. Those who would become gallae were frequently flogged into a high-endorphin altered state by their Cybellean sisters, and then they would sever their genitals with their own hand.

The do-it-yourself aspect and the public viewing were necessary to show the people that their choice was completely voluntary. Besides, the custom was to fling the severed bits out into the crowd, and if they were caught by a bystander or flew into the door or window of a house, it was good luck for the entire household. The family who was blessed in this way would show their thanks by caring for the new galla while she healed, and providing her with her first set of women's clothing.

Although throughout most of the history of the Cybelline temple the castration was reported as being a complete removal of all external genitalia with a pottery shard, by the time of the late empire they were using bronze clamps decorated with figures of Cybele (some found as far north as Roman London) and the castration may have been reduced only to removal of the testicles.

Current scholars of gay history are frequently stymied in their attempts to interpret the gallae as homosexual men when they are forced to consider the ritual castration custom. Although they are characterized as having sexual encounters with men (and occasionally women), and though female garb was often donned by male prostitutes, the castration set the gallae apart in more ways than just religious ones. Psychologically, removal of the organs of sexual pleasure are usually either due to an ascetic distrust of pleasure as evil, or that old bugaboo that no one but a transsexual understands, body dysphoria . Since the Cybelline cult was not an ascetic but rather a hedonistic religion, I don't believe it's too far a leap to assume that these castrations were what passed for SRS in those days. While I don't know a single gay man who would sacrifice his genitalia for any reason, I know more than one male-to-female transsexual who took a razor to themselves in a fit of adolescent dysphoria.

Records of the sex lives of gallae, while often hostile and sneering, show that they enjoyed sex with both men and women. There are writings referring to gallae getting "married" to traditionally masculine men, as well as some who apparently lived as "hairdressers" and "kept lovers" of rich women. Straight male Victorian scholars (and a few modern gay male ones) often had trouble with the concept of feminized, castrated "men" having physical relationships with women; they either leapt to the assumption that a femme role merely masked homoeroticism, or they lacked the imagination to understand how a woman could be satisfied by someone with, effectively, no functioning genitalia. Sexual activity, however, comes in a variety of forms that may not even involve the genitalia of both individuals.

While much criticized by the Roman government, the gallae were apparently revered and appreciated by the common people. The worship of Cybele was one of the most widespread in the Middle East during Roman times, from Spain to Anatolia. Gender-crossing women, as well, were associated with the cult; many writings of the time refer to "amazons" or female warrior-cults as being worshippers of Cybele.

There is also the myth of Atalanta, a Greek princess who chose to hunt and dress in men's clothing, and refused to marry. Her father, who wanted an heir, demanded that she marry someone. In defiance, she staged a racing contest, declaring that she would marry whoever beat her at a footrace. A young man, Melanion, knowing that he could never beat her, set out to outwit her by throwing three golden apples in her path as they raced together. Atalanta swerved to retrieve them and lost the race. The two were married, but Atalanta's father refused to make Melanion his heir; he found the young man unsuitable for some reason. The reason can be inferred by the next part of the story; Atalanta and Melanion "are turned into lions" (become guardians) of the temple of Cybele.

The scholars' confusion around sacred castration echoes modern doctors' and researchers' confusion around the insistence of transsexuals on hormonally and surgically modifying their bodies. Many students of the changing currents in social gender believe that if gender roles were looser (or even nonexistent) no one would be driven to change their bodies. However, the experience of many transgendered people through the age denies this theory.

"Gender dysphoria", a term coined by the medical profession to describe a feeling of dissatisfaction with one's gender, has two separate and unequal parts to it—role dysphoria and body dysphoria. Role dysphoria is basically disliking the social gender role one is forced into due to one's birth sex. The level of role dysphoria an individual person feels can be linked to the rigidity of the roles in any given society; in really strict cultures half the population is probably suffering from a certain level of role dysphoria.

Body dysphoria is different. It makes no sense, even to those of us who suffer from it. It doesn't have anything to do with lipstick or ties or privilege; it's more like longing to be able to stand naked on the street corner and have everyone who passes know nothing about you (except that you're the sort of person who would stand naked on street corners) and say, casually, "Oh, yeah, that's a guy (or girl)." Contrary to popular idea that the body symbolizes the cherished role, the truer reality is that the trappings of the role—clothing, movements, speech patterns—are crutches to help the sufferer pretend that their body is rearranged differently.

Body dysphoria has been likened by transsexuals as a kind of "phantom limb" syndrome, except that the body parts in question were never actually there. Medical researchers have theorized that the developing fetal brain was accidentally programmed to "believe" the body has one set of genitals, and to instruct the central nervous system to react as if it were so, causing confusion and psychological difficulties in the sufferer. And if there's one thing I've learned from being transgendered, it's this: the body is more plastic, more easily altered than the brain.

In our phallus-centered society, where the penis is both biggest taboo and biggest gift, most of the owners of these phalluses have a very hard time imagining how someone could pray to all their gods, night after night, to take away this dangling thing that does not feel right and replace it with a "mere" hole. The idea that transwomen would not only willingly give up that organ but also their privileged place in society for a lifetime of being harassed on the street is mind-boggling to them. At least some of the violent reaction of some men toward transwomen is this sense of their being traitors to their sex; one wonders if transwomen's willingness to give up what these men so value somehow calls that value into question, and violence is the only way not to think about it.

So assuming that justification for body-altering surgery is irrelevant, and that people have been performing this surgery in one way or another throughout history, what is needed is not to change the brain (which doesn't work anyway; transsexuals are notorious for being incurable via therapy) but to see the bodily transformation as a sacred act, a rebirth.

Medical procedures today are treated as anything but sacred. Doctors see the body as a machine to be fixed as quickly and efficiently as possible, and often seem to feel that the inhabiting spirit of this "machine" is more of an obstruction to their work than the reason for which the body is being healed. It may be up to the individual awaiting the knife to create the ritual space and bring it with them internally to the operating room.

One of the important lessons that we can learn from the gallae of Cybele is that they banded together and created their own families. Even though there was a ritual place in society for them, that didn't mean that they did not lose ties to their blood kin. Part of that was expected; when one became a priest/ess or other sort of sacred person, one was set apart, much like when one becomes a monk or nun today. Your family might be proud or disgruntled, but even the supportive ones would recede in favor of the life of the temple. In the cases where becoming a galla meant giving up family, kin, and even citizenship, one's fellow gallae would be all that one had. The gallae themselves referred to each other with familial titles—Mother, Sister, and so forth.

We can see this echoed in the *hijra* of India and their living structures. While *hijra* might have had a respected place in society once, today after centuries of European influence and modern social pressures, they are basically an embarrassment ... and yet younger members keep joining their ranks, although with less frequency. The *hijra* custom is also to create chosen family, to adopt each other as mothers, sisters, and aunts in a matriarchal system. To become a *hijra*, the youth chooses a guru (teacher) and becomes a *chela* (student); the guru shows the *chela* the ropes and protects them from making bad decisions and getting in trouble. In return, the *chela* helps to support the guru financially and helps them in their old age. The *hijra* themselves characterize it as very much a parent-child relationship.

While most Western transwomen may not want to live in intentional communities with each other, it is still important to have strength in numbers. One alone, going into a new situation, is vulnerable. Two are less so. Three make people stand back, and give each other confidence. More than that and the traditionally gendered people no longer feel that they have the majority vote in the situation. It should never be forgotten that Stonewall was begun by a bar full of drag queens ... because they had nothing to lose, and everything to gain.

Discussion questions

How do you feel about a possible future when we could all change sex like we change clothing? Would you do it? More than once? How would it change the way men, women, and ambiguously gendered people are seen and treated?

What would you—and wouldn't you- sacrifice for inner peace?

In this chapter I deal with the surgery and ritual preparation of the male-to-female; in the next with the female-to-male. I realize that much of the gender community tends to pay attention to its femme members first, and that many of the FTMs feel left out. The subject order here is due less due to this kind of overlooking and more to the frustrating fact that this kind of pseudo-reverse-sexism is historical as well. Scholars—both ancient and modern—seem to be much more interested when men change roles than when women do, and there is far less information on the latter.

Discussion questions part 1 (for transwomen)

What is femaleness? Physical? Mental? Biological? Social? How well do these things cross cultures? (If you don't know, it's time to do some studying.) What is femininity? Is it the same thing as femaleness?

How much do you think that the female psyche is bound up with the cyclical nature of the female reproductive organs—the uterus alternately ovulates and bleeds, but the changes in organs during sex are more subtle? Not at all? Some? A lot? When you ask your biowoman friends about this, what do they say? (If you don't have any biowoman friends, try to remedy this situation ASAP. You will learn a lot from them, even if some of the lessons are hard.) How will you learn about the mysteries of the female cycle, and how it affects how women think? Have you actually observed female organs in all phases of their cycle? Did any part of it disgust you? How are you going to work on that, even if you don't expect to have those organs?

Which parts of "women's mysteries" apply to you, and which don't? What parts of traditional femininity can you relate to, and which leave you bewildered or cold? What sort of women are your role models? What sort of women are you repelled by, and why? What do you hope your relationship to women will be in the future? To men? To other transwomen? To transmen? To transfolk who have not yet or are not intending to transition? What commitment will you make to help your sisters, like the gallae before you?

What do the women and men in your life tell you that you have to work on the most?

Inner world activity

If you are getting ready for surgery, list the things that you think it will gain you. Reread your list and ask yourself how many of them are realistic. For example: Genital surgery is not going to affect how you are viewed on the street, nor is it going to make prospective partners overlook the fact that your genitalia once looked like something else. It may not allow you access to gender-limited groups, unless you are willing to lie and run the risk of being found out. Talk to transsexuals who have had surgery at least 5 years ago or more. How do they feel about it this far down the road? What good things did it do for them, and what things did they expect of it that they never got? Make sure you have no unrealistic expectations before you leap in.

Outer world activity #1

Sex reassignment surgery and other specific-to-transsexuals surgeries are only performed by a few doctors, in this country and others, and these doctors have discovered that it is terribly profitable and guarantees them work, as transsexuals are basically a captive market. Many of them have less-than-respectful attitudes towards the people that they may be exploiting. If you're shopping for a surgeon, ask hard questions. Don't be put off, and if the doctor sidesteps or glosses over certain things, consider it a warning sign. This is your body that you are going to lay down on that table. Do not settle, no matter how much you want this. Get hold of medical manuals and read about the surgery that you want, until you can practically do it yourself in your own mind. Knowledge is power. Anyone who goes under not knowing exactly what is going to be done to them, and what every risk is, deserves what they get.

If you don't think you want a traditional sort of surgery, tell them. If they feel that the way you want it done (assuming it's possible) isn't morally right or "normal", hold fast. You are the consumer, and you are the one holding the checkbook. You should have what you want. If you want designer genitals, you should be able to get them. You can always find another doctor. Tell them so.

Outer world activity #2

Surgeons have conventions to discuss methods and techniques. SRS doctors have them, too. Find out when they are happening and go to them. No one will check your M.D. credentials at the door; anyone who registers can come. Once there, speak up. Don't let them talk about transgendered people as if they were freaks or experiments without letting them know that one of them is present, takes offense at their attitude, and is willing to call them on it. Tell them how it feels to be what you are and in the position you are in. Tell them what you want from surgical procedures and ask about new improvements. At the last such convention, jokes were made about the sexual habits of post-op transsexuals in the middle of a presentation, and the brave transgendered folk standing unnoticed in the back of the room felt humiliated.

This helps, of course, if there are quite a few of you attending such conventions. Remember, there is strength in numbers. One person might be dismissed, but a whole bunch is harder to overlook.

The Rituals

Not all transsexuals—and here I use the word to describe people who make permanent changes in their physical bodies in order to ease a long-term discomfort with certain somatic sexual characteristics—are going to have any kind of surgery. This needs to be accepted in the community as a normal variance, without any judgment placed on those who choose to forgo surgery, or certain types of procedures. Vaginoplasty is unnecessarily expensive, painful, prone to complications, and may leave an individual orgasmically impaired. Phalloplasty is all those things as well as being even more expensive and prone to shriveling or rotting off. If anyone in the gender community does not feel that the benefits of these procedures outweigh the disadvantages, their feelings should be respected. And if people may just enjoy their androgynous bodies they way they are and do not want to change them, this too should be respected.

On the other hand, surgery can be, as it was in the days of the Gallae, a great and holy sacrifice to the gods.

Sanguinaria: A Rite of Passage

This is a pre-surgery ritual for male-to-female transsexuals. It has been used for transsexual women opting for orchidectomy (removal of the testicles only) or full vaginoplasty. It should ideally be performed the night before, but if circumstances prevent, it can be done some days before. The original date of the Sanguinaria was March 25; we do know of at least one galla who convinced her surgeon to perform it on that date, so it isn't impossible. Perhaps if more and more transsexual women request it, it will become a custom.

You will need: Drums and cymbals (we used pie plates for some of them). A ritual blade. White roses with good-sized thorns. Milk and fragrant bath oils. Fresh-baked bread. Wine or cider. Red altar cloths and hangings. A piece of white yarn. A smooth stick about 6" long. A new dress, robe or gown in white. A dish of *moretum*, sacred to the Goddess Cybele. (This consists of feta cheese with garlic, celery, vinegar, olive oil, and a pinch of coriander and rue. It's very good, especially for vegetarians.) Wild game bird such as pheasant or quail (chicken can be substituted instead).

The new galla is bathed in a bath with milk and scented oils added to it. Outside, in the main ritual area, the participants should be drumming, banging, chanting, and otherwise making noise and/or music. Assistants that she trusts bathe her and then bring her forth—either naked, or wrapped in white cloth, depending on the modesty of the individual galla.

Someone should be acting as priest/ess, which should ideally be an older MTF, but can in actuality be anyone she trusts. She is given a knife (or a broken potsherd, if you want to be really authentic) by the priest/ess, and asked if she is ready to start anew, in spite of pain and trouble. When (we assume) she assents, she makes a ritual cutting gesture where her genitalia are. Then the priest/ess pricks her finger with one of the thorns on the white rose, letting blood drip onto the white thread. This is then wrapped around a stick, and she is told, "This is your woman's blood, shed for the Goddess." Then she is clothed in the white gown and the knife is given to a friend to throw into a river afterwards.

The new galla can recite the following piece from the hymn to Cybele:

Sing to me, oh Muse
of the Mother of all gods
and of all men,
in the din of rattles
and in the sound of pipes
She delights.
In the howl of wolves
and the roar of glaring lions,
in resounding mountains and wooded glens,
She finds her joy.
And you and all the God/desses
delight in my song.

Open the wine and pour it into the cymbal; the new galla should drink
first, then any other gallae present, then the rest of the company. The lingam-
shaped breads are laid in the drum and passed around similarly. At the finish of
the ceremony, everyone should howl like a pack of wolves in honor of the
Goddess of the Wild Ones. The organs removed should, if possible, be arranged
to be brought home from the hospital and returned personally to the earth.

Accepting the Chalice

This second ritual is more modern and draws less upon specific myths. It is for a transwoman in order to prepare her for a vaginoplasty, and is much simpler than the Sanguinaria ritual. For this one, you will need a large cup or goblet, some kind of special drink (wine if there are no problems with alcohol, perhaps juice or spring water otherwise), three long scarves the color of the sea, a bottle of a scented oil (your choice), and a small cup of salt water. This should be seawater at best, but if you don't live near the ocean, put salt into water and perhaps add a seashell. You will also need someone female-identified to officiate in the ritual. Some transwomen will prefer it to be a genetic female, who knows intimately the mysteries of female shape and biology and can pass them on; others may prefer it to be a post-operative transwoman, who knows the ordeal that she is about to go through and the rewards and trials of the time afterwards. Either way, the initiate should be clothed in red for blood, and be freshly washed in a long, quiet meditative bath with salt in it.

Everyone forms a circle around the initiate, with the priestess in the West. If your tradition invokes the elements, someone at each point of the circle should bless the directions in the name of appropriate female deities—for example, Iris in the East for Air, Hestia in the South for Fire, Aphrodite in the West for Water, and Gaea in the North for Earth. She should face the priestess, kneel, and say, "I come before you now to offer my sacrifice. As the God is sacrificed to the Goddess, so I give up the last manhood of my body, and I come home to myself."

The priestess says, "You have come down a hard path with many twists and turns. The first step in your journey was clarity, realizing what Destiny expected of you, and having the courage to begin." She anoints the initiate's forehead with a drop of the scented oil, and then continues, "The second step was to take into yourself the magical essence of a woman's body, to flow through your brain and change it, to teach you the experience of a woman's magical chemistry." Someone form the circle steps forward and ties the first scarf around the initiate's head, like a headband.

The initiate says, "I have learned why a woman's mind is like the sea, eternally powerful and eternally changing, spreading over all borders, ebbing and flowing with the tides, giving up life from its depths."

The priestess says, "You have taken the third step, which is to take into yourself the woman's sign of nurturing and sensuality." Someone from the circle steps forward and loosely ties the second scarf around the initiate's chest, over her breasts.

The initiate says, "I have learned why a woman's heart is strong, knowing when to stand firm and when to yield."

The priestess says, "Now you must learn what it is to be the chalice of the world, the source of the ocean, the doorway to the soul." Someone from the circle steps forward and ties the third scarf around the initiate's hips. The priestess continues, "The path will continue to be difficult, but the rewards may yet be greater. Are you ready for the joy and the responsibility of womanhood?"

The initiate says, "I am."

The priestess says, "There is one last thing that you must do. Before you sacrifice the last manhood of your body, you must mourn for him, for he sustained your life while you were in hiding and he deserves mourning. Weep for him, so that you may go on with a clean heart." She marks the initiate's face with the salt water as if it was tears; if the initiate can shed a few tears of her own, it would be good. All join in, weeping and wailing, which should slowly change to a chant or group sung note, guided by the priestess. When it is done, the priestess holds up a chalice and presents it to the initiate, saying, "Drink of the lives of the millions of mothers and sisters and daughters who have come before you, and will continue after you are gone." She drinks, and is raised to her feet by the hands of all present, who congratulate her and open the circle to feasting and a party.

Interview with Julia Cybele Cachia (2001)

(Julia is part of a revived metro'on *or temple to the Great Mother Cybele. The* metro'on *is even online in cyberspace as we speak, proving that this is no dead religion, but a living, inspiring faith. The* gallae *have not died out; they've gotten webpages. Hail Cybele!)*

How do you conceive of your gender?

Julia: I'm a post-op transsexual woman who recognizes SRS (sex reassignment surgery) as essentially cosmetic, something of a powerful ritual, yes, but not an event that made me other than the person I've already grown to be. Nature, nurture, destiny ... who claims the wisdom to separate these? Not I, surely. I live and work as a woman, neither particularly concealing my "past" nor imposing it in a manner which I would find overbearing in others.

What is your current spiritual path?

Julia: A good word for it is "Paramythia", derived from the Greek word for "consolation". It seems to me what Marcus Aurelius meant by the exhortation, "to live with the Gods". Not in the worship of an external presence, not immersion in doctrines, nor following self-appointed leaders, but seeking the truth of the spiritual quest in all human history. As my partner said, we began with a child's love of Mother, and the memory of those feelings persists across the generations. I find Cybele within me, archetypal, and reflected in gradual understanding of the cosmos from childhood to this day ... perhaps a profound mystery, perhaps none at all.

How do you see being nontraditionally gendered as affecting—or becoming—your spiritual path?

Julia: It is a great gift, truly a "gift of the Goddess" if one comes to maturity at last. One either receives the crown in self-realization or is shattered along the way if buying into the subtle and not-so-subtle controls of "conventionality". It is a gift to be able to know something of the wholeness of the human experience, as the two "halves" are also good in themselves. Yes, transgendered people who attain wholeness have bridged the worlds and bring living expression of sacredness.

What do you feel that nontraditionally gendered people have to offer to everyone else?

Julia: A return to the Source of Mystery, which means crossing the thresholds of categories: female and male, sacred and profane, all the dualities. Conventional religions are lamps with only the memory of light. And that light may have been some remarkable person long ago whose nature built a bridge across dark spaces.

Interview with Reverend Battakes Cathryn Platine (2008)

(Cathryn Platine is head of the Matreum of Cybele in New York state, a living temple and abbey of Cybele which can be found online at http://gallae.org.)

Tell us about your gender identity.

Cathryn: My gender identity is woman/female. Sounds simple, doesn't it? It is far from so. I've been told by both intersexed people and trans people that I don't exist, that the conditions of my birth are impossible or at least impossibly rare enough I could not possibly be who I am ... and yet I am. Up to now I have mostly kept these things private to myself and those who came to study with me for this reason. I was born a tetragametic chimera, born during the sign of Gemini. In simpler terms, I am, literally, twins in a single person with two different sets of genetics in one body. In my case fraternal twins, one male and one female, that combined around the second or third cellular split. At my birth I embodied Agdistis. I was born at a "cottage" hospital in 1949 and presented with both an apparent penis and labia; the doctor sewed up my labia and declared me male.

From the time I was first able to grasp the concept of male and female, I knew I was female. The circumstances of my birth having been kept from me, when I ran across the concept of "transsexual", I thus assumed that was what I was and "transitioned" as an adult within that context. It was only after I first transitioned that I learned of my own nature, although I had suspected so my entire life. Today my body reflects the Divine Feminine.

Tell us about your spiritual path. How did you get to where you are now?

Cathryn: Again, simply put, I was called from my earliest memories. Once again that sounds simpler than the reality. Around the same time, age three to four, while I was becoming aware I was not the boy everyone said, I was also having very vivid dreams, many of which I remember to this day as if I had them last night instead of some 56-odd years ago. I had a lot of nightmares and quickly learned the technique of lucid dreaming to turn them around and make the "monsters" into allies instead of enemies. But the most vivid dreams that reoccurred over and over were of an enormous, larger-than-life beautiful woman dressed mostly in white robes. In those dreams She comforted me, told me things I could never quite remember upon waking, but those dreams were incredibly peaceful and soothing and had a profound effect on me. Today I know that is the traditional way She calls Her daughters.

Up until kindergarten, my childhood was relatively free of gender policing and playing dress-up with the girl from across the creek was allowed and not discouraged. By the age (in those days) that children were allowed relative freedom from constant parental oversight, I was spending almost all my time in whatever wild area was nearby, and thus spent most of my early childhood in forests and woods. The adults I sought out to learn from were the women that today I would call crones in the best sense. My family tree on both sides is mostly old New England, my father's side the pragmatic and down-to-earth, my mother's side the eccentric free-thinkers, spiritualists and proud as punch of our ancestors. They include Susanna Martin, a Salem witch trial victim from Amesbury, Mass. and William Wood who wrote the book "New England Prospects" that launched much of the immigration to that area in the 1600's, but had his own property taken away for going too native. I grew up with spirits, ghosts, tales of witchcraft, and devoured any books I could find on those subjects. I grew up a Pagan, in other words, hidden in plain sight. I had a personal feminist awaking around 1958 just as second-wave feminism was in it's birth, as a reaction to my own father's patriarchal treatment of my mother. While the world saw me as male, I was always female within my own head, and made as much peace as possible with that.

At age fifteen, our family moved to India, traveling leisurely through Rome, Greece, Turkey, Egypt, and the Middle East both on the way to India and the way back. I "knew" all these ancient places we visited. My father leading the way with an outdated *Europe on Five Dollars a Day* book, we found ourselves over and over off the beaten path of the tourists. We vacationed in Kashmir, I was allowed to travel alone to places like Dehra Dun, Agra and Jaipur. I explored wild places infinitely wilder than I had before, and an India which at the time was closer to the India of the British Raj era than the India of today. I met and spent long hours with "gurus" and Muslims and Hindus of all social classes. I was aware that I would not have been allowed to have any of these experiences had the world seen me as female, while knowing the inequality of that. Strangely enough, my actual gender seemed to be clear to many of the Indian people I encountered, who reminded me that my auburn hair would get me in trouble in many remote villages I visited if I were seen as female, as it was considered the mark of a witch-woman. Our live-in cook never called me by my birth name, but only "Jackie" after Jackie Kennedy who occupied a place in world culture immediately after JFK's assassination. It was his way of telling me he knew who I was and that was fine with him. I most likely met some *hijra* during that time, but was unaware of who they were. Had I been aware, there is little doubt in my own mind I would have gone native and joined them.

My college years were at the height of the counter culture movement of the late sixties. Paganism was coming of age at this time as well and more and more material was coming into my hands, so much so that by the mid-seventies I found myself teaching a course at the Free University at Ohio State on the history of Paganism and the Occult. It was around this time I discovered a sporadic wealth of material on the Mother Goddess traditions, but it was years later before the specifics about Cybele Herself came to hand, as my eventual path was one of the most ruthlessly suppressed of all the Pagan traditions.

Throughout my lifelong studies, I was far more interested in the essence of Pagan theology than I was in the trappings, and abandoned ceremonial magick as a personal dead end in favour of a gnostic approach. In 1989 I ran across a copy of Merlin Stone's *When God was a Woman* in a flea market, and suddenly things clicked into place. I started going back and re-reading the occult "classics" with new eyes. I suddenly kept seeing the name "Cybele" literally leaping from the pages for me in one semi-vague reference after another. The thing that struck me more than anything else was that all the Mother Goddess traditions, presented as totally different religions, weren't. They all shared the same symbols, the same essence and many of the exact same trappings of practice for literally thousands of years.

At the same time, my final bout with the dysphoric imperative was also coming to a head. I had previously managed to come to an accommodation with it short of out-and-out transition; I had learned that I could "be" a woman and have others see me as male. By this time, that had stopped working entirely, and those I met were seeing me as a woman regardless of how aggressively male I tried to appear. Further, it was becoming very distasteful personally to be seen as male. So I transitioned and the Mother Goddess started knocking me around whenever I strayed from Her path. I was directed to establish a reclaiming of Her worship in the form of Cybele, and then move to the Catskills of upstate New York and establish a centre for that tradition. When I balked somewhat at that last, She took away my ability to disobey by handicapping me physically. When the Goddess directs you, She will prevail.

The Cybeline revival began with what Roman and Greek materials we had easy access to. Since then we have expanded that further back to the essence of all Mother Goddess traditions and advanced our theology to reflect what we would have been today without the 1500-year interruption resulting from our wholesale murder by the early church. We are not a reconstructionist path, sticking only to Roman or Greek practice, but a living extension of our own traditions throughout the world and history. As our knowledge of prehistory expands, we absorb and embrace that.

What's the most important thing for trans people to know about spirituality?

Cathryn: Balance, the single most important thing for anyone, but especially trans/intersexed people. It is the concept of walking between the worlds and standing in balance. That is the position the Mother Goddess occupies and She is within all of us. "Walking between the Worlds" is so much more than just gender/sex. It is the intersection of science and magick, the living and the dead, the seen and unseen worlds, the darkness and the light. The gift of being different, and I do see it as a Divine gift and obligation, is the ability to understand what it means to actually put yourself in the place of another and see through their eyes.

I teach from within the concept of the Mother Goddess, but often those very words are misunderstood today. "Mother" brings visions to the modern mind of stay-at-home moms, all-nurturing and devoted to children. Goddess implies a larger-than-life version of the Christian God somewhere out of reach, perhaps sitting on a cloud watching our every move. Both fail if you believe this. The image of the Mother Goddess in every tradition I have studied is the Divine Feminine principle. The image is one we can grasp, but She is also the

Mother who never gives birth, the Goddess of wild places and of lions and birds of prey. Her essence is present in the fact that all higher level life starts off first as female as the default setting in fetal development. She is that within ourselves, male, female, other, that is the spark of Divine, and if you do not find what you seek within, you shall never find it without, because She is with us from the beginning.

The word *Namaste* is a Hindu word now seeing wider use in the West. Literally, it means "the Divine in me acknowledges the Divine in you." Trans and intersexed people have a rich and ancient connection with the Divine as teachers throughout almost all cultures of the world. Several years ago I wrote a series of essays on the transsexual priestesses of the ancient world (http://gallae.com) as a gift of heritage to those who followed me. Today I would write a different version given additional information, gained insight, and having witnessed attempts to turn my own hard-won path into a "tranny" religion when it never was any such thing. Balance is the key.

What do we have to teach the rest of the world, spiritually?

Cathryn: We have the power to challenge gender roles merely by being. This is vastly different from destroying the essences of male and female by rendering asunder all good about maleness and femaleness, but rather teaching others it is possible to become fully human whatever that means to any particular individual. As a dyed-in-the-wool feminist, my opposition to the patriarchy is a given, but my beef with the women's spirituality movement born of Pagan radical feminism has been the desire to replace the patriarchy with a matriarchy and a rewriting of history, particularly of the Goddess cultures, to reflect that. Two-thousand-plus years of a total patriarchal ascendancy over the world can make equality of men and women appear matriarchal, but my own lifelong journey into ancient history and spirituality teaches me that it was equality, not female dominance, that was the hallmark of those cultures.

And thus we return to the concept of balance and standing between worlds. Once you truly accept that everyone and everything around you is also a part of yourself linked by your own Divine nature, you do not need rules to tell you harming others and all around you is harming yourself.

Chapter 12
The Quest: Stories of Manhood Around the Fire

> Graceful son of Pan! ...
> Your fangs gleam,
> The curve of your breast is a lyre;
> Tinklings vibrate in your blond arms,
> Your heart beats in those loins
> that cradle a double sex ...
>
> *–Arthur Rimbaud*

I think that there are blessings and challenges in taking into our lives as men what we learned and experienced as women, as being raised and identified as female. One of the profound ironies I felt in my transition was a female co-worker who worried that I wouldn't be able to make it in the "tougher" world of men, and at the same time, accused me of now having it easier because I now had access to the "old boys' network". I thought of all the things I had been through as a woman, and how strong those things had made me ... and that if I could make it for 30 years in the sexist world as a woman, I could surely make it in a world of men. At the same time, no one is giving a trannyboy a free ticket into the old boys' network.

The mystery I see is how to take that strength with us and into our lives as men, without forgetting where we got it. To be men and to live, with those experiences and the knowledge that we gained, in a way that furthers justice and equity in our lives and in our world, and honors our spirits and journeys.

> *–Justin Tanis, FTM clergy*
> *Metropolitan Community Church*

This chapter doesn't begin with one single myth, because I haven't found a single myth that adequately describes the female-to-male transsexual experience wholly and completely. Instead, I find snippets, patches, tatters, bits; tantalizing fragments of story that I long to patchwork into a quilt to cover us.

In a sense, the FTM transsexual experience is even more a creation of modern technology than the MTF one. In ancient times, priestesses like the *Gallae* stopped the onslaught of their hormones with self-castration, but although there are many records of women who dressed and lived as men, none of them had access to the kind of surgery or body-changing medications that we do today. While a castrated male might occasionally pass nearly naked as a flat-chested woman, latter-day FTMs would have had to hide their bodies fairly thoroughly. They would have had to conceal such things as breasts and menstruation, and be constantly seen as boys through their more delicate features and lack of facial hair. Some might have been able to pass for normal even in carefully controlled sexual situations with women—certainly individuals such as Sean O'Neill, an FTM teen who was prosecuted for having heterosexual sex with unwitting teenage girls, managed to do it—but by and large there probably would have been more limited opportunities.

Testosterone changed all that. While certain cosmetic surgery techniques have been able to help disguise the masculine bodies and faces of MTFs, a sizeable percentage still don't "pass" perfectly (not that "passing" should necessarily be anyone's real goal) and are still perceived as androgynes. Testosterone is powerful stuff. Its permanent effects bathe the bodies of those exposed to it young like an indelible stain, and conversely serves to transform anyone exposed to it later in life so completely that they would not recognize their future selves in a mirror. Nearly all of us FTMs pass perfectly as men, not androgynes, after the stuff is through with us. It's almost frightening, or would be if we didn't want it so much.

We pass except for our crotches, that is; in most cases anyway. Nine out of ten of us don't opt for genital surgery; phalloplasties are expensive and often give poor results and many of us are waiting for better technology. In that one sense, MTFs are slightly better off than we are—vaginoplasties have at least a decent percentage of success these days. In one generation, we have passed from being people who might be perceived by clueless strangers as masculine women to people who those same strangers would perceive, ironically, as castrated men. What does it mean to transform, not away from, but into, a penisless man?

Of course, many FTMs do not choose to transition, and there is a whole range of people who wouldn't call themselves FTMs, who live as butch dykes, boychicks, FTVs (female transvestites) and other folk clearly still in the original mode of manly women. If there's a single clear dividing line between us, it's the moment of the needle in the arm, the start of the physical transformation, and yet even that line is pretty fuzzy. Butch dykes like Leslie Feinberg, who took hormones for years and passed as male, yet who calls hirself a "passing woman" and accepts either pronoun, blur the simple concept of pre-and post-transition still further. The question still remains lurking in the back of our minds, though: Does someone living as a butch woman share the same spiritual mysteries with someone living as a penisless man with a female history (or, for that matter, a man with a female history and a reconstructed phallus)? Do they share some, perhaps, but not others? None at all? There are no answers, yet, to these questions, but I'd sure like to hear them discussed. They are as ambivalent as the fluttering, swirling ambiguity of the archetypes I've dug up.

There is the Jack-A-Roe, the woman wearing the horned mask of the earth god, Giver of Ecstasy, recalling both the stone butch who gives her partner pleasure while sacrificing her own, and the testosterone-enhanced libidos of the frolicking FTMs in the porn flick *Alley of the Tranny Boys*. So many of the vaguely FTM deities that I see are extremely sexual in some way, or have to do with sexuality; this is from figures created long before exogenous testosterone, as well. Perhaps this may be related to the social stereotype that men have "real", initiative sexuality and women's sensual natures are more passive and dependent on the attitudes of the partner. However bogus this idea is in and of itself, it may have been internalized over the years by women who found their internal masculinity to be a freeing doorway to aggressive sexual exploration.

The Jack-a-Roe also touches on the figure of the cross-dressed wandering woman, since there have been several folk songs and tales of "hir", including the popular one performed by the Grateful Dead. Usually the woman in these doggerels lives as a man in order to be a soldier or sailor, to search for and rescue a lost beloved, or to enter a traditionally male trade. That "Jack the Deer" or "Jack the Stag" was the woman designated to play the male role of the Horned God in early witch-covens (see chapter on Baphomet) reflects the idea that such cross-dressing is magical. (Ironically enough, the medieval Inquisitor Jean Bodin was apparently convinced that male and female witches frequently changed their sex by exchanging clothes with each other. Such is the lingering efficacy of ritual transvestism.) The name Jack is curious as well; it is traditionally the nickname for trickster figures, "knaves", the hero who outwits rather than outfights the enemy in fairy tales.

As discussed in chapter 7, the figure of Baphomet does indeed seem to be a figure with breasts and an artificial-looking phallus—one recalls to mind the allegations of Inquisition-tortured "witches" that the Devil's phallus was as cold as iron—and the few remaining ritual items linked to hir worship show not only Baphomet's androgynous figure but that of bearded women, wearing open robes and carrying caduceuses. There are certainly records of leather and metal strap-on phalli in use going all the way back to ancient times; a "passing woman" in Germany centuries ago was executed for using one on her wife. The satyr-god is always Giver of Ecstasy, no matter whether he is framed as Pan (entirely male), Baphomet (androgynous), or other creatures such as Marsyas or the satyrs associated with the Dionysian revels. (Indeed, the "satyrs" on pottery depicting such revels have not only enormous false-looking phalli, but suspiciously false-looking beards as well. I recall some sources saying that no uncastrated men were allowed into the Dionysian orgies, and I wonder.) Those of us who have issues with our genitalia may be a bit taken aback or uncomfortable with the idea of taking on any patron who is associated with sexual ecstasy, and yet here they stand, dicks erect, waiting for us to notice them.

For some of us, the testosterone-induced increase in libido takes the "edge" off of our genital dysphoria; suddenly any erogenous tissue is useful, whether it's the right shape or not, and occasionally we can even fetishize our in-between state. For others of us, the dysphoria does not abate, and the tidal crash between the feelings of genital wrongness and the looming libido is like being crushed between Scylla and Charybdis. The mystery, says the Giver of Ecstasy, is not about sexual denial. He forces the issue, right into our faces, making us deal with it. It is hardly an easy gift; the Horned God with the giant strap-on is no pleasant fairy godfather. His unashamed lust and pride—verging on arrogant swaggering—is something that we, socialized as female, were taught to avoid. We were instructed, often too well, that this was not a power that we were allowed.

Susie Bright wrote tellingly about how disappointed she was by the FTM transition of a butch friend—she perceived him as going from a hard-edged, dangerously sexy butch to a soft, overly polite man, and thus he was no longer attractive to her. Another friend of mine, an intersexual raised and living as male, follows his bisexual girlfriend into lesbian space and is immediately assumed to be an FTM ... because he is by nature quiet, retiring, soft-spoken, and unassertive.

This bit of information bothered me, and kept me up nights for a while thinking about it. For many of us, having listened for years to tirades of what women hate about male behavior, as well as sometimes getting the brunt of that behavior personally, taking on manhood is something we can only ethically do by rejecting everything we or the women around us disliked about men. In some cases, we overcompensate by becoming too soft, too polite, too passive, so as not to offend women (whom we perceive as easily offended). We may be well aware of the double standard that arrogant behavior that is acceptable in queer spheres in a butch is not acceptable in someone perceived as male. Or we may simply have had so little training in being assertive—especially sexually assertive—that we may have no idea how to do it.

It doesn't help matters that in the sexual-appeal hierarchy FTMs are definitely on the bottom of the heap. Even after taking out of the mix all the heterosexuals who will only be attracted to fully male or female bodies, the only genderfuck seen in any kind of mainstream porn is MTF bodies. When the average person says "hermaphrodite", they are usually picturing MTFs. Although being pictured in tacky she-male mafia porn is hardly a fate to be avidly desired, the fact that we don't even exist sexually for nearly all of our society can be pretty hard on one's sexual confidence. When I showed photos of naked, post-mastectomy, extremely built and (to me) quite attractive FTMs to a variety of people, a number of gay men and heterosexual women were disturbed by what appeared, at least at first, to be an otherwise normal, attractive man with no male genitalia in evidence. A few men even instinctively grabbed their crotches as if to save them from this fate. Perhaps if we weren't so sexually invisible, folks might have some kind of mental template to work with in order to consider us attractive and sexual beings. Perhaps we need to learn something from the Giver of Ecstasy about how to reclaim our swagger, how to flaunt our bodies with pride, to make them believe that we're really something worth drooling over. Certainly we won't get anywhere by being polite and retiring about it—except to get shoved even further back in the invisibility closet, that is. At this point, we may well have little to lose.

There is the troubling and difficult figure of the woman warrior, as well. "Amazon" is the word that is popularly used, but so many myths have grown up around that term for the last 3000 years that it is very difficult to separate them from the realities of any actual bands of woman hunters and warriors wandering the Anatolian plains. The ancient Greeks claimed that Amazons cut off one breast in order to better draw their bows, but there is no such evidence of this whenever they are pictured in ancient art. (Of course, most views of Amazons in ancient art are actually just excuses for the sculptor to be able to draw or carve athletic, half-dressed women, so depicting such a mutilation might be counterproductive in an aesthetic sense.)

There is some evidence, however, that tribal people of the areas said to be the original homes of Amazons sometimes pictured their deity as an androgyne much like the Hindu Ardhanarisvara, who is divided vertically down the middle with one side male and one side female. It is possible that any such mutilations were done to make one more like the Divine Androgyne physically, or (more likely) that the myth simply came down as a tangled story from the sight of such statues.

Historically accurate or not, the myth of the Amazons has a powerful pull in our subconscious. By tilting one's head sideways and trying to see a transgendered aspect to it, one courts danger, for it is hardly accurate to label the archetype of the woman warrior as "masculine", and much has been done in modern woman's spirituality to reclaim her as just as feminine as mother and nymph. To assume that boldness, courage, and even violence are naturally the attributes only of males is to make a huge error. Granted, there have been societies where the warrior role was such a province of men that women may have had to assume other male trappings to get it, but that may or may not have been in the eye of the beholder.

And yet there is a segment of women warriors who did seem eager to take on those male trappings, not only as a way of cementing their role, but of embracing their masculine natures. From Athena to Joan of Arc, there is a magical tradition of a woman cross-dressing in male clothes in order to gain powers of victory. The skein is tangled, and the line between warrior woman and "male" soldier is blurred and vague, as blurred and vague as the similarly debated line between butch and FTM.

An example of a Native American "amazon", so to speak, is the Hopi Pohaha, a mythical woman warrior who was so fierce that she saved her tribe from neighboring enemies several times. Her name comes from the words "po", meaning "wet", as it was said that killing people gave her a sexual thrill; and "haha" meaning laughter, because it was also said that she always laughed gleefully while in battle. Pohaha exists still among the Hopi as a *kachina*, a symbolic protective figure created in mask and figurine, and like her MTF counterpart He'e (see chapter 3), carries a bow and arrow in one hand and a sacred gourd rattle in the other, balancing male and female.

Traditionally, the most frequent reports of cross-dressed female-to-males in history have been in and around the military. Women have masqueraded as men in order to be soldiers and sailors seemingly more often than they have done it in civilian life. One could make the argument that war has been such a guarded male preserve that it was the only way that women could take part in it, but this sidesteps the fact that many of these women became career military men—and thus career transvestites. Perhaps being a soldier or sailor or military doctor was worth living in permanent disguise, or maybe there was something else going on in their minds. At any rate, these women were not only good at what they did, many were very good, being given awards for bravery and courage under fire. Some were "discovered" only after having received terrible wounds. There does seem to be something very powerful about donning the (specifically male) warrior mask, as opposed to the equally powerful but less culturally pervasive female warrior's face.

One myth that seems to have grown up organically in the FTM community, such as it is, is the "typically" male story of the Great Quest. The Quest myth in general has taken a lot of heat from some mythopoets, who point out that in the quest stories that do not end up with the quester as King and Dominator, he inevitably ends up at home, finding in his own back yard what he set out to find in the first place. If that's the case, they reason, why bother to quest at all? It's just foolishness, a waste of time. I would argue that sometimes you have to grow a foot or two before you can reach the golden apple that hangs on that tree in your back yard, and until you leave home, you can't grow any taller. The experience of the Quest changes us forever; although we return home, we are not the people that we were when we left, and we can see—and reach—things that we couldn't when we left, and if we'd never left, we never would have noticed or achieved. The Quest forges us, and gives us the edge to be a keener tool for our own use.

The Great Quest imagery is rampant in FTM community ... slogans like, "The Journey Begins"; "The Journey of a Lifetime", etc. abound. More than any man born with a penis, we have to struggle for manhood, a project often requiring leaving home and family behind, perhaps permanently, and creating our lives and support systems anew. This is not to say that the Quest can't be experienced by a MTF (or for that matter a non-transgendered man or woman), because it can. However, in this culture, manhood is seen as more elusive than womanhood; women become women at puberty while most biomen wonder vaguely their entire lives if they're really "man enough". Part of the undercurrent of the quest is the threat that *you could lose*, that you could spend the rest of your life wandering about stupidly and never finding what you're after. If it's that elusive for a factory-equipped male, it may seem a galaxy away to someone raised female, without the benefit of naturally-grown male parts.

The man in the Quest story is sometimes a warrior, girding on sword and shield, but more often he is a fool, in the sense of the Fool in the Tarot deck—a wide-eyed, innocent beginner with the handicap of naïveté and the resource of untainted instinct. Sometimes, the Jack (funny how his name is so often Jack) in question takes along the sword of his dead father, a sword that he is not trained to use. FTMs may recognize this sword, the verbal, physical, and strategic weapons of our own fathers and male role models; something we may have seen used but were not encouraged to practice with against our brothers. Ironically, in many of these stories, the Jack never actually ends up using the borrowed weapon, but has to outwit the enemies along the road, who are always better armed than him.

One interesting archetypal behavior growing up in the queer and transgender communities, and especially in their wide overlap, is the proliferation of female-bodied people who prefer to think of themselves as "boys" rather than "men". This seems to be especially true for FTM crossdressers, butches, and other people on the spectrum who do not choose to change their bodies, although there are a few transsexuals who see themselves that way as well. Men, they reason, are the ones who've spoiled the world, the authority figures against whom we rebel. Boys get all the fun and have little responsibility. (Ironically, my own personal feelings were just the opposite—to me, boys were the immature, and therefore dangerous, creatures who beat me up after school; men could be held accountable for their actions, or at least the police were more willing to arrest them.)

Being boys (or, as they are sometimes spelled when referring to FTMs, "boyz" or "bois") puts one squarely on that Fool's path, the Quest of the Jack who sets out, not for the warrior's goal of rescue, battle, or some other service to a goal, but to Find His Fortune. Girls in myths do sometimes go on quests, but it's almost always to rescue someone else, like the female heroine of Hans Christian Andersen's "The Snow Queen", or the sister in "The Seven Swans" who rescues her brothers. Jack and Fools have no such agenda. Their journey can go on for as long as it needs to; a lifetime if necessary, ambling from one adventure to another. As long as they are boys, they have the mythical permission to continue that quest. The Fool's Journey is less goal than process; a wild ride during which they gain skills and learn how to be better at being themselves. Sometimes it is scary or dangerous, but the Fool can make it through—as long as they only have themselves to worry about; as long as no other inconvenient people get in the way with their needs or goals. Transition is a lot like that.

June, 1994: I don't like the idea of transitioning; I'm afraid of it. I have made many excuses as to why I can't do it; can't leave home. They are all good excuses. No one could possibly fault me for them.

Then I dream one night that I am seized by a strange band of people. They wear bizarre tribal masks; they beat drums and shake rattles. Ragged strips of cloth and strings of beads swirl around them. They take me up a mountain on a forced march.

Near the top, we approach a cliff, at the bottom of which is a great lake. The sun is bright overhead and I can see the clear blue water below ... very far below. The strange people take a long log, a tall felled tree, and they push it out over the cliff many feet. They all hold down and anchor the end that is still on solid ground. The leader takes a big shining sword and throws it over the cliff. It sails down, down, turning end over end like a silvered thunderbolt, until it hits the lake and vanishes into it.

With a sinking feeling, I know what my job is. I have to retrieve that sword. There isn't even any promise that it will be mine afterwards, but I have to go down after it and bring it back. They don't force me, but I know it has to be done. I crawl out on that log, over the impossible drop, and look down. I will have to jump, fall all the way down into that lake, and live. Then I will have to swim underwater until I find that one item in the depths of the lake. Then everything will be all right.

I jump, I hit the water in a great splash, and I wake up. My first coherent thought is, "Swords! Water! Geez, psyche, couldn't you have been any more original than that?"

The warrior's quest is slightly different. There is usually little in the way of lightheartedness when he sets out; the mood is one of grim determination. This is no place for boys. The warrior is well armed and skilled; the test remains to see if he will be able to prevail against equally well-armed or skillful opponents. Usually he takes on his quest in service to some greater goal: a rescue, or a search for a way to save his kin and clan, those he loves dearly. Other people are depending on the warrior's quest to be successful; failure means suffering for more than just himself.

I've found that this kind of quest is the sort of thing that tends to happen after transition, when you think that everything is going to be fine now, and then you realize that the battle has just begun. Maybe it's discrimination, or being beaten up on the street, or the struggle to find a mate now that you've redone your chassis, or finding a job with some woman's work history on your resume. Perhaps it is the fight against social expectations, or the fight to find one's own brand of masculinity. At a recent FTM support group meeting, several of the post-transition FTMs who had chosen not to have phalloplasties wanted to talk about dealing with post-change body dypshoria; the problem being that it doesn't go away completely, it just gets better, and sometimes flares up. A new boy, just considering the idea of a change, heard them speak about their ongoing and permanent struggle and burst into tears, running from the building. It had not occurred to him that reaching that faraway personal goal would not fix everything, but only bring on new challenges.

The warrior has been through the fire, and been tempered, and is out to change more than just himself. There is an implication that he is not just a loner on a journey, but part of a community, whether it be the majority rule that he defends, or a tiny minority that he protects. Not only that, but he has already experienced the fact that the Quest ends at home, or in a new place which you then make your home. He expects to finish at home, wherever that is or may become, if he lives and succeeds. The thought of that peace is what keeps him going. I found that once I had changed enough that I was finally feeling some comfort in my body, I could develop a sense of inner peace and balance that had been previously lacking. Before this ability to reach a comfort zone, every crisis threw me off. I felt as though the world could go wrong at any minute; I had no trust that everything would eventually be all right. Afterwards, that comfort zone and my trust in its existence—even when I was temporarily off balance—helped me face crises with less panic and both feet securely on the ground, which is every good warrior's best stance.

Another myth that at least a few FTMs found similarities to is that of the werewolf. In the post-Victorian folklore of this society, women are seen as the civilizing force, an idea that is present both in old-fashioned views that "the hand that rocks the cradle rules the world", or "men always need a woman to look after them or they will behave badly"; and also in some modern feminist ideals of women as the "peaceful" sex. Men are seen as wilder, less controlled, having a less-restrained sexual or aggressive urge that might "leap out" and wreak havoc. Women are supposed to be less wildly sexual, more self-disciplined with their own aggression (or as just plain non-aggressive), and non-violent. I've seen this myth used both by women to bolster feelings of low self-esteem by claiming moral superiority, and by men to slyly excuse or justify uncontrolled violence.

The idea that men are more "animal-like" is also linked visually to the physical fact that men have more body and facial hair. This is especially true for Caucasians, who may have the strongest indoctrination in the aforementioned myth. When I did a poll of my heterosexual female friends, more than three-quarters preferred men who were hairless to moderately hairy, not extremely furry; in fact torso-shaving among men is becoming the fashion not only in the gay community but among heterosexuals as well. The women in question did, true to form, suggest that extreme hairiness seemed somehow less "human" and thus indicative of a violent, carnal nature.

When FTMs start taking testosterone, they often experience the simultaneous sensations of facial and body hair growth, a rise in aggressive feelings, and a spike in libido. Yet we come from an upbringing that taught us to repress (and if possible not to feel) our anger, to suppress our assertiveness, to value romance over lust. Ironically, although many of the FTMs I've spoken to (myself included) did notice that our anger was quicker to rise and harder to get around, none that I know became assaultive or beat our domestic partners. I have to wonder if the effects of the testosterone simply forced our assertive instincts up to a healthy level where we were required to overcome our early programming. I also noted that although many of us complain (or crow) over our enhanced, "rabid" libidos, we don't seem to be becoming rapists. There is a lot of fear there, though, around the twin urges of sex and violence; we speak in whispers about how it's difficult to rein them in, as if there was a beast suddenly leaping within us, clawing to get out.

An FTM friend came back from seeing a movie starring Jack Nicholson as a mild-mannered executive who gets bitten by a werewolf and suddenly becomes hairier, stronger, more athletic, more sexual, more likely to attack and rend those who threaten him, and gains keener senses. "That's just what testosterone was like for me!" he exclaimed in wonder. To my eyes, of course, he himself was still a mild-mannered sort, not the type to savage anyone in the park; this was simply an internal awakening generated by the mind-and-body-altering chemicals. "Boy juice", as another friend calls it, is an intense experience—turning up the volume on emotions such as lust, anger, and joy. I also noticed that it changed my sense of smell—for the first time in my life I could perceive specific bodily odors of other humans, and tell them apart by their scent. (The garbage can, however, remained the same.)

Of course, I have to lay in a disclaimer that the FTM chemical experience is a very individual one, and different FTMs will have differing reactions. Not all have discernable mood changes, a few will not notice an enhanced libido, hair growth patterns vary with race and genetics, and my change of smelling ability is by no means universal. Therefore, the issue of the Beast Within may not seem familiar to every one of us. On the other hand, I've seen it come up as a topic too many times in FTM support groups for it to be an anomalous experience. One single FTM admitted half-shamefully that he had been reduced to combing the late-night Internet for more and more "perverse" pornography to satisfy his new masturbatory urges; another one, married, recounted how the moment he came home from work every day during the tumultuous first year of his transition, his wife would send him off to the bedroom to masturbate before he was allowed to touch her, in order to take the urgency out of their later lovemaking.

It is certain that even if a specific FTM is not terribly troubled by said Beast, their female partners fear that they will be. (Male partners of FTMs tend to be less bothered by such things.) The single most common worry I hear from female partners of would-be FTMs is that "testosterone will make him violent and abusive". In some cases, I've also seen this fear exacerbate the problem, as the female partner anxiously scrutinizes every aspect of their metamorphosing partner's post-testosterone behavior and creates a climate of distrust that may actually trigger outbursts or withdrawal. The Beast is a potent visitor, even when he doesn't actually show up.

This is not to say that an FTM's loved ones are necessarily imagining all changes in his behavior. We may well become snappish or argumentative as we navigate our new emotions. Many FTMs report that they allowed themselves to spend a certain amount of time—usually a couple of months—indulging in a certain amount of "bad" stereotypical male behavior on a small scale, which gave them the "elbow room" they needed to come to terms with both chemical changes and social expectations. All report "getting over it", and that it made their adjustment period that much quicker. In FTM support groups, there is a certain level of understanding that FTMs have to learn about the more physical—and animal—side of things, something that they were not often allowed the way boys are in childhood. A term that has grown up to describe FTMs who transition at the same time, and support each other throughout that difficult time, is "litter-mates", implying a rebirth into a phase of strong scents, bouncing, nuzzling, and physical play.

Wrestling with the Beast isn't an easy task, especially for those of us who were not trained to expect it. Genetic men, it seems, are taught to deal with the onset of this chemical that makes our feelings so much harder to ignore by getting rigorous, brutal, almost crushing training that frequently forces them out of contact with all their feelings. This is akin to using a nuclear warhead to restrain a werewolf ... surely there is a better way?

The Beast Within lives in everyone, regardless of gender or hormones; he crouches in the trees or the tall grass of our DNA, with only one thought, and that is Survival. Anything that threatens him or that which he loves is worthy of fight or flight. Struggling for dominance and territory is his lifeblood. He is akin to the prehistoric ancestors who donned the skins and masks of animals in order to bond with, hunt down, and become like their animal brothers. When we meet him, eye to eye, in our psyche, we need to react not by trying to put him in a cage, which is the instinctive response of many a female faced with a male "monster", nor by attempting to kill him, which never works anyway. Running away is also not a good response, because Beasts of any stripe will chase you if you run away from them. The way to deal with a Beast is to speak to them in their own language, and wrestle them if necessary, and show them who is the Alpha—namely you. Not your politics, or your socialization, or the needs of your loved ones ... you.

Discussion questions part 2 (for transmen)

What is maleness? Physical? Mental? Biological? Social? How well do these things cross cultures? (If you don't know, it's time to do some studying.) What is masculinity? The same thing as maleness?

How much do you think that the male psyche is bound up with the physical nature of the male reproductive organs—the penis thrusts forth, quests for sensation, climaxes in a burst of creative seed, and then is limp and withered; the testes give forth hormones on a steady basis rather than a cyclical one? Not at all? Some? A lot? When you ask your biomale friends about this, what do they say? (If you don't have any biomale friends, try to remedy this situation ASAP. You will learn a lot from them, even if some of the lessons are hard.) How will you learn about the mysteries of the male body, and how it affects how men think?

Which parts of "men's mysteries" apply to you, and which don't? What parts of traditional masculinity can you relate to, and which leave you bewildered or cold? What sort of men are your role models? What sort of men are you repelled by, and why? What do you hope your relationship to men will be in the future? To women? To other transmen? To transwomen? To transfolk who have not yet or are not intending to transition? What commitment will you make to help your brothers?

What do the men and women in your life tell you that you have to work on the most?

Inner world activity

When faced with the Beast, first you need to learn his language. He may not speak in words. He may converse in gestures, or noises, or imagery, or just raw emotion. Think about what sounds he might make when he is triumphant, or frustrated. Close all the doors and make them. Then imagine that you are facing him down, eye to eye. Growl at him, in your mind. If he growls back, growl louder. Make yourself bigger. Do not back down. If he looks like he's about to leap, don't panic—leap first. Imagine getting your teeth around his throat. Imagine bowling him over, letting him scream and snarl, holding him down. Be patient. Endure. You are not going to kill him, you are going to wait until he shows throat, however long that is. If he fights you, just hold on. You can win this battle. (Biting a pillow helps with this exercise. Make sure it's an old one you can afford to destroy.)

When he rolls over on his belly and submits, however grudgingly, let go. Make a triumphant noise, something he'll understand. Then explain to him, in his language, that you are the alpha in this body. You feed first, and you'll decide when he feeds, when he gets his needs met. If he acts up, you'll put him down again.

Now that he's submitted, he is now your dependent, not your enemy. Your job as alpha is to hunt for him, make sure he gets at least some of what he needs, whatever that is, when it's appropriate. Don't neglect him, or he'll get uppity again.

Outer world activity

How do you deal with conflict, especially physical conflict? Perceived as a male on the streets, you will be challenged by other men, sometimes physically, especially if your particular expression of maleness is less traditional than most. For that matter, you will be challenged verbally by other males who will assume that you know the rules of this game. If you lack confidence, get together a group of FTMs and start a martial arts or at least self-defense training group, so as to get through any last vestiges of female passivity training. You don't have to play the male challenge game, but you at least have to have the courage to stand up to it, and the awareness not to be taken off guard and knocked into a position of passivity and confusion.

The Rituals

The FTM experience is generally marked not by one but by two major surgeries, of which the majority of transmen only get the first one. Unlike MTFs, who can grow breasts with estrogen, no amount of testosterone will completely flatten fully developed breasts and they need to be removed. "Chest surgery", in fact, is the single most common FTM surgery, and when transmen ask if you've had "the surgery", they generally mean a bilateral mastectomy.

Genital surgery, be it phalloplasty (construction of an artificial penis), metaoidioplasty (the procedure where the enlarged clitoris is moved upwards on the pubic mound and testicles formed from the labia), hysterectomy (removal of the uterus), vaginectomy (removal of the vagina), or some combination of the above, is much rarer. About half of all transmen get hysterectomies and half don't bother. The other surgeries are expensive and yield varying results. Thus, this chapter contains two rituals, one to celebrate chest surgery and one for lower surgery.

Ritual #1: The Opening Of The Heart

Ancient Egyptians performed a ritual on the mummies of deceased loved ones called the "Opening Of The Mouth" ritual that supposedly gave them eternal life and happiness in the afterlife. Similarly, after I had had my bilateral mastectomy, which was an extremely painful event that required a good deal of stamina to endure, I discovered that a part of me which had been dead for some time was slowly coming back to life.

The breasts are symbols of nurturing, positioned at the level of the heart chakra. In women, breasts give nurturing to infants and pleasure to their owners, both associated with love and warm feelings, appropriate to the area of the heart. For transmen, however, breasts are a source of difficulty ranging from ambivalence to downright hatred. Most women would cringe to hear the kind of things transmen say about their breasts in support groups.

When I transitioned and began taking hormones, I felt a whole range of feelings that had been veiled in a grey pall of depression before my chemical adventures. Still, I had trouble expressing them, and difficulty in getting past my thirty-year habit of pushing people away if they got too close, both physically (so they wouldn't touch my ambivalent body) and emotionally. My friends had long ago been trained not to offer me an embrace unless I offered it first. Yet after surgery, when I looked in the mirror and thought, yes, this is how it's supposed to be, my heart began to come out of its shell. I realized that for me, breasts were a weight on my chest, keeping me from breathing freely, using my whole lung system, veiling and imprisoning my heart chakra rather than being part of it. With my flat chest, I felt emotionally naked, as if there was no longer anything between my heart and the world. Yet after years of repression, it felt wonderful.

Cutting off the breasts is, for women, a sad and mournful action, usually associated with disease and the possibility of death. Even Amazons supposedly only mutilated one breast, and there is nothing positive in those scars, except perhaps a kind of triumph that one is still among the living. "Were you depressed afterwards?" a female student asked me worriedly. No, I told her, I found I could fill my lungs entirely for the first time since puberty, and I kept getting myself into dizzy, euphoric states through accidental hyperventilation. After the pain passed, I spent a lot of time giggling. I could suddenly hug my loved ones closer, could press them against the beat of my heart without vague embarrassment or discomfort. For most people, yes, it would have been a mutilation; for me it was a stripping-down, a removal of the unnecessary, and a way to peel back layers and show myself.

I have a dream, just after surgery. In it, I was talking to my ex-lover, who had been pretty invested in seeing me as female. We were eating peaches, and I held out my hands to him with a ripe peach in one hand and a naked pit in the other. "When you met me," I said, "I was like this," and I indicated the ripe peach. "And now I'm this," and I held up the pit. "And I know that you liked the fruit better, that it was attractive to you, and that what I am now isn't something that you have much of a use for. But what you have to understand is that the beautiful flesh of the peach isn't the really important part, not to the tree that bore it, or to the Earth it sprang from. The important part is this pit, this seed, which is going to grow a new tree. The peach is just something the seed grew to get it where it needs to go."

For this ritual, you will need the following items: A knife, any size; body paint in different colors; some kind of fruit with a rind or peel (we used an orange); a separate paring knife if the fruit is an apple or thin-skinned type (not a peeler); and a piece of red cord. There should also be someone male-identified to officiate. Some transmen may prefer that it be a genetic male who knows the mysteries of the male body; some may prefer that it be a post-operative transman who knows what they are about to go through and can empathize.

Start by gathering people together in a circle, and create sacred/safe space however you prefer to do so. If your tradition invokes the elements, you may want to invoke a male deity for each direction, such as Hermes in the East for Air, Shango in the South for Fire, Neptune in the West for Water, and Pan in the North for Earth. The transman who is about to go through surgery should stand naked to the waist; I know that this is a hard thing for many FTMs, so choose the members of your circle carefully to minimize embarrassment and maximize supportiveness. The priest/officiant begins to paint the transman all over his torso and face with the body paint, in whatever swirls or stripes seems appropriate. He says, "Warrior of the Sacred Third! You have fought long and hard against many enemies, you have won many battles, and you are close to winning your war. You are facing your final (*or next to final, if there is more surgery to come later*) ordeal, when you heart shall be laid open to the world. Are you afraid?"

The transman says, "Yes, but it will not stop me."

The priest says, "Have you faced opposition?"

The transman says, "Yes, but it did not stop me."

The priest says, "Has your heart been wounded?"

The transman says, "Yes, but it is healing."

The priest says, "Has your will been tested?"

The transman says, "Yes, but it is still strong."

The priest says, "Has your body been alien to you?"

The transman says, "Yes, but I am winning it back."

The priest says, "Has your face been alien to you?"

The transman says, "Yes, but now I know who I am."

The priest hands him the fruit and peeling knife, and asks, "What lies at the center of this fruit?"

The transman names all the parts of himself that he has hidden or buried over the years. This is an entirely personal list, and should be worked out beforehand. Everyone's will be different.

The priest asks, "Are you ready to share all of this with your tribe and community?"

The transman assents, and walks around the circle peeling away the rind of the fruit and giving pieces to each member of the circle, saying, "This is my gift, and it is worthy, as I am." As he does this, the folk in the circle are passing a red cord from hand to hand, so that as he steps to each new person they are handed it by their neighbor.

Each person ties a knot in the cord, not on top of but next to the last person's knot, and says, "I receive your gift, and give you back_____" They name something that they want him to have. When it circles back to the priest, he gives the cord to someone previously selected, who kneels and ties the cord around the transman's ankle. (Ankle jewelry is the least likely to interfere with any kind of surgery.) The designated person says, "Your heart is valuable to us, and we will help you to protect it."

Then the priest takes the knife and says, "This is the first stroke, but not the last. With this, I begin the opening of your heart." He makes three slashes in the air above the transman's chest, in an upward-pointing triangle.

This point in the ritual is a good time for applause, and congratulations, and hugs, and breaking the circle for food and a last party before the trip.

Ritual #2: Seizing the Wand

This second ritual is for FTMs who are having phalloplasty or metoidioplasty, and it is a counterpart to the Accepting the Chalice ritual in the last chapter. Again, it is up to the transman in question as to whether he wants the priest to be a genetic male or a post-operative FTM. However, it is important to the ritual that there be at least several factory-equipped bioguys present and willing to help, although no one need be restricted from the circle for their gender. For this ritual, you will need a wand or staff, or other long thing. It can be as short as a foot long, like a talk stick, or as long as a six-foot staff; it can be phallic or not, but it should be highly decorated and a good deal of time should be spent in making it interesting. You will also need a small cup of salt water, and a vial of scented oil, any scent that you like. (Good suggestions for not-too-sweet scented oils are citrus or pine.) The initiate should be freshly washed in a long, meditative bath, and should wear red for blood.

Everyone files in and stands in a circle; create sacred/safe space any way you would like. The initiate comes in and kneels facing the priest/officiant, in the center of the circle. He says, "I come before you now to offer my sacrifice. As the Goddess is willing to give up her life to bear her Son, so I give up the last womanhood of my body, and I come home to myself."

The priest says, "You have come down a hard path with many twists and turns. The first step in your journey was clarity, realizing what Destiny expected of you, and having the courage to begin." He anoints the initiate's forehead with a drop of the scented oil, and then continues, "The second step was to take into yourself the magical essence of a man's body, to flow through your brain and change it, to teach you the experience of a man's magical chemistry."

The initiate says, "I have learned why a man's mind is like a flame, leaping and bright, burning in its intensity and clarity, giving warmth to all who come near it."

The priest says, "You have taken the third step, which is to open your heart."

The initiate says, "I have learned why a man's heart is strong, knowing when to stand firm and when to yield."

The priest then raises the wand or staff, and says something personal about what the phallus means to him; how he sees its joys and responsibilities, and he passes it over the head of the initiate to someone else. Everyone, male or female, can speak about what it means to them. (Keep it short and concise; it's up to the priest to make sure nobody rambles on.) It is passed back and forth over the initiate's head, and at some point when everyone has spoken who wants to, someone in the circle calls out one of the many names for the phallus, and hands it off quickly, in the air, to another person, who calls out another name for it, and passes it off again. The initiate, at this point, can leap up and start grabbing for it; the ritual becomes rather like a game of keep-away, with the wand or staff quickly passed from person to person too fast for him to catch it. As each person grabs it, they call out another name for the phallus. Don't be afraid to use them all, no matter what their connotation; someone who wants a phallus must not be frightened of all its many names, no matter how obscene society considers them. Of course, the initiate is going to grab it eventually, and when he does, he roars out his own name, and everyone yells is back at him in unison. Then, grasping the wand or staff, he kneels again before the priest.

The priest says, "There is one last thing that you must do. Before you sacrifice the last womanhood of your body, you must mourn for her, for she sustained your life while you were in hiding and she deserves mourning. Weep for her, so that you may go on with a clean heart." He marks the initiate's face with the salt water as if it was tears; if the initiate can shed a few tears of his own, it would be good. All join in, weeping and wailing; the wailing should gradually change to a chant or group sung note, and then to laughter, guided by the priest/officiant. Then all seize the initiate, lift him up as a group, chant his name, and then hie themselves off to food, drink, and celebration.

Interview with Gary Bowen (2001)

(Gary Bowen is an FTM Ghost Dancer of Native American descent. He is also the founder of The American Boyz, a national support network for FTMs/butches/masculine women, etc., and the yearly True Spirit Conference for transgenderfolk.)

Please describe yourself and your gender identity.

Gary: I accept the term "female-to-male transsexual" as the label the dominant culture puts on me, but it's not culturally appropriate. I am a mixed blood Native American, and each Native culture has its own terminology. Because we are mixed blood, my family has inherited a fragmented tradition and I don't know what the word is in my ancestors' language. However, I did grow up with strong female gender role models like my great-grandmother, a mannish woman who was described as "the old battleaxe", and "we always know who wore the pants in the family". It took me a long time to understand what feminism was about, because the women in my family had always gone ahead and done the things that feminists were fighting for the right to do.

Unlike many transgendered people who reject their families of origin, I feel very much a part of my family, and the elders in my family accept me as a unique individual. They are delighted with my interest in the family history, and are busy passing on information to me.

How do you feel about having a nonstandard gender? How has it been for you?

Gary: It is a gift of the Creator. Creator is a hermaphroditic being, and He/She/It created human beings like itself; men, women, and hermaphrodites. In Native American English, the word "hermaphrodite" refers to people who are spiritually part male and part female. The hermaphrodites, since they resemble the Creator, are believed by many traditional people (but not all) to have a special connection with Creator. The role assigned to them varies by tribe; they have lived and served their communities as doctors, nurses, counselors, foster parents, warriors, hunters, dancers, etc. Since this is a gift from Creator, it would be sacrilege to turn my back on it, or to denigrate it.

When I was young and didn't understand much about the world and didn't know much about Creator, it troubled me a lot; but the trouble was not from within me, it was from members of the dominant culture who persecuted someone who was different. Being from a culture outside of the mainstream, I can see that a great deal of transphobia is motivated by xenophobia; the dominant culture, for all its claim to be "colorblind", in fact operates on the assumption that the dominant culture is the only legitimate one, and it is colorblind only as long as people of color act like white, middle-class people. I have personally witnessed quite a lot of abuse directed at Native American people who assert the validity of their indigenous cultures; they are assaulted with a combination of xenophobic, racist, homophobic, gender-bashing language and exhorted to "get over the past" and to join in the mainstream culture. Give them some silver body paint and they sound an awful lot like, "We are the Borg. You will be assimilated."

Describe your spiritual path and how you got there.

Gary: My spiritual path is Ghostdance ... When I was twelve, I went to powwow for the first time—it was 1973. The drums spoke to me and I had my first Vision. In it I saw myself as who I truly was: a Native American traditional man. This was something that baffled me for a long time as I had no grounding to explain what had happened to me or what it meant. The beads that make up my hairpipe choker were obtained at that time, and I wear them with pride. Elder Native Americans remember how things used to be, and they recognize history in my choker. This is important because ever since *Dances With Wolves* came out, it has been chic for people to try and "reclaim their Native American heritage".

Unfortunately, you can't "reclaim" something you never had. I am mixed blood, I don't try to "reclaim" anything. I try to come to terms with the elitism, racism, culture bashing, mixed messages, and shame that I grew up with about my ethnic origins (combination Native American and rural Southern "cracker"). Each time I take a step in the right direction for dealing with my culture, gender, religion, family, or other issues, the Great Mystery reveals another piece of the puzzle to me. Four years ago, when I went in for my hysterectomy, I had my second Vision. I was standing in the hallway at 6:30 a.m., waiting for my chance to register, when it happened. I can't tell you what it was, but as a result of that Vision I pledged myself to the Ghostdance.

Describe how your gender identity affects your spiritual path, and vice versa.

Gary: Spirit is universal There is no piece of it that is specific to any person or type of person. No human being can have a monopoly on Spirit, though many people claim to do so. What I think you're really asking here is if there are any rituals specific to FTMs. Rituals are the ways people use to open themselves so that Spirit can illuminate them. Rituals are not religion; they are the outward expressions of faith that we use to remind ourselves where we came from, who we are, and what we believe about the Great Mystery. Rituals are specific to particular cultures and have meaning within those cultures because they are the accumulated wisdom and experience of that culture.

An FTM has to grapple with their place in their religion, and to understand the lessons it has to teach. But these are human issues, not spiritual issues. The Spirits are not like human beings, although they are often transmogrified into a human form to help people grasp some facet of their nature. When Spirits look at human beings, it is like human beings looking at birds. Can you tell whether a bird is male or female? Most people can't. And generally speaking, it doesn't matter. When Creator gives gender-specific rituals, it is doing so to satisfy the tremendous importance gender and sex have for human beings. Creator is opening a path that people can follow to the Great Mystery—no matter how compulsively they are wrapped up in the activities of the flesh.

What do you think that people of nonstandard gender have to offer everyone else?

Gary: An example of faith. Each of us has the ability—and the duty—to transform our lives in order to live in accordance with the Great Mystery. It isn't necessary to explain, or even understand how it happened. The thing about "mystery" is that it is mysterious. If we can get past the rationalizing part of our brain, then we can accept that there are a lot of things we don't understand and don't need to understand. I don't need to understand nuclear physics—the atoms whirl around whether I understand them or not. And I don't need to understand Mystery; as it unfolds itself little by little, my own understanding grows, but I can never understand it all.

This is the thing Native American elders have taught me; No one can encompass the totality of the Great Mystery; therefore Creator has revealed unto each people the rituals and ways of believing that work best in their culture. While they appear to contradict one another, and some seem more attractive than others, no way is superior to another. Therefore it is contingent upon people to examine the religion of their own culture, and to come to terms with it. Many people reject their religion of origin because they are so closely associated with it that they can see that people are imperfect. They call them "hypocrites" and blame the religion for hypocrisy, when it is only the inadequate understanding of human beings that makes it so. Disillusioned, they do not try to penetrate the mysteries of their own religion; instead, they look for somebody else's religion to see if it would be more appropriate. Being on the outside of that other religion, they don't see the bickering and conflicts among the people within that religion. If they learn enough about the new religion to realize that it is practiced by imperfect human beings, they are disappointed and move on to find yet another religion. But they will never find a suitable faith until they have the faith to believe that even though people are imperfect, there's nothing wrong with them. I doubt that anyone can achieve religious faith until they start tolerating human frailties.

Interview with Haverl (2008)

(Haverl is a shy-until-you-get-to-know-him kind of guy. He spends his time studying, brewing, and crafting all and sundry things usually Heathen-related, but not always.)

Tell us about your gender identity.

Haverl: I am an FTM. At 16, I decided to transition and bend my body to my own will. Between the ages of 20 and 22 I got a hysterectomy and oophorectomy, started testosterone, and had a double mastectomy with masculine chest contouring. I am now a hairy-shouldered, deep-voiced, flat-chested man born out of a smooth-skinned, alto-voiced, and breast-bearing (but never female) person. I am a consciously created work of human sculpture forced into the shape I have chosen.

I identify as male, but never regret my female upbringing. I am still a feminist, but a tad bit mellowed from my teenage years of being a man-hating-Hot-Head-Paisan-loving-baby-dyke. Being raised as a woman has made me an infinitely better man.

I am omnisexual, and attracted to different genders for different reasons. I love very feminine non-trans-woman for how different they are from me. Their bodies are echoes of what mine would have been had it not been mine. Their curves mirroring the shadow of who I was that still lingers in the back of my head. They are who I might have become had I not extruded myself through my own mould.

I love transgendered men for how closely our bodies resemble each others. Ours is a nakedness of what we are now and a testament to the force of our wills. We have similar scars, and similar outlines that compliment sweaty, naked coupling in a way nothing else can.

I love non-transmen out of adoring envy because I will never be them. I look upon their unscarred bodies and floppy exposed dicks and take in with my breath the scent of testosterone home-brewed instead of mass produced and injected. They have massive hard erections and are unable to hide their desire behind folds of flesh and secrecy.

Tell us about your spiritual path, and its contradictions.

Haverl: What I wrote above is my external world, the part of me that is my body and flesh but buried under everyday life and the mask of just another guy at the office. My internal world follows the path of my ancestors. My family is of Germanic stock; English/German with some Irish in there as well. I practice Heathenry, the religion of the old Norse/Germanic people. I was pulled into this path by the lure of the Runes, mysteries given to us by the All-Father. They are incantations of truth, whispers of intent, and vertical, horizontal, and diagonal lines that have been drawn by knives, fingers, and pens for years and years and years. They encode the secrets of a culture long past and tease and taunt me with hints of my Gods and Goddesses and the world around me. They are paths to the lands of my forefathers and road maps into my very own self.

My religion holds men to a high standard of *uber*-masculinity, and a code of warriors and Kings and fathers. The traditional family structure places the man at the head of the household, lord of his own castle, and leader of the family's spirituality. I do not fit in their vision of society. But just as in any society, there are those that do not fit, nor do I believe are they supposed to. There are those that skirt the borders of "acceptable" and step into the world of darkness and the Other. The Other is that which is called on when the norm has been shattered and something else must be explained or fixed. The Other masters the hated but necessary parts of society. I do not believe that because I am a transsexual that I hold any monopoly on any Sacred Otherness, but that I am just a single point in a vast universe of Otherness and we all have our own special roles.

I strive to emulate a God of liminality, a male deity that practices a woman's sorcery but that gathers the slain warriors in a hall for the battle at the end of this world. A god that twists words, and warns of treachery, but is treacherous himself; the Father of the Aesir that is bound by blood to the trickster and instigator of chaos himself. He holds the mystery of the ecstatic trance and the knowledge gleaned from a deadly sacrifice. His tools are thought and memory, and his art is the refinement of the self. He is a warrior god for the berserker but the magician god for the intellectual. I try to worship him by knowing because he is the God of Knowledge. I try to blot to him by teetering on the edge of acceptability and accepting my self for who I have made myself to be. I was drawn to him because he is outside of society like I am, but still functions with power and confidence.

What would you say that we have to offer the world?

Haverl: Because I am a transsexual, and I identify as a Heathen, and choose to move in Heathen communities, I will always be on the boarder of their society, but that is where I feel I belong. I have gained knowledge of the path of both man and woman and it's not something everyone can, or wants to, understand. I will someday serve my community as a more whole person because of my transsexual history. Right now, I serve my community by learning, I serve my Gods and Goddess by honoring them in the manner of my ancestors to the best of my ability, and I serve myself by accepting my *wyrd* and weaving it anew with each of my choices and actions.

Chapter 13
The Trickster: Laughing Through the Pain

> A brave world, Sir, full of religion, knavery, and change!
>
> –*Aphra Behn*

The Myth

Long ago in medieval Europe, the first of May was celebrated by a parade of costumed performers. The figures became set in tradition—the hobby horse, the May Queen, the Green Man—but strangest was the "Betsy" or "Teaser", a man dressed as a woman. The Betsy is a clown figure, mocking the spectators and the other participants, fighting a mock battle for the Green Man with the Spring Maiden, which she loses, symbolizing the barren winter (another symbolic mention of the deferred fertility of transgendered people).

Among the Native Americans of the Southwest, the most famous trickster figure is of course Coyote. In one story, Coyote falls in love with a man, and in order to sleep with him, temporarily removes his penis. The Northwest tribes have Raven, the trickster deity who castrated himself, pounded his penis to a pudding, and fed it to the Earth Mother in order to fertilize her.

Ancient Palestine was named after a pre-Judaic deity named Pales, a bi-gendered trickster deity. The guide and guardian of wandering herders, Pales was shown as being hermaphroditic and bearing the head of an ass. Imagine how the political situation in modern-day Israel might change if the energies of this mischievous, braying third gender deity were invoked to upset the current balance of anger and vengeance!

Astrologically, the Trickster figure is represented by the planet Uranus, named after a castrated god. People with strong Uranus aspects, according to astrological thinking, tend to be forward-thinking, nonconformist, driven to tear down rules and structure, tricksy, and often androgynous.

The trickster turns everything on its head. Nothing is safe from them, and no custom untouchable. The ultimate goal of a conscious trickster is, indeed, to teach; putting the message into a medium that may work when reason has been ignored. Cross-dressing, on its own, is a blatant example of turning the world upside down, which is the simple answer to all those cross-dressed "fools" in the old parades. There's a more complicated one, as well.

Tricksters often play with gender; in societies where gender is a rigid entity, they are often the only ones allowed to do so. They don't have to "prove" their manhood or womanhood; since society can laugh at them, society allows them that freedom. Indeed, when anyone does anything that is gender transgressive, the most common reaction is to laugh at them, thus defusing their threat to the average person's world view.

While this is certainly a slightly better reaction than the second most common one, and the one that is usually reverted to when the humorous defusing doesn't work—hostility—it can take a hard toll on the self-esteem of the average gender transgressor. Sometimes it's hard to refrain from taking any of it seriously and still stay sane. We have to work harder to keep our perspective, but that's what being a trickster is all about—a change in perspective.

Being a trickster has long been a method of teaching the rigid or defensive to change their perspective as well. Traditionally, it's the jester who could tell the king he might be wrong when all the king's counselors were shaking in their boots with fear of beheading. The jester's privileged position of never being taken quite seriously gave him the ability to slip in the occasional bit of criticism and let it simmer. It's a careful and masterful balancing act.

In one story of a West Coast Native American tribe, a female *heyoka* or sacred trickster was disgusted by the way that her people traded their valuable products with the white traders for cheap beads and trinkets. She felt that they ought to demand a better price, or at least stop wasting their furs and carvings on such fripperies. Her tribesfolk, however, would not listen to such criticism, so she set out to change their minds a different way. She set up a rough stall next to the traders and mimicked their way of hawking their wares, only she offered for sale random rocks, twigs, and piles of feces, claiming that they were valuable jewels. Her people grew shamefaced and stopped their trade. Unfortunately, the white traders realized her trick and killed her. Some people have no sense of humor.

Violent ending aside, this kind of satire is the trickster's sacred duty. True tricksters of any stripe can't resist doing it. If there's fun to be poked, they'll find it. If a sacred cow walks down their street, they'll attach a KICK ME sign to its butt. It's a calling, and at the bottom of it is an urge to ask why. Why do we take this as gospel and never question it? Isn't anybody else wondering about this? Wait a minute, what are we doing?

The part that scares most people about the Trickster's role is the idea that, at bottom, there is nothing too sacred to be questioned, and questioned again periodically. Most people like the idea of there being at least some certain precepts that one wouldn't even think to question. It's a nerve-wracking idea, the thought that there's nothing to stand on that isn't a flimsy human-built construction, easily dismantled by some clown who happens to point a finger and yell, "Why?" In Umberto Eco's *The Name Of The Rose*, a dogmatic monk defends his hatred of laughter by pointing out that if men can laugh at the devil, there will be no more fear of God.

Gender is one of those unquestioned certainties, and as such, nothing needs questioning more. If it can be done with laughter, so much the better. Even the most comic and clumsy crossdressing is still breaking the taboo that we shouldn't mix genders. Sure, sometimes it's meant to be insulting, but sometimes that's an important first step. This year, the bigot will laugh at the guy in a dress. Next year, he'll laugh at a bunch of guys in dresses and a woman in a tuxedo. All the while, though, he's being slowly desensitized, so that in five years there's nothing more to laugh about, it's just ordinary background, and he's found something else to occupy his amusement. This kind of frog boiling doesn't always work, but I've seen it work often enough that I count the Trickster's way as a valid path for change.

Many crossdressers take a lot of flak from the rest of the gender community for not being "serious" about their transgender expressions, for merely "playing" with gender. Personally, I think it's good that someone, anyone, is playing with gender. If we can play with it, it ceases to become a huge, monolithic, immovable object and becomes instead a pile of glittering toys to play with, pass around, trade off, recombine, and dispose of when you're done for the day.

Like shamans, tricksters are often shapeshifters (see chapter on shapeshifting) with many forms and masks to help with their performances. Coyote has a veritable menagerie of critters that he can become, male and female, in order to infiltrate his way into the lives of his various victims. In one story, he lends his penis to a friend and sneaks into a gathering of women as a woman, but then discovers to his chagrin that his friend has made better use of the borrowed organ than he had himself. I can't help remembering friends discussing the positive attributes of having a strap-on dildo, including the ability to pass it around to friends, and to throw it at the ceiling and see if it sticks. Penises are yet another thing that our culture takes far too seriously. Their presence or absence dictates such things as class, clothing, upbringing, and pay scales. Their size, or lack thereof, often has a large effect on self-esteem. Indeed, the assumption that self-esteem will be negatively affected by the absence of a whopping schlong is so ingrained that doctors who alter intersex children often make the decision to amputate a small phallus and build a vagina on the basis of size alone. The idea that the penis is, in essence, just another piece of costume that can be strapped on, grown with hormones, grafted out of an arm, or otherwise acquired with various levels of ease is a particularly uncomfortable one to many people. The ones who suffer the most discomfort with it are often the ones who count most heavily on the privilege that they were promised due to being born with a socially-adequate one.

This is not to say that the phallic symbol isn't sacred. It is a symbol of growth and hope and exuberance, and the idea that phalluses can't be seen or shown in public, that they are somehow obscene, is in itself an obscenity to me. But keep in mind the deities in different cultures whose symbol the giant penis actually was, and you'll find something interesting.

In ancient Greece and Rome, the great stone phalli were known as "herms", and were dedicated to Hermes/Mercury, a trickster god if ever there was one. The *herms* were great pillars, often with a face carved on them where a "head" would be, placed at crossroads to honor the travel-loving nature of this quicksilver messenger god. While still a child, Hermes stole his brother Apollo's herds and then lied about it, becoming the patron deity of thieves, merchants, and fast talkers. Hermes had two other attributes: he was a psychopomp, a guide, the only deity able to pass in and out of the underworld at will, and he was identified in the alchemical mysteries as being the embodiment of the sacred androgyne. Indeed, he is the father of Hermaphroditus. Does this combination of traits—trickster, psychopomp, androgyne—tell us something about how we as bigendered tricksters can be guides out of social darkness? And ... what about those big stone dicks?

In another non-coincidence, the Afro-Caribbean Yoruba pantheon also has a deity (or *orisha*) whose symbol is the disembodied penis, and who also happens to be a trickster entity. His name is Legba in Haiti, and Ellegua in Brazil, and he is also associated with crossroads. He is the most insidious prankster in the whole array of *orishas*, referred to by Catholic writers as "a very demon", and yet he is the first and foremost orisha, the spirit that "opens the door" for communication with all the others, and so must always be propitiated first.

Various phalli decorate traditional altars to Ellegua, and somewhere in Africa there is a nunnery of women who are his "wives", celibate save for the huge stone phallus they ceremonially take turns mounting every night. In spite of this apparent maleness, though, Ellegua is suspiciously nonstandard in his gender. He also takes many forms, and one of his most popular is that of a little girl with a hideous clay-and-cowrie-shell head. In ceremonial parades, he is often played by a girl wearing a huge oversized phallus. In Brazil, Ellegua has a wife, Pomba Gira, whose name comes from the Nigerian *mpambu nzila* or crossroads. She is rumored to be not so much his wife as simply another form of Ellegua, as she shares an altar, colors, preferred offerings, and other attributes. She is the *orisha* of lust and is appealed to for aid in achieving sexual connections; she is pictured as a beautiful woman in black and red lace, and is the patron of drag queens, by whom she is sometimes played in parades.

The same picture of oversized and seemingly artificial phalluses appears in amphora pictures of ancient Greek Dionysian rites. (See chapter on Dionysus.) The "satyrs" who romp through these vases also have suspiciously false-looking beards as well. I read in writings of the period that no uncastrated men were allowed into the Dionysian orgies, and yet here appear these "mythical" creatures with their too-rampant organs. I have to wonder if some of my gender-crossing butch friends might recognize themselves in these "satyrs".

The message between the lines here seems to mean that when the phallus is exaggerated beyond normal proportions, both physically and in a psycho-social medium, it ceases to become a simple biological organ for aiming semen and urine, and becomes a symbol that can be borrowed by anyone of any sex, and functions as an automatic temporary change in gender status, a way to take on ceremonial maleness and yet satirize it at the same time. By growing larger than life, it passes out of the realm of true manhood and into the transgender mysteries, and those of the trickster who waves it in your face, forcing you to rethink the simultaneous combination of taboo and privilege that it supposedly confers.

One rather feminine friend, certainly not butch at all, had a strap-on made and, in a moment of whimsy, wore it to her job as an apartment desk clerk. She described her feelings on the subway en route to her work: "Everyone I looked at, I wanted to bend over and screw. I found myself looking at women and thinking, *Yeah, she wants it.* And those cute boys! I imagined them getting down on their knees and sucking it. As soon as I got home, I was shocked at myself." Nothing had changed in her gender presentation (she was still wearing skirts) or her hormones, yet the presence of the phallus mask allowed her to play with and mentally satirize the worst of stereotypical male behavior. In a truly Coyote-like twist, she sprained her ankle on the way home and ended up in the hospital, still packing her toy and unable to get to the bathroom to remove it. She found herself going to all sorts of trouble to keep the medical staff from winding bandage too high on her leg, and thus discovering an addition that would have to be explained. "I know just how a pre-op transsexual feels now!" she commented to me later.

Discussion Questions

What things do you hold so sacred that you can't laugh at them? (If you can't think of any, ask your friends to make affectionate fun of you and see how many minutes it takes before you bridle and become angry.) Do you feel that you need to change this? Would they have as much of a hold on you if you could laugh at them? How can you use humor to defuse difficult situations? Are there places in your life where you've been being vehement where humor might have gotten better results? What sort of "mask" would you have to wear in order to do it?

Inner world activity

Make a list of all the fools and tricksters you can think of who bend gender in some way. (Yes, Bugs Bunny counts, and so does the Widow Norton.) Claim them as your role models and learn from them. How can they teach you not to get bogged down in the seriousness of what they are doing? How can they teach you how to react when people laugh at you (which they will, sooner or later, it's inevitable)? How can they teach you to teach those laughing people something important—and make it easier to swallow than a lecture or an attack? Create a big, silly, lush, overblown hymn to all of them. Recite it whenever it's needed.

Outer world activity

Comedians have always used gender crossing as a fertile field for jokes, but they have often been painful and humiliating. With your friends, put together a collection of video moments featuring transgendered jokes of any kind. Discuss them and figure out where the fear comes in, where the humor becomes a vicious put-down. Compare this with what humor you can find by real transgendered folk. Write and perform new humor about the actual flaws and foibles of your own local transgendered community. Don't pick on people; make them laugh. We as a community must not fall into the trap of either allowing others to define us through vicious, hurtful humor or of being so oversensitive to our dignified appearance that we can't laugh about the really laughable things in our existence. The one trap makes us into doormats, the other into stiff posts just waiting to be toppled. Be neither. Be flexible, and bend in the wind of laughter.

The Ritual: Tricksters, Fools, and Reversers

(This ritual was beta-tested on a Uranus conjunction with Q-Moon, a Boston-based group of queer pagans. It is an act of magic first, and activism a far second. Remember that as you go about it!)

You will need: A whole bunch of people who are willing to be tricksters and fools. The crazier you all dress, and the less repressed you are capable of being, the better. Remember, there is strength in numbers! Wild cross-dressing is especially effective.

One person to trail along and be "speaker to police and other authority figures". This person is not to attempt to throw cold water on the schemes of the tricksters; they are there to interpose themselves and *protect* them from authorities, without interfering. Not an easy job!

A whole bunch of small (or not-so-small) trinkets—jewelry, bric-a-brac, flowers, stuff out of gum machines. Every one of these items should be labeled with bit of taped-on paper that says, "Whosoever receiveth this shall change or be changed!" The more of these, the better. A few large pieces should be saved for leaving at the places you intend to visit. You will also need several boxes of thick colored sidewalk chalk.

A list of places around town that you think could use a change of perspective. We created an itinerary of such places as City Hall, the State House, the IRS, various political campaign headquarters, and a few churches of exceptionally rigid worship.

The first step is to gather and invoke the protection of the Trickster. Don't underestimate the power of the Trickster's nature! Under the Trickster's protection, you can do anything and get away with it—as long as it works toward a positive goal and isn't just a reflection of your own hang-ups (in which case the Trickster will turn it around on you). Make a circle and call out the names of Tricksters everywhere: "Coyote!" "Bugs Bunny!" "Pales!" "The Cat In The Hat!" "Murphy!" "Puck!" "The Warner Brothers—and the Warner Sister Too!" "Hermes!" "Legba!" "The Roadrunner!" "Reynard the Fox!" "Hail Lady Eris, All Hail Discordia!" (You'd better not forget that last one, or *you'll be sorry.*) Don't be afraid to invoke the names of real, living tricksters, especially drag kings and queens and your crazier friends.

Throughout the entirety of this ritual you must *have no fear*. The Trickster has a special place in reality; they are allowed to make fun of the authority figures without fear of retaliation. If you invoke this archetype, you too will magically slide by. Believe this! It works, far more often than you'd imagine. Of course, actually breaking the law is not a good idea and is liable to get you bounced out of your circle of invulnerability.

Plan your itinerary beforehand, and how you are going to get from place to place. We used public transport (singing bawdy songs through the subway) but if you're more rural you may want to arrange for cars and vans. Once on your way, act weird, strange, hilarious, but not threatening or angry. Don't get in people's faces, yell insults or invade their spaces. You don't need to do that; your magic is strong enough without it.

Hand out your trinkets at random, to anyone you pass on the street. Explain nothing. Justify nothing. Do not be goaded into anger or made afraid. Laugh, frequently, at everything. If anyone demands an explanation, glossolalia is always an alternative. In the event you run into proselytizing members of some of those religions that could use a change of perspective, try drawing chalk circles around them and giving them the Erisian Turkey Curse.

(**The Erisian Turkey Curse:** *Walk around someone in circles while flapping your arms and gobbling like a turkey. Do not explain your behavior.*)

At each place on your itinerary, assemble on the sidewalk in front of the building (don't trespass; stay on the public walkway) and draw, with sidewalk chalk, the weirdest symbols you can think of. Don't write angry slogans or complaints; that's not the Trickster's way. Make bizarre symbols that symbolize these things to you; no one else has to understand them. You're trying to change things magically, not with direct action. After each drawing, hop or dance around, sing magical songs (*Fish Heads* or *Dead Puppies* work well, as do TV commercials sung backwards), leave a big, visible and clearly-labeled trinket at the door, and move on.

Change or be changed!

Interview with Hal Fuller (2001)

(Hal Fuller is the emcee for the Boston-area radio show Gender Talk, *a bi-gendered cross-dresser, and a trickster in his own right.)*

Tell us about your gender identity. What do you call yourself?

Hal: Aaaah ... pin myself squiggling to the page with a single word? Sorry, can't do that. I am Bi-sexual certainly, but primarily attracted to the feminine in whatever flesh it breathes. Bi-gendered? Two-souled? Trans-gendered (well, yeah)? I've worn too many faces and played too many roles to think there are only two states of anything. My lover Marcia calls me Shapeshifter, among other terms of (mostly) endearment. A stone with a thousand facets depends a lot on the light. What I may be becoming though, I can maybe guess, and I believe it is a more femme creature who still does the things this moment's spirit does. I am just beginning to grow, don't know what color my wings might be.

Vague, huh? How 'bout ... Hot Bi Cross-Dresser in Boston, feeling very playful!

How I spent my hetero life getting to be here and queer? Discovered Mommie's drawers—literally; whalebone-formidable rubber stuff, corsets, girdles and stockings. Found I liked the feeling of them and in them, and so discovered sexuality, sensuality, masturbation all wrapped up in those silken treasures ... and dropped all this shit some few years later because life suddenly got interesting—college, theater, altered states of whoopee. Thus began a pattern.... In—Out. Purge—Splurge. Know the dance? Heavy helpings of shame and remorse. Till WHAMMO SOCKO ZAP, Life Fall Down Go Boom due to drinking and suicidal depression.

I walked myself to the brink of death and life, and chose to live, but to do so left almost everything behind, friends, possessions, a goodly chunk of cognitive abilities. Was real, reduced to blank slate, what a gift. I call it My Black Hole. To truly start over, Unlearn and Learn. Reconnect with Spirit. Find and Follow the little sweet voices of my own truth and self. And one of the constant truths was the dressing and gender experimentation. The Fates practiced their notorious sense of humor, and gave me what I needed. Like a Radio show; great thing, cheaper than therapy, everybody should have one.

Describe your spiritual path, and how you came to it.

Hal: *(singing)*
> Bringing in the sheaves,
> Bringing in the sheaves.
> We shall come rejoicing
> Bringing in the sheaves.

Nice harvest time kinda hymn, and redolent of the velvet upholstered wood-framed God-voiced preachers who could shake the windows and make the stained glass dance. Them's my roots. Southern Baptist. So Dull we were almost Methodists. But there is a spirit voice in there, and if ya listen it can touch you and fill you. In fact, my assigned fate in too many eyes was to be a minister of same stamp. I actually was Youth Minister of a Baptist Church for a week. But from it all I got some rhythm, the beginning of a spiritual foundation, and found the weapon, the tool that my voice and words can make.

But there is nothing so handy as a good old fashioned life/death trip to goose up spiritual growing. I spent 28 days eating, talking recovery, relearning to bathe and brush my teeth, and staring at the trees change colors in a slow cool New England autumn. If you can see that and not feel the hand of the Divine, the Spirit in it, then I grieve for you. I've dabbled in Behavior MOD, biofeedback, past life regression, witchcraft, 12-Step, polyamory, one scary session of EST, healing by touch, an obsessive fling with D&D, fantasy role playing, erotic roleplaying, and a lot of just being open so I can hear the whispers, touch a tree so I can hear it laugh in the June sun., find like souls to play with. Lord of the Rings meets The Matrix meets Sartre meets La Cage meets a Hairy Rama ... mmmmm...

What do you think that we have to teach or give to single-gendered individuals?

Hal: We teach possibility and a wide range of gender expression. We ask a freedom to breathe ourselves into the world, to Be as Our spirit and our dreams, live Our flesh and our questions, challenge the chains, the rigid gender roles, or if wurst comes to wurst, We can paint on Our draggiest smile, pack them slacks, slide on in wearing Our best outfits, and just Party. DAMMM! Being a sexual minority does have its perks; you have so much to live DOWN to.

Chapter 14
Shapeshifter: Chameleon With A Calling

(Transcript of an interchange between the author and an unnamed dissenter at a panel on female-to-male transsexuals and their needs:)

SHE: I just don't understand it. To cut off your breasts? It isn't right. I mean, I don't see what you've gained.

ME: I suppose you won't get it if I was to say that we don't miss them. We're usually glad to see them go. They don't feel right. But surgery is a hard thing, yes. But testosterone is great.

SHE: But it puts you at a higher risk for stroke, heart attack, high blood pressure...

ME: Yeah, but what it did for my crotch is worth the whole deal.

SHE: What? *(Taken aback.)*

ME: You know what happened down there? Look at your pinky fingernail. That's the size of most women's clitorises, isn't it? Now look at the end joint of your thumb. That's how big it would get if you shot up with testosterone. Yes, really, actually mine's even bigger than that. The foreskin pulls right out into a shaft. It looks like a perfect little penis now, except without a pee hole. And it feels great! It's the best sex toy I've ever had. The nerves are more spread out, so my orgasms are twice as long and twice as intense. I'd never give it up, never.

SHE: *(pauses, then says, blinking with a strange expression on her face)* Really?

The Myth

The earliest shapeshifting was undoubtedly done as a way to commune with hunted animals, the tribal members wearing the skins of those creatures whose spirits they wanted to propitiate into being willing to sacrifice one of their own. Ancient caves are adorned with crudely painted images of dancing figures wearing horned animal headdresses; this idea of taking on a specific animal's powers and properties by wearing its skin or head must have slowly grown into the concept of "totems", both personal and tribal.

As discussed in the chapter on Dionysus, shapeshifting or otherwise communing with animals is a function of shamanism all over the world, right next to dying and being reborn, perhaps with a bit of madness in there with it. In his book *Shamanism*, Mircea Eliade notes that shamans-in-training in many cultures must learn to commune with spirits, and the first spirits that they deal with are usually those of the animal world. Often they must learn a "secret language", which originates in animal cries and noises, in order to speak to them; this is especially important for learning to communicate with birds. Once this language is learned, the shaman decorates themselves with skins or feathers, and proceeds to make noise and act like their "target" spirit, attempting to bring it into their body.

When one thinks of shapeshifting, one generally thinks of it in terms of turning into an animal, but many of these same shamans did ritual cross-dressing to enable them to take on the characteristics of another sex, exactly as if it were a bird or elk or bear. Some changed permanently, like the "soft men" of the Chukchi or the "bear women" of the Inuit; others did it periodically for reasons of magic—some spirits preferred to speak to a shaman of a certain sex, so any shaman worth his or her salt ought to be able to shapechange, at least ceremonially, in order to please them. There did not seem to be much difference for most shamans in changing species or changing sex; either way, it was another example of their role as Walker Between Worlds.

In a reverse similarity, many of the gender-ambiguous deities are themselves shapeshifters par excellence. Many male or female deities are quite capable of taking on an animal form as well—certain of them, such as the Egyptian gods, are normally shown as half animal—but it is the in-between figures who often have the widest range of random animal shapes—Ellegua becomes man and woman and little boys and girls and chickens and goats and snakes; Lilith takes forms of asses, goats, owls, and dragons; and Athena disguises herself not only as owls, hawks, and seabirds, but often as the male companions of her chosen heroes in order to advise them; and so forth. One could even theorize that the ability to shapeshift leads to gender ambiguity as well as the reverse process; after all, once you've been a member of a different species, being a different sort of human is practically a walk in the park.

The most famous shapeshifting mortal in the Greek mythic tradition is Tiresias, whose story has suspicious elements of shamanism in it. His sudden change into the body of a woman has two posited origins: in one tale, he has a vision of serpents coupling, which is reminiscent of the psychotic/ecstatic visions that often accompany the onset of a shamanic altered state; in another, he is enjoined by Zeus and Hera to undertake an experiment. They change him into a woman for seven years and order him to report back with the sure knowledge of which gender has more pleasure during sex, an issue which seemed to be an ongoing argument with them.

When Tiresias comes back in seven years, she tells them that the female has more pleasure, and begs to be allowed to remain one. Both Zeus and Hera are furious: Zeus because his masculine ego is wounded, Hera because her secret is out; and they deny his request. As a consolation gift, however, cross-dressing Athena steps in and gives Tiresias various shamanic gifts, such as the ability to tell the future and to understand the speech of birds.

Gender-crossing, as discussed in the Dionysus chapter, is a valid way to create an altered state. It certainly creates an altered state of *perception,* as anyone who's done it will tell you. When you cross-dress and walk out on the street as someone else, you are treated differently. You may find that the character you are portraying takes on a life of its own, with its own mannerisms and preferences; often these are elements of yourself that have always been a part of your psyche but which have been unable or unwilling to express until given the freedom of another shape.

Cross-dressing is the kind of quick shapechanging that is reminiscent of characters such as Coyote or Ellegua or Lilith. Coyote turns into a bird, turns into a beetle, takes off his penis and becomes a beautiful young woman, twines dried grass in his hair and becomes an old woman, walks around with a dog's face and human body and hair under his cowboy hat. It is the shapechanging of human theatre: the costume becomes the shape, the mask defines the aspect of the soul. Indeed, the word "mask" comes from the earlier *masca,* which referred specifically to an animal mask. Cross-dressing is mask magic. Some might call it a fetish, but as we've discussed in Baphomet's chapter, the word "fetish" has an alternate meaning which is more magical.

Then there's the other kind of shapeshifting; the long, slow, transformation of our bodies by the force of our wills and modern technology. Those of us who actually choose to get sex changes have the unique ability to watch our bodies slowly change into something "other", different, alien. The only time when there is more rapid change to a human form is during puberty, or possibly a severe illness. Hair growth patterns alter and body fat redistributes. Skin softens or coarsens and muscles form differently. With each passing month, we come closer to the divine androgyne; we become mythical beasts. It is a wondrous process for us to watch.

There's also the other issue of hormones, which is even more controversial. They also change our minds. Whatever doctors (who usually haven't done it themselves) may feel or say, hormones are mind-altering substances. They do not react the same for everyone, but everyone that I've ever spoken to who has had the opportunity to experience different types of hormones in their lifetime has admitted that yes, they are different on the brain. Sometimes the differences are immediate and obvious, sometimes subtle and long-term, but they do exist.

This is not to say that a shot of testosterone will create the kind of behavior in everyone that I see in the roosters that strut around outside on my farm, attacking each other and committing gang-rape, or that an estrogen pill will turn anyone into a meek, docile hen. For one thing, we're far more complex than chickens. However, it is foolish to assume that just because we're arguably the most intelligent animal on earth means that we do not react to hormones in the ways that most other animals do. We can't disown our animal heritage, or our animal brains. The effect, certainly, is somewhere between "like my rooster" and "not at all", and calibrating it is the source of much disagreement, but the fact still remains that hormones do change our minds. They are really mind-altering substances. I know for myself that how far away from depression I am varies directly with where I am in relation to my next shot. I know that my body was having mood-altering effects from estrogens, when I was put on them at puberty. I know that the way I respond to estrogens and androgens is completely different from the way they were experienced by my male-to-female transsexual wife, but I also know that they mind-altered her just as dramatically. In fact, every one of the transsexuals that I know reported a serious mood-altering stage directly upon starting hormone therapy, regardless of whether or not they had changed their bodies or social roles at that point.

More testing needs to be done, without an agenda behind it that demands certain results, and we shapechangers are in the front lines of the probable answers. Of course, we all hate being under a medical microscope, which is likely a good reason for more of us to get together and do our own research more respectfully.

In the meantime, it's also a sure thing that dramatically changing one's body, and radically altering the way you are perceived by others, is also likely to result in a change of headspace. If you are a shapeshifter, make sure that you keep a journal of your feelings from day to day. Describe how you a re treated differently by different sorts of people, and what it teaches you about them.

Discussion Questions

How do you change your shape every day, as you get ready to enter different environments? Does your version or presentation of masculinity or femininity alter as you don these masks? Can you list them? Do you like all of them, or are some stifling?

If you take hormones, what was the experience like? What did it teach you about male and female? How does it compare with the experience of other transsexuals, especially those going in the opposite direction? Compare and contrast. How did it feel to watch your body shapeshift into something different? Did you have a hard time recognizing yourself in the mirror, or did you recognize yourself for the first time?

Inner World Activity #1

If you aren't transgendered, cross-dress for one day. Don't make it a spur-of-the-moment thing; do it right. Treat it like a ritual and put the same amount of preparation into it as you would any other ritual. Carefully collect whatever clothes and makeup you may need for the transformation. Ask other cross-dressers to help you if you aren't sure how to go about it. The end result isn't to look perfect, or even to pass, but to spend a period of time discovering what it's like to cross that border, even if only externally. Don't do it alone; plan to be around people, although you can choose them and create a safe space if necessary. Honor your inner male or female and let them have the day for once.

Inner World Activity #2

If you're in the process of morphing your body, photograph it in each stage. Do this even if you hate the way you look. Someday, you'll look at those pictures that make you wince now and be glad you took them; they'll be a record of the magical act you performed. Be sure to include nude photos, with genital shots if your genitals are going to change. If you've already changed, it's not too late to start taking pictures. You will change still further as you move through life.

Inner World Activity #3

If you're transsexual and have already transitioned some time ago, commit yourself to spending one day cross-dressed (perhaps with friends) either in the persona of the person you once were, or in a new and different one who shares only the "putative" sex of your original gender. This may seem like a strange thing to do, after all that work to get over to the side of the table you're now on, but once you've been too long in one form you may well forget about the shapeshifting magic, and how it gives you the power of altered perception. Once in a while, it's good to visit the other side of the table again, just for a day, although no one will ever force you to stay.

If the prospect, even in play, makes you profoundly uncomfortable, explore why that would be. If playing with your gender gives you the willies, it could be that you're still not firmly and confidently settled in your new space; that you have insecurities about it. This might be a good exercise for rooting them out and examining them.

Outer World Activity #1

If you're in or attached to a school, college, or university, request or help sponsor a cross-dressing seminar. Encourage people to get extra credit by coming in cross-dressed, perhaps after a workshop on how to do it properly and some help from an expert. Contact your local cross-dressing organization to get assistance for such a workshop. Drum up as much enthusiasm as you can; make it a fun rather than serious thing. It's the sort of thing that's much more fun to do in droves, with backup and safety in numbers. Make sure that everyone gets to go out somewhere, to a club or restaurant, in order to try their new "personas" in public.

After you've spent all day cross-dressed, get together and talk about what it was like. One suggestion might be to take photos of people before, after and during their "transformation", so you can discuss the dynamics of shapeshifting and what it felt like. Have people exchange feedback on whether they acted/walked/spoke any different when "transformed" or not. Write up an account of the experiment, complete with photos, and see if the school newspaper will take it, or give it out as a handout.

Outer World Activity #2

Organize a theatrical production of a traditional play, perhaps Shakespeare. Have all the parts played by individuals who are not living in the sex of the characters. Present it, with a discussion period afterwards so that the audience can talk about how it came across to them.

The Ritual: Circle of Masks

This ritual requires a lot of preparation. The people in charge of running it should start making masks some time in advance, and creating tapes. The physical requirements are some sort of stereo or boom box tape player, a whole lot of appropriate tapes, a big mirror, and as many masks as you can put together. These masks should be reasonably easy to put on and take off, should fit a variety of head and face sizes, and are created to be archetypal figures. The list of masks we ended up with were:

The Face of Fire
The Face of Air
The Face of Water
The Face of Earth
   (these first four were highly decorated half-masks that were brought up first
   to do the elements, acknowledge the four directions, and create sacred space)
The Face of Dreams (lots of chiffon!)
The Face of the Old One
The Face of Night (lots of trailing black)
The Face of Power (a big dragon's head made of papier mache)
The Face of Respect (a furry skunk's head with a long tail down the back)
The Trickster (a Coyote mask similar to the skunk mask)
The Face of Prophecy (very mysterious, lots of swirls of DNA)
The Face of Sacrifice (stark white with drops of scarlet blood)
The Face of Gaiety (a feathered Mardi Gras mask)
The Face of Gaea (motherly, green and leafy)
The Face of Pan (very male, laughing, feathered eyebrows and beard)
The Face of the Maiden (innocent and pretty)
The Face of the Warrior (a helm with a grim face fixed in it)
Top Dog/Underdog (two masks fixed together under one fedora—the Top
   Dog has the clean side of the fedora and is young and grinning; the
   Underdog is old and dirty under the messy side; the mask is switched
   around halfway through the person's presentation)
The Face of Love (lots of pink and jewels)
The Face of Anger (enraged scarlet face)
The Face of Chaos (crazy face, Picasso-esque)

I'm sure you can think of more. This is just to start you off.

Decide on some song or piece of music that best describes the feeling of each mask and put it on a tape, cued up to the first note. Put them in order, clearly labeled. Get a deck of cards—we used Tarot trumps, but regular playing cards will do—and assign each mask a card. Use only the assigned cards; put the others aside. Stand a large mirror where everyone can see it clearly.

It's good to have three or four people helping with this ritual—one to run the tape deck, and two to get masks on people. When everyone is present, have each person pick a card—you can let them each take only one, or keep going until all the masks were used up. The point of the cards is that no one knows exactly which mask they're going to get. They must portray the mask that Fate hands them, regardless of its appropriateness to their gender, size, mood, or station in life. Inevitably, I've found, the Face of the Maiden ends up on some big football bruiser and the Face of Pan will go to the most man-hating woman in the lot. Sometimes the masks will fall so well that you won't know what happened until afterwards; the first time I did this ritual, the Face of Sacrifice (whose tape featured a folk song about a woman who dies in childbirth) went to a woman who had just had a miscarriage, and was two weeks sober after twenty years of alcoholism. She had a psychotic break in less than twenty-four hours after this ritual.

Each person, in turn, hands their card over to the person running the tape player, who puts in the correct tape. The maskers tell the person to close their eyes, stand them in front of the mirror, get the mask securely onto their head, and say, "Behold the Face of (whatever)!" The music starts, and they have the whole period of that song to do whatever they want. If they choose to sit and stare at the mirror, that's fine. If they want to dance, or mime, or interact with the crowd, that's fine too. The idea is not to entertain others with a performance, but to find the spirit of that archetype deep within you, wherever it may be. Don't give in to the temptation to direct the person or give them hints; let the chips fall where they may.

If you have the time, and have cycled through all your masks and want to do more, a second part can be placing the archetypes in situations together. Have a stack of cards with various situations, such as "Getting Your Oil

Changed," "Holding Up The Convenience Store," "Trying To Seduce A Married Person In Their Spouse's Presence", "Selling Door-To-Door", and so on. Decide in advance how many people each scenario needs. Then have a neutral person draw cards to see who gets to do what. Can you imagine the Trickster and the Face of Chaos trying to Hold Up The Convenience Store, with the Face of Anger behind the counter?

Afterwards, everyone should sit down and pass a talking stick around, and discuss what their feelings were about their mask experience, about how it felt to change their shape temporarily. Watch for people who seem withdrawn and distressed; this can be a heavy ritual and buried feelings may arise. You might want to have someone capable of a lot of unconditional positive regard talk to them afterwards, just to see if they're all right.

Interview with Halley Low (2001)

(Halley Low is a shapeshifter, drag queen, and Radical Faerie, a genre of earth-centered gay male spirituality.)

So how would you describe yourself and your experience of gender?

Halley: First and foremost, I would state that I am a human being, and like other humans I have a body which flows with living blood, and I am a living manifestation of the Spirit, but I am an individual. My thoughts and dreams are my own, as is my body, which is defined anatomically as male—I have a penis. Yet that in no way negates the naturalness of my feminine experience of gender. I did define myself as transsexual for many years, but I was never quite comfortable using a medical diagnosis to name that which is most natural to me.

Also, I never really bought into the notion that doctors, through the miracle of surgery, could change your "sex". Even early on I thought that concept served to deny both my reality and the naturalness of gender variance, but feeling the pull of cultural conformity, and not having any other language than the alienated and authoritarian medical/psychological babble, I accepted the accumulated "wisdom". That was until, in my passion for the study of religion, I discovered other words and cultural views—words like *winkte, gallae, hijra,* among many others. With these words I was able to re-discover ways of seeing myself as a true part of Nature and as having a role in the social order. No, I'm not a *winkte* or a *galla* or a *hijra,* but I have come to understand that we are linked, and I find inspiration and courage in their histories.

So what label would I use to describe me best? I could say that I am a gay transgendered male, or a fem-male, or a big old queen, but I prefer to be seen as a whole human being, so the word to describe me best is simply my name— Halley.

Could you tell us how you got to the place where you are now, experientially and spiritually?

Halley: The symbolism of the Tarot helped to reawaken my spiritual life, and opened my eyes to the all-inclusive gender of divinity. I started to read a wide range of works on metaphysics, theology, Jungian thought, and feminist spirituality. Though I have read many scholarly and popular works, I guess I would have to say that the simple books by a simple man named Scott Cunningham brought me to Neo-Paganism and natural magick. I have always considered myself a solitary (in truth we all are in the end) and I am not interested in a "coven", so I think I should not use the term Wiccan because I am not schooled in any of the "traditions". So maybe simply Pagan is better.

So to answer your question in a nutshell: theologically I am pantheist, and philosophically I am a Taoist. I practice Nature magick and work in alignment with the earth. I am a Light-Worker.

In the early '90's I became involved with the Radical Faerie movement. On a very personal level this was an important step in my unfolding. Primarily, my involvement with the Faeries has helped further to heal the culturally imposed split between my anatomical sex and my gender identity. I have become more aware of the fluidity of sex, gender, and sexuality. the bonds of rigidity and dogma have been undone, and I have come to see the femininity inherent in my hairy male body, and embraced it as it is, rather than accepting culturally imposed self-hatred and the mad pursuit of doctors with messiah complexes. I have come to understand the truth that I possess, and I define my body, not the other way around.

I have also come to accept that aspect of masculinity that lives within me— my Animus—which for so long I thought of as non-existent or alien. This has freed my energies and expanded my understanding of myself and my fellow humans. It has also brought me to a new place of many questions—which I believe is the beginning of the next stage in my journey.

How does it feel to change shape? Is there a spiritual or magickal use of the power to transform?

Halley: I have always been struck by the term "trans". Trans-formation, trans-figure, trans-illuminate, trans-personal, trans-sexual, trans-gender, trans-theistic, trans-cendental. The dictionary defines "trans" as "to go across, beyond, through, so as to change". I think the heart of the trans-experience is the ability to cross and go beyond so as to perceive and experience like from different perspectives. This ability allows one to see how conflicts can be resolved. No wonder so many trans-people have held the role of counselor and healer in traditional cultures—this ability can open one to deep levels of understanding of the trans-communal nature of Life, and this understanding leads to compassion.

I am not saying that all transgender of gender variant people experience this potential as natural within their lives; we live in a culture that does not nurture the gift. Western culture feels threatened by our power, because it challenges the neatly boxed social constructs that establish its social order. The ability to transform, to radically change perspective, and the understanding of Self (individual and communal) that can come from this experience can lead to the realization of the unity of the multiplicity of form known as the Universe.

So to answer your question—is there a magickal bent to using this ability—in rituals, particularly Radical Faerie rituals, I use the transformative power of gender-crossing to evoke the hermaphroditic nature of Divinity. By channeling this energy, I work to heal the wounds of division that mar our human souls. How does it feel to change shape? In ritual or when channeling it is a powerful and ecstatic experience that takes me beyond ego-self. "Ritual drag" is different for me than the personal or mundane experience of transgender living. On that level there is power too, the power to be comfortable with oneself. And there is fear; fear of a hostile society, a fear that can paralyze, but can be overcome by the sense of freedom that comes with self-acceptance, which is the core of compassion.

What do you think that differently gendered people have to offer the rest of the world?

Halley: I could say that we can help people see the multiplicity that is gender, and that by virtue of our unique perspectives we might have a special place as counselors and healers like in days of old. Surely those of us so inclined should pursue such a path—all that best psychics I know are differently-gendered in some way—but I am hesitant to simply re-hash our roles in by-gone days. Nor do I wish to peg trans-people into a limiting social role, however noble. Rather, I think the heart of the gift we can offer is to be true to our visions and gifts, whatever they may be, and to utilize them to the benefit of self and other. Only by being true to our own nature and abilities can we as individuals ever achieve what is our heart's desire, and hold our place and express our purpose in the grand scheme of things.

Chapter 15
Turquoise Boy and White Shell Girl:
A Place In The Community

Dear binarists, for you are dear to us and part of us,

Forget this note. Don't even read it. It's only trouble, you don't want to bother. We are dismissible. We aren't an important voting bloc, we don't have lots of influence with the powerful, and we're rarely organized or organizers. Forget us. Stop reading now.

We can't even agree among ourselves: many of us demand nothing less than the demolition of your cozy and false 2-party gender system, while the rest of us shore it up and demand to join, only in places you'd forbid. We don't define well. We do work hard and make great allies, except that you lose more of your other support by including us than we replace. Many of us, scarred from being radically disenfranchised, are unreliably flaky, even as many of us are astoundingly talented. We are easy to make deliberate fun of and easy to inadvertently insult; we may make ordinary conversation (under your old assumptions) difficult, and the above demands show how hard we are to please.

So forget us. It won't even take any effort for some of you, since you already have. Some of you, while meaning well, always did, never considering that we might exist, or considering us as variations on the theme. The theme of both Eden and Noah: always and only two types of human, as if your two-party system were divinely ordained. Sometimes the same ones ridicule astrology for positing only twelve types of humans. Some of you are queer and still redefine us away.

You may not know you have a system for pigeonholing people, but what's the first question you ask about a newborn? How many kinds of restrooms are there in public? How are Olympic and other sports events segregated? How are pronouns segregated? Ever bought clothes or filled out a form? Who is in a marriage or a family? How many ways are there to enforce our erasure? The problem is, we aren't going to go away. Oh, we can and often do hide, but a vocal minority of us (already a minority within a minority) refuse to. You may believe you've never met us. We exist; we have existed as long as humans have (maybe longer?), and we will exist as long as humans do, since we are an integral and inseparable part of what it is to be human. Since we're so few and such trouble, the only reasonable thing to do is omit us.

Omit us at the peril of losing your own humanity.

Some of you who believe in the binary paradigm do so by default, swimming in the same unquestioned cultural waters as everyone else. Which fish discuss water? (Answer: The drowning ones.) Some of you believe in it for admirable and noble reasons: hoping it can more swiftly bring justice to your oppressed gender, or hoping it can ease your transition from a gender assigned to you to a gender you feel you belong in. I support your goals and do not wish to do anything that hampers your progress, and I request that you not run over us along the way. Find out more about mullerian and wolffian ducts, and the relatively late embryological differentiation of structures having a common origin. Find out about the real range of chromosomal and phenotypal variation. The binarist supposition is not only disproved by the physical, medical, and biological evidence; it also produces an artificial pair of polarized camps more suited to continued unequal conflict than to reconciliation.

Yes, solidarity is necessary to struggle, but let's base it on our goals, not something that crumbles upon close examination. Must we again relearn that separate is inherently unequal? Positing some of us as Other works against imagination and against opportunities to influence. It would de-emphasize or even deny our common humanity, an ingredient of the scapegoating found to be a requisite for genocide in Staub's *Roots of Evil*, which examines five genocides and extracts their common roots.

Evolutionary pressures favor phenotypes adapted to local pressures, yet in every human generation lots of "superfluous" traits are expressed, from musical ability to a capacity for awe and wonder. I submit that we who are omitted from your binary scheme are useful to the species and to the ecosystem (this may be one reason we keep popping up), and we should be respected and honored as such. It may be about diversity- after all, the Nazis had it exactly backwards. The evolutionary strength of a population comes from its ability to weather as many kinds of stressors as possible, so the widest variety of functioning individuals ensures survival, since the pressures of natural selection will shift in unknown directions. I invite you: let all our thinking evolve along with us all."

*   –Zot Lynn Szurgot*

The Myth

The Dineh (Navajo) people of the Southwest tell of the beginning of the world, when First Man and First Woman started the human race. The People multiplied, but still had much to learn. They traveled from the primitive First World to the Second World, which they quickly outgrew as well. Passing to the Third World, they met two *nadle*, or third gender people, named Turquoise Boy and White Shell Girl. They invented pottery, weaving, and created the first hoes and grinding stones. All these gifts they gave to the People, and the People thrived.

No one knows exactly how the trouble started, but the men and the women began to quarrel, and the fighting spread throughout all the people until the two groups split and lived in separate camps on either side of a great river, meeting only to mate so that there would be more children. Turquoise Boy did all the women's work for the men, and White Shell Girl did all the men's work for the women. The two *nadle*, however, grew tired of this state of affairs and eventually decided to bring the people back together into one tribe.

They noticed that the river was rising, and realized that all would be drowned if they did not unite and think of a solution. With pleas and flattery and tears, they wheedled the People into working together again, men and women side by side. Turquoise Boy placed a huge reed on top of the highest mountain, and the People scrambled up to the Fourth World, but the flood waters followed them and threatened to sweep them all away. White Shell Girl then brought a second reed, with which they were able to climb to the Fifth World, which was dry and safe, and where the People live today.

What is it like to read a myth where third gender people not only create all the useful arts but save the very human race? There is a lot to learn in this Dineh picture of the world that in so many ways resembles ours. First, in the myth, Turquoise Boy and White Shell Girl are the source of all nonprocreative creativity, inventing all the arts necessary to daily comfort. This is reminiscent of the astrological principle of the asteroid Pallas (see the chapter on Athena) which symbolizes both creativity and androgyny. It is as if the human psyche feels that by damming the procreative force, you get a diverted and much more intense outpouring of creativity not attached to physical fertility. This kind of mythic thinking stereotypes the gay community as being full of artists and other creative people—or is it a stereotype?

The third gender people in the myth are also shown as being mediators in the war of the sexes. It's almost redundant to point out that those of us who know both sides end up being the intermediaries, the ambassadors, again and again throughout our lives. As children and adolescents, we may have played with the opposite sex—or if we played with the members of our own sex, we often ended up being the ones to explain the mysterious motivations of the opposite sex to our compatriots. As adults, we were often the apologists for that opposite sex: "No, they aren't *all* bad, some of them are fine people, they were just brought up to believe thus-and-so..." For some transgendered people, it was their constant apologies, their perceived ability to "identify" with the opposite sex, that triggered their understanding of their own natures.

On the other side of the coin, there are the androgynous progenitors, who bore all of humanity from their merged natures. Unfortunately, most of these are fairly abstract, like the depersonalized androgyne on the Tarot card of the World, who symbolizes completion. The most personified and least abstract (besides Obatala) is Zurvan, the primal androgyne in Persian myth who bore the twins Ahura Mazda and Ahriman, light and dark, sun and shadow, constantly struggling with each other. Zurvan hirself is pictured as an elderly, wise figure; Barbara Walker in her book *The Crone* (Harper&Row, 1985) refers to hir as "a half-masculine Crone figure" and points out that hir name, Zurvan, translates to "Infinite Time", the same meaning as that of the Hindu Kali.

The great Progenitor Zurvan was said to be the keeper of secrets that would not be understandable to mortal men and women, something that we transgendered people often irrationally feel in our childhoods of shame and hiding, only our secrets are perceived as being not only incomprehensible to others but dangerous to us should they be found out. Our irresistible draw toward what we needed, however, is echoed in Zurvan's other titles, "Destiny", and "Fate".

Zurvan was also referred with an additional title that translated to "decrepitude" or "extreme age". Human beings are most androgynous at two periods in our lives: pre-pubescent childhood and old age. When we become elderly, secondary sexual characteristics often become obscured beneath wrinkles and white hair; men gain sagging chests and women grow facial hair and sometimes bald. As our reproductive abilities disappear and our physical strength wanes, our gender becomes far less socially important; we are considered to be elders first rather than men or women. We may well also, by this time, have outgrown the need to restrain ourselves within socially acceptable gender roles. I remember my grandfather discovering that he had a talent for rocking babies to sleep when no one else could get them to be quiet, and an elderly woman friend who decided, at the age of eighty, to become a loud and aggressive activist. Zurvan may well be the archetype that embodies such a state, being the wise crone and the wise elder statesman in one being, with the combined knowledge of years of both male and female understanding.

We in the transgender community are just starting to get to the place where we have actual elders. The brave individuals who started applying for sex changes 30 years ago are now sporting grey hair and wrinkles; and the formerly closeted cross-dressing elders are coming out of the closets with retirement, feeling that they have little to lose. As sex changes become more and more common—a record number of SRS surgeries were performed last year—and as even those staying in their birth slot are playing with gender roles, many of these elders are surprised at the younger generation looking to them to find out what it will be like for them.

Growing old as a transgendered person produces its own difficult situations. For one thing, all that work that you did in order to pass as an attractive member of the opposite sex is kind of, well, societally useless now. On the other hand, you pass better in general because of the elder-androgyny-thing, but you may well have ceased to care by then. You'll be subject to the discrimination that elders in general get in this society, as well as transgender discrimination. On the other hand, you may by that time be pretty well immune to the opinions of the peanut gallery. You may be under pressure by your relatives to act "normally", or with more "dignity". It is unlikely that elders in nursing homes are allowed much in the way of gender leeway, either, which is a situation no one seems to be addressing much, perhaps because of the nasty idea that there's not much point in wasting activism on people who will just be dead in a few years anyway. Historically, many a "passing woman" who lived her life in men's clothing was forced in old age to don the shawl and skirts of the old woman, forced on her by the proprieties of old age homes.

We must take great care not to let the transgender movement become, like some other movements, a creation largely of the young and beautiful, or would-be beautiful. We must let our elders know that it's OK for them to have grey hair and wrinkles, and that we respect their opinions. We must value the fact that they suffered with clueless doctors, manipulative researchers, experimental surgery, archaic morals, isolation, and even less protection than we did, and that we have what we have built largely on the backs of their sufferings. We must never let ethics become overrun by aesthetics, or at least not the aesthetics of the larger society. Never swallow Society's favored aesthetics without a hell of a struggle. It's already proved it can't be trusted with them.

Then there are those in our community who are basically damaged goods. If years of living in the wrong body don't grind you down into insanity, being discriminated against in the workplace, assaulted on the streets, and having difficulty finding partners and friends might well do it. There are an appalling number of transgendered people on mental disability, and even more living on the streets or clinging to a subsistence life because of mental problems. It's not that transgender is caused by mental problems, it's that it creates them—and they are compounded by society's gauntlet. We laugh and make jokes about "FNTs"—fucking neurotic transsexuals—but the truth is that just living a transgendered life is enough to give some people a bad case of post-traumatic stress disorder. We, as a community, need to start thinking about what it will take to heal our broken and protect our fragile. Currently, to be transgendered is, in most cases, to be isolated. There are no shelters or halfway houses or transitional housing situations for us, even though we are extremely vulnerable in mixed living situations with strangers. No one is going to create these facilities for us. If we don't do it together, we're basically out of luck.

There's also the matter of violence towards us, a matter touched upon in other chapters. We are stuck in the center of the gender war, caught between two warring tribes, our bodies their closest battlefield. Before they take the war onto each others' land, they have to trample us, and they do it frequently. Our only hope of survival is becoming the diplomats between them, loudly and boldly, even if the only thing they can agree on at first is that we are the enemy. The only way our dead will be honored like the wartime casualties that they are is if we remember them loudly, protest visibly, make people know who they were and why they died. Do the memorial service at the end of this chapter on a regular basis, in public places. Make them see that we are human, not inhuman vermin whose killing can be justified. Unobjectify us.

One of the best ways we as a community can make a dent in how people perceive us is to do volunteer work out of the closet. All too often transgendered people are so busy just staying alive, or obsessing on our problems, that we allow ourselves to become introverted and blank out as much of the outside world as we can. We see ourselves more as victims than as people who can make a difference, adding to our feelings of helplessness. Yet the most important thing we can do is to be seen, exactly as we are, making a contribution out of the goodness of our hearts, showing that even with all that is stacked against us, we are still big enough to be able to afford to be generous.

So go out and find an organization to volunteer for, and do it as "out" as you possibly can. If you're a TV, make a commitment to do it dressed. If you're a transsexual, tell them all. If you're afraid of bashing or need moral support, do it in a group. As we've found, while a lone gender transgressor may be fair game, a whole group of us together tends to make tongues freeze and eyes glaze, and allow us to walk on by unmolested. Very few people are foolhardy enough to take you on when you're in a group.

Volunteerism in the larger community can be difficult if you're openly transgendered. Even if you offer a free pair of willing hands with an open heart, organizations who up to the last second are bemoaning their lack of volunteers will suddenly find a reason to turn you down. One MTF that I know tried to volunteer at several different organizations before one of them deigned to allow her to do scut-work. She was openly incredulous at their hypocrisy. Of course, what they're thinking is that if someone sees you working there, and it's known that you are "associated" with them, they might lose funding from more conservative benefactors. However, there are still groups out there that will take anyone up to and including the Elephant Man should he resurrect and offer to help, and they should be the ones rewarded for their tolerance with your earnest efforts.

The first thing you should do, upon walking in the door, is to make yourself invaluable. Show them what a gem they have in you. Yes, some of them may attempt to exploit you, but you can walk out whenever you like and you should let them know that if you feel exploited. Since volunteer groups often network with each other, good works that you do in one place may reverberate through to others. When you're volunteering, it's important to be proactive and not just sit around twiddling your thumbs waiting for someone to tell you what to do. Look for things that seem to need doing, and ask, "Can I help out with this?" This also gives you the added benefit of possibly being able to choose your venue, and answers the problem of the bewildered volunteer coordinator who may not know what to do with the strange bird that's fluttered through the doorway.

Discussion questions

What are our traditional roles, both in communities around the world and here, in this society? Are they fulfilling? Restrictive? Are they what you want to be doing, and if not, how can this be changed? How can we create new sacred roles for us? How can we rehabilitate old and forgotten ones? Remember that what is forgotten on the surface may still exist in what Jung called the "collective unconscious", and may still somehow strike a strong chord of recognition in people, which they may welcome or fight.

Outer World Activity #1

What communities do you belong to? How can you bring transgender awareness to them? You don't necessarily have to come out yourself, although hopefully part of the results of such transgender awareness would be that it would then become safe for you to come out. Arrange quietly to have someone come and speak, or at least be visibly standing up against discrimination should a nontraditionally-gendered person be fired or a denied a job. Sometimes all that is needed is for enough people to get up and protest. If you do nothing else, report such incidences to the ACLU and other groups concerned with fair employment practices, so that at least there is a record of the events. This may help them to create background for a case later.

Outer World Activity #2

Grapevine with a vengeance. In your area, set up a list of service providers and companies that are, in order: Transgender or Transgender-owned. Transgender-friendly (and will put it in writing). Queer or queer-owned. Queer-friendly. Circulate this list, and keep adding to it. Every time you meet a transgendered person who has their own business or an influential position in a company, put them on the referral list. When you need a plumber, go for the list rather than the Yellow Pages, and encourage others to do so as well. Publish the list in various places; make sure that as many people as possible have access to it. Transgendered folk are extremely discriminated against in hiring practices, especially if they are "out" or don't pass well. We need to help our own.

If the entry is that of a company who has hired a transgendered person, but you're not actually going to be using that person's services, make sure when you call that you inform them that they were chosen because they were willing to employ (and treat decently) people of nontraditional gender expression. Make sure they understand that their willingness to do so got them customers. This provides job security to the transgendered person in question.

Outer World Activity #3

Volunteer to work for political candidates. They need all the help they can get. Usually they're one of the groups who'll take the Elephant Man, because you're not just a person, you're a constituent! They generally can't afford to look bad, unless they're serious conservative right-wingers, and you don't want to go near them anyway. Keep your eyes open, make contacts, keep your "gaydar" going. The name of the game in doing volunteer work is networking and gaining social capital thereby. In the human service world, it's so often not what you know but who you know, so personal contacts will do more for your reputation than anything else. Let them know your issues while working your tush off to show how valuable you are.

The Ritual: Memorial Ritual For the Dead of Our Tribe

About one transgendered person per month dies by murder or suicide in this country alone. At the Year 2000 True Spirit Conference, some of us decided to create a memorial for our transgendered dead—friends, lovers, or just people who shouldn't have gone down. The ritual was amazingly simple, and can be done anywhere you all have enough space to stand in a circle. All it takes is a ball of black yarn, a knife or scissors, and someone to read the invocation, which Bella and I wrote the night before doing the ritual.

Unroll the yarn, handing it back and forth across the circle so that everyone has one or two pieces to hold on to. It should make a giant web across the circle. The person officiating says, "This is the web of life that we are all connected to." Then they read the invocation. Then they read a list of the names of dead transgendered folk—it might be a good idea to pass around a piece of paper first to get names from all the participants. Another person walks around the circle with a knife or scissors, and cuts a strand as each name is read.

Afterwards, we took the various broken strands and twisted or braided them together, and wore them around our arms like black armbands, or around our necks, or elsewhere visible on our persons, for the rest of the conference, to show our solidarity.

Memorial Invocation

This is a heart's song for our fallen
brothers and sisters
whose bones lie scorned
beneath markers
memorializing lives they had discarded
under names not their own
buried by relatives
who refused to know them
for who they were.

This is a heart's song for our
brothers and sisters
for whom the world proved too harsh
too painful for their sweet fragile spirits
who chose to open the door and go
with their own hands.

This is a heart's song for our
brothers and sisters
who fought, stubbornly,
day after day
mile after mile
and who finally gave out
from exhaustion
and bad brain chemistry
and soul-eating stress after
the world's final blow
and lost what sanity
this cruel time had left them.

This is a heart's song for our
brothers and sisters
who were hunted like animals

down narrow city streets
whether out of fear or sport
or both
who became prey
kissing the rifle's slug
clubbed to death like seals
on a beach.

This is a heart's song for our
brothers and sisters
who only wanted a night's comfort
and trustingly invited in
the keepers of raging inner demons
who saw those demons in their ambivalent bodies
and tried to snuff them out
stabbed, shot, beaten
anything
to make us cease to exist.

This is a heart's song for our
brothers and sisters
who survived the nights of comfort
only to take home silent invaders
who ate them out
from the inside -
who sang them in with needles
trying to drown out their own pain.

This is a heart's song for all our
brothers and sisters
who fell by the wayside
to pave our road with tears
to wash us with their blood
to wash us clean

their blood lives in us
we carry their memory
under the skin of our faces
under the skin of our hands
every time we look in a mirror
every time we reach out and touch each other
we will see them
and we will remember.

Chris Darcy ~ Tacy Ranta ~ Tyra Hunter ~ Robert Eads ~ Sabrina Von Betz ~ Marsha P. Johnson ~ Brandon Teena ~ Nicole Seely ~ Rita Hester ~ Fitzroy Green ~ Vianna Fay Williams ~ Elizabeth Short ~ Louis Graydon Sullivan ~ Chanelle Pickett ~ Debra Forte ~ Michelle Downs ~ Richard Goldman ~ Christian Paige ~ Jesse & Peggy Santiago ~ Carmen Marie Montoya ~ Harold Draper ~ Cameron Tanner ~ Francisco Luna ~ Marcelle Cook-Daniels ~ and many more...

Between: A Song for the Day of Mourning

2. Between the door to the Dead and the living,
We are the warrior Dead of your tribe,
The ancestors lost to the hand of the foe
Between the storm of their hate and desire and fear.
You hold all of our dreams under your skin,
Your body's memory keeps us alive,
For you are the children of our hearts and our souls
And there are more of us
Every year.

3. Between the ice and the steam is the ocean,
Between the day and the night is the dawn,
Between the song of your voice and your face in the mirror
Is the life of the Earth and the flash of the star.
Between the woman and man we were caught here
But the blessing we held will live on,
As long as the children of our hearts and our souls
Keep remembering
Who you are.

I wrote this song in honor of the transgendered folk who died by violence, whose names we call on the Transgendered Day of Remembrance, November 28th. It is my offering to them, and my gift to this community. I provide here the sheet music for groups who want to get folks to sing it; if you go to my website at http://www.ravenkaldera.org/activism/between.html you'll find an informal recording of me singing it, so that people will know what it sounds like.

Who can sing it in public? Anyone! Who can record it? Anyone, so long you ask my permission first (email me at cauldronfarm@hotmail.com), send me a few free tapes for giving out as gifts, and send me a .mp3 of the recording to go up on this page. In other words, any recording of it by anyone will be made free to all eventually. That's what "gift" means.

May we remember, always, our beloved dead.

Interview with Cynthya BrianKate (2008)

(Cynthya BrianKate is one of the few people who have taken on the title of Speaker for the Transgender Dead. In the face of all her disabilities, s/he puts herself out in various communities, reminding us of where we came from and how far we have yet to go.)

How would you describe your gender identity, and how did you get to this point with it?

Cynthya: I'd say your quote about being "so much of both you're practically neither" is a good start, though I'm not sure that even exactly fits my gender. I was assigned male at birth and my family tried raising me as a boy. Thankfully they also raised me to treat people decently, so I can say they succeeded at one goal. The funny thing is that they'd wished for a girl when I was born, so I tease them with "Careful what you wish for!" because they got half that wish with me.

I never exactly had a sense of myself as being a little boy or a little girl. Most of my childhood playmates were spiders, and when I did play with neighbor kids I was always the crash-landed space mutant. When I started school all the gender segregation, with separate bathrooms and all, scared and confused me, and still does. Everyone told me I was a boy even though I didn't feel like one, so I tried being one. Not to say I did that well at it, especially once regular gym started. I had some clues that I wasn't quite a boy, but I didn't feel I could tell anyone. Part of it was not having the words to understand, let alone express this. I was getting beaten up by other kids, and the only person who even dared ask if anyone ever had dreams "of being the opposite sex" was laughed into silence. By junior high, I'd started thinking about and questioning my gender. I was the odd kid to begin with, and the class sissy, and most of my friends were girls, and they seemed to see me as one of the girls. I was also getting beaten up a lot for not being macho enough. I got through until the beginning of high school by picking up friends and bodyguards, most of whom were butch girls.

But by the end of high school I knew I was not a man no matter who said I was. My intersex condition bloomed, and while I have only one set of genitalia (can't have everything we want, I guess) I had at least two puberties. I have male genitalia, though they're nonstandardly proportioned. My first puberty was beyond unusual, and painful. My gonads overdescended and felt like they were trying to rip themselves off of me and run away to Mexico. That lasted over five years. My second puberty was much more fun. I grew breasts without taking any hormones to get them. Imagine my surprise when one week my nipples started swelling outward. I noticed the lettering on my shirts bending out at the sides, and eventually I figured out I was growing breasts. Those came with a year and a half of hot flashes, mood swings and most of the hormonal signs of PMS. These days I'm a B cup, smaller than Dolly Parton but bigger than Björk.

By the time I was in college, I was living as almost militantly androgynous. I was still going by my birth name, but was telling everyone I met that I didn't feel like either ... which, of all things, gave me some freedom to explore being girly. My first girlfriend, a goth chick named Lenore, got me my first Wednesday Addams dress, my first set of fishnets and first set of makeup, and got me into Rocky Horror. I've come to see that for me wearing either typically gendered clothing is cross-dressing. I am partial to pretty foofy girly things so I go more with that. I've ended up with several names and all of them work and yet don't work at the same time. My parents named me Brian, which the family still pretty much uses. For a while I went exclusively by Kate, till I saw so many transwomen using that one, so I combined the two to make BrianKate. I've also always liked the name Cynthia, which has had to do with having a connection with the night and the moon. I often feel like I've traded away having "one true name" in order to be myself.

In addition to all the years I tried living as a man, I also tried living as a woman for about five years. While I lived in Ann Arbor I lived almost exclusively as a trans-identified intersex woman. I even spent a couple of those years in the local lesbian community. After a while I just didn't feel any more like a woman than I did a man, so I stopped identifying as one. An amusing irony is my while I was trying as hard as I could to be a woman my then-girlfriend was trying equally hard to be genderqueer. Each of us finished where the other was hoping to go. Another irony is that when I was going out of my way to live as a woman I never felt all that feminine, and ever since I stopped living as one I've gotten a lot girlier. These days I'm somewhere on the femme side, although as I've had to tell even a transgender priestess friend, just because I use a girl's name, wear dresses, and have breasts doesn't exactly make me a woman.

These days I use omnisexual to describe my sexuality. I'm not exactly a man or a woman, or 100% male or female, so the whole gay or straight thing doesn't quite apply, and "bi" doesn't quite fit as most of the people I see using that seem to mainly be looking for men or women, not someone who's both and neither. Instead of the whole gender system I actually see more sense, and certainly more fun, in kink, and that's a community I do pretty well in. As for me, I'm attracted to all sorts of people as long as they have personality, an open mind and respect me.

How would you describe your spiritual path, and how did you get to this point with it?

Cynthya: I've had an initiation that I don't recommend anybody ever try, anywhere, by nearly getting murdered. In 2000 a mob of queer-bashers nearly killed me because they couldn't handle someone of unclear gender walking through their neighborhood. They hunted my friend and myself through the streets of our hometown, screaming "Get the fags!" They nearly caught us. As they gained on us, a liquor bottle went through my friend's beehive hairdo, and I knew that if they caught us, they'd kill us. We ducked under a parked car. I could hear them searching for us, and at that moment I uttered my first real prayer ever— "Any power in this universe that doesn't want to see us murdered here damn well better show up now!" Moments passed as we huddled under the car ... and suddenly the bashers scattered and ran away from us. The spirits of the transgender dead, especially the murdered ones, had stepped in directly.

Before then I had no spirituality, no politics, and cared only about hanging out, clothes and makeup. I consider the event something like a shamanic death and rebirth. My body didn't die, but everything else about the person I was did. I know I'd be dead if the spirits hadn't intervened; in several senses they brought me back from the dead, so I spent the next three years on transgender and intersex activism in gratitude. While this included helping create the Long Island Transgender Day Of Remembrance (TDOR), it was purely political ...

until I started encountering the ghosts. At first, I felt vague presences around me while I did TDOR or spoke on behalf of dead transpeople. Then I started hearing voices, and felt the spirits more clearly. This really messed with my "everything is rational science" view. I'll admit I freaked out and did the whole "This can't be happening! Am I going crazy? There are no ghosts!" deal. All the while, the spirits kept trying to talk to me, and I finally realized that something saved me that night, so after a while I started listening.

At first I had trouble understanding the ghosts. For the longest time they mostly sounded like Charlie Brown's teacher — "wah wah, wah wah wah wah" —to me. It took a shamanic journey to the Deathlands and the Death Goddess installing a psychic "Babel fish" translator in my head for me to start really being able to understand what I heard. Now it's clear, though I never know whether it will be English words or just knowing, like a feeling, like intuition. I mainly hear and feel the dead, though I've seen some as well, so I can use that "I see dead people" line from *The Sixth Sense* and mean it. I've seen my late friend Sylvia Rivera at a point where I needed advice; she's shown up to kick my butt a few times when I felt like I couldn't go on. I've even seen one murdered transwoman show me her murder through her eyes. It's all part of the work I do helping the transgender dead, along with speaking on their behalf, telling their stories and trying to comfort their spirits.

Along with my path as a deathworker, I've also discovered other aspects of my spirituality. I've realized being trans and intersex is sacred. That may sound like a "duh" statement for someone helping dead (and some living) trans and intersex people, but it took me until a few years ago to understand this. I use the word hermaphrodite to describe my body rather than intersex because there's spiritual power in the word—I don't know any god named "Intersex", but the word hermaphrodite is the name of an actual deity, Hermaphroditos. I also work with a pretty eclectic mix of gods. Many are death deities, some are third gender gods, and some are animal spirits like Tarantula and Carrion-Beetle.

Ever since I learned of Agdistis I've been working with hir, even before I knew hir story. At my last college, a clique of transphobic students attempted to harass me into silence for being too trans, too intersex, too proudly public for them, and a year after I graduated every single one of them either came out as gay, went mad, transitioned gender, or did all three at once. One of the ringleaders is now a transman trying to make up for how he treated people while living as a woman, and another went from being a stuck-up gayboy to being so ultrafeminine she can't leave the house without full makeup, stiletto heels and the right shade of pantyhose. It's the power of Agdistis, working through me.

Even my energetic anatomy is third gender. I've tried astral shapeshifting into a man and a woman, and only got about halfway there. I've 8 major chakras, 3 connected to sex, the two usually associated with men (root) and women (second) and a third most people I've asked haven't heard of in front of the second, which often shows up as a blue ball with a pink core. For most of my life I had no energetic connection to my lower half, because a doctor removed two toes out of an original twelve against my will when I was age 10. I've had several soul retrievals to reconnect the lower half of my astral body and so far one of the missing astral toes. Until recently, I only knew I had genitalia when something physically touched them; otherwise I felt like a Barbie doll. I couldn't ground energetically and I had almost no sex drive. If this happened to me over toes I shudder to think of the spiritual effects for intersex people whose genitalia were messed with.

I've also learned about the power of third-gender blood; I use my own to charge certain ritual objects. I now use pomegranates and almonds to represent Agdistis, and as being sacred to third gender people in general. I've explained the myth to a lot of people, and I make sure to keep either pomegranate juice or almonds in the house. I use them as my form of holy communion, as they are the sacrificed body and blood of Agdistis. I eat and drink a lot of each, and I have special ritual uses as well.

Every year, in commemoration of my having nearly been murdered, and in thanks to the trans dead for saving me, I have an unfuneral/rebirthday, where I sit down to share a meal of almonds and pomegranate juice with my ghosts. I make sure to have some multiple of the number of years it's been since, and I set one plate and cup for me and one for them, and I have mine, I leave them theirs for the night, and the next day I put their portion outside as respectfully as I can. I've used pomegranate juice as an offering to the trans dead for the last few years, and I've helped with a group ritual to do this. At the most recent

Crucible trans spirituality gathering we did a ritual to honor all the trans dead we know of. To an unintended (but welcome) musical accompaniment by a radio playing, of all things, the Grateful Dead channel, we gathered in a circle, and as the names of the dead were read we poured a drinking-horn full of pomegranate juice into the earth, to symbolize the blood of our people, which has been spilled far too many times.

I work a lot with the power of third gender blood, both the spilled blood of our dead and the blood flowing in the veins of us living. When I work with TDOR events I usually do so wearing a Gwen Araujo t-shirt I got at Camp Trans. The person who gave me the shirt almost didn't because "we had a printing error and you see all those dark smudges." I insisted on choosing that shirt because to me those marks symbolize the blood of my people, and I've swum in the blood of my people during a guided meditation. We were told to go through the World-Tree and see where we went, and (big surprise!) I went to the underworld. I found myself in a tributary of the River of Blood where I could hear and feel the voices and screams of the trans dead going through me. This vision has made me realize that I'm covered in the blood of my people.

What does your title "Speaker for the Transgender Dead" mean to you, and how do you manifest that?

Cynthya: The trans dead saved me so I can help them, both as a sort of caseworker and as an interpreter and a representative among the living. Part of what I do involves being there for the my ghosts, making sure they know someone on this plane cares and wants to help. I've been learning about this as I go along. Sometimes it's easier, sometimes it's hard. Some people are more traumatized than others, especially the violently murdered ones. I've helped reacquaint my intersex friend John/Testika with a murdered friend of his. Chris didn't identity as transgender, but he played with gender and was killed for that. Chris has been watching over John ever since, and is relatively coherent and sane for someone who's been brutally murdered; ze even seems to have a fun sense of humor. Ze's not stuck here because of trauma, instead ze's chosen to stick around as a guardian angel. One of my hardest cases so far was a three-day-old murdered intersex baby who didn't seem to even be verbal. I'd just hear a baby screaming without words at all. I didn't know I could ask death deities for help in such a case, so I muddled through and just kept telling this child's story and hoped that would help. In the end I had to ask the rest of the trans dead for help, and they showed the child how to move on.

A large part of what I do is speaking for the trans dead among the living. This means telling their stories, a lot. One of my qualifications for the work is a very good memory for stories and details. I tell friends who envy this if they want to borrow my brain they'd also be borrowing an encyclopedia of the trans dead and all the graphic details of the murder cases. While I do a lot with TDOR, for me it's not one day out of the year as it is to some. For me, I know that at any time and place I may be called upon to tell the stories so people don't forget them. That's a pretty important thing, being remembered. The more people hear the stories, the more they're aware of transpeoples' lives and deaths, and the more they hear about the unpleasant details of the murders, the more people see that kind of violence as unacceptable. So I do a lot of storytelling on their behalf.

The other title I've ended up with is Speaker for the Forgotten Transgender Dead. There are always transpeople whose stories just don't make the official lists of our dead, so I tell their stories too. This includes actions from making sure that event organizers know these peoples' stories as well, to showing up at a TDOR or Samhain event and saying "Sorry, you haven't mentioned these people," and telling their stories. I've decided to start a website for these stories which don't make the official radar at "All Our Dead," found at www.allourdead.weebly.com

What do you think that third gender people have to teach the world?

Cynthya: By existing in the first place, we prove that there are people like us in the world, and always have been. By telling our stories and being visible, we make this truly evident and spread the knowledge and power we have to the rest of the world. By being visible we reclaim the power of being third gender from the people who've tried to keep us silent ... and we have the potential to change the world around us, by making room for ourselves in it, and by showing and teaching the lessons that being third gender has given us. We show that there are not just two genders in the world. We show that gender isn't necessarily about genitalia or clothes or all the other things gender lines have been based on.

We also show that people don't have to live inside the lines they were told to if they don't want to. Almost every other day non-trans women come up to me to tell me they're freaked out because they don't feel 100% girly-girl every day of the week, or they want to do or wear something butch. They feel they can tell me this because I'm third gender and I won't think they're crazy for wanting to go outside the boundaries they were taught to expect, and I usually tell them that I hear this often enough that it can't just be me and them, which seems to comfort and encourage them to express themselves. After I did a drag show as a clearly trans spoof of Shania Twain to a trans-punk remix of *Man I Feel Like a Woman* at my last college, half the football team came up to me for weeks saying "Wow, I wish I could be as out about who I am as you are." I think we can show people that they can be themselves.

Interview with the Crucible Attendees (2001)

(The following is a partial transcript of a workshop on creating community relations at Crucible, a yearly transgender spirituality retreat held in New England. The participants spanned the entire spectrum of transgender experience. Instead of identifying them, I chose only to repeat many of the ideas we came up with in our brainstorming session.)

"Be situation-appropriate. Take control of subtle clothing perceptions, especially those that are forms of sexual display. If you're careful, you can be androgynous and most people will be more curious than threatened."

"Don't work under the table! If you get fired or abused on an under-the-table job, you can't use the labor board and the non-discrimination laws!"

"Move in packs!"

"I've had good results employing tremendous courtesy. Seek victory through superior manners. Act noble; then when you do throw a royal hissy it will be that much more impactful."

"Be a person first."

"Infiltrate and alter existing organizations. We need to make ourselves valuable. Try local government and unions. I did a lot of subtle education simply by serving on the International Brotherhood of Electrical Workers central labor council as an out transgendered person. Don't so much tell them where they're wrong as show them the way. Labor, feminists, gay groups are our natural allies, even if they don't know it."

"Be serious and a hard worker. Work with co-workers, gain their respect as a person."

"Volunteer! A lot. Work for their cause and *then* ask them to work for ours. And offer to do the scut work! You get lots of points for doing boring volunteer work that nobody wants to do."

"Be known in your neighborhood. You may be the only one they know. You can't go for normal, but you can go for community—like, 'They're weirdos, but they're *our* weirdos.'"

"I really think people remember the ancient sacred roles for transgendered people, even if only subconsciously. Use that. They will be more comfortable with you in traditional roles: mediators, caretakers of the old, keepers of the sacred, and so on. We can even be sacred clowns and it works."

"When faced with actual enemies, you can sometimes learn their fears and address them directly. Like, if they say, 'We'll lose membership because of you,' you say, 'How do you know?' and ask around. They might be proven wrong. For typical fears, like recruiting, have answers ready."

"Well, this is going to sound harsh, but there is a small minority who are just not going to hear us. And some of them are figuring out that, yes, we really do intend to change the world. We can downplay that goal, but we can't deny it, not and be honest. For the really intractable ones, the ones who will never even listen, all we can do is keep in mind that they will die sooner or later. Culture changes funeral by funeral."

"You know, people come down on public figures like Dana International, RuPaul, and so on, but one thing they do provide is desensitization; there are fewer people out there who have never seen one of us. If there's only one of us, it's an aberration. If there are two, it's a fad. If three, it's a movement. We should grab a little coattail action there."

"Remember that we have heroes and be one."

"I think we need to remember that we have—or rather, that societal hostility has produced—casualties, and not just people who can't get jobs because of discrimination. Many of us are on disability, addicted, too screwed up to take care of themselves. There aren't any statistics, but I'm seeing it as about a quarter of the TG community. These people can't be expected to do community service, but we can't disown them. There but for the Powers That Be go any of us, y'know..."

"We should spend more money on our own community. There are a lot of valuable skills in here, and often they go to waste because those of us who have skills can't get hired. We should make the effort to hire our own, to check around to see if there's an out-of-work transgendered plumber before we call the first ad in the Yellow Pages. I've always said that there are so many talents in this community that if we pooled our resources we could have our own space program!"

Interview with Zoltana Moon (2001)

How would you describe yourself and your gender?

Zoltana: By medical standards, I am called a "male pseudo-hermaphrodite". I was born with Complete Androgen Insensitivity Syndrome (CAIS). I am a genetic male, but a physical female. I was born with a small vagina and no internal female reproductive organs. I had my undescended testes removed when I was 19 years old. I was told that my "ovaries" were to be removed because they were cancerous. Basically, I was lied to.

How do I describe myself? My heritage is part Mexican and part Apache Indian. I identify as female, but I have always had very "masculine" mannerisms, and people perceive me as an aggressive female because of that. As a child, I was very aggressive. I enjoyed bullying and fighting with my sisters and felt they were too "prissy". When I received dolls as a gift, I would cut off all their hair and take their clothes off. I preferred to be outside playing football and basketball with my brother, and I hated being in the kitchen cooking or doing other household chores.

I feel I had more gender dysphoria as a child than I do as an adult woman. I am very comfortable in my womanly skin now, and I have acquired or "learned" how to "act" as a woman and take advantage of my looks. I enjoy being complimented by men, and I enjoy being made to feel feminine and beautiful by my husband of 17 years. I did not feel so comfortable as a child.

I am also comfortable with my intersexuality. Being intersexual is a responsibility for me. Not too many people out there know the term. I feel intersexuals should educate others when given the chance and the voice. When I found out I was an intersexual I felt, "Ahh, at least I understand myself now." My search for enlightenment and my path are clearer now because of my knowledge about myself.

Tell us about your current path.

Zoltana: My current spiritual path is to locate my comfortable place within myself. At the age of 36 I have found the need to feel selfish. I am learning to be selfish with my time, my energy, and my love. I am learning to think positive about my being here in this world. I am learning how to draw within myself and take care of me. For now, I feel that this is more appropriate to my intersexuality than the path I was raised in. I am gleaning my knowledge acquired through my Catholic indoctrination and using my faith to have faith in myself. I am also trying to shred the feelings of guilt that the religion placed on me for so many years, but at the same time embracing the positive affirmations I learned in the Catholic faith. I am learning to love myself so that I can truly love others.

I am my own religion. The world is my temple and I worship myself. I sometimes get knocked down in this struggle I call life, but I patiently and persistently let others know that I am here, that I am special, that I am beautiful, and that I have my place here in this organism we call Earth.

How does your intersexuality intersect with your spirituality?

Zoltana: I see the spiritual aspect of being intersexed as a gift. I feel I am a sacred being. I am very perceptive and empathetic, which I attribute to being intersexed. I can enter a room and somehow "feel" what was said or what occurred prior to my entrance. Some people might not think this is very special; however, it does help to have those powers which I feel are important to my self-preservation. If I feel an overwhelming, stifling, or suffocating atmosphere around me, I will not subject myself to that environment. When my body senses something or someone evil or bad, the hairs on my arms and neck stand on end. I can feel when someone is watching me, even though that someone maybe behind me or out of my line of sight. My mother says I am a "witch", but I tell her I am just intersexed! I am sacred because I am dedicated to myself, dedicated to what I feel and know, to having faith in myself. I don't know whether I would have come to this level of spirituality if I hadn't been intersexed, because I can't fathom anything other than being this way.

What do you think nontraditionally gendered people have to offer the rest of the world?

Zoltana: We have much to offer today's spiritual paths and teachings. One of the most important things intersexuals can teach is acceptance. Another thing that can be taught to other paths/teachings is that intersexuals have their place in this world; that there is a "grey" area in the proverbial black and white spectrum. This is all tied into acceptance.

Interlude III: Meditation on the Hermaphrodeity

(This can be done as a personal visualization, or as a guided meditation for groups. Thanks to Siren for the inspiration.)

You are walking down a long road that stretches out in front of you for miles, all the way to the horizon. It goes on behind you all the way to the other horizon. You are alone on this road.

In the distance, you start to see movement. Someone is coming toward you on the road. Looking over your shoulder, you see movement in the other direction, also coming your way.

As the figures come closer, you see that one of them is the most beautiful man you have ever seen, and the other is the most amazing woman you have ever seen. One is behind you and one ahead of you. They come closer, and closer, until you can see them clearly. They wave and call out to each other.

They are very close, now, one coming up behind you and one coming right up to your face. And then, as if your body is made of air, they smile and embrace, standing on the same spot you stand on, embracing each other through you. For one moment they are both within your boundaries, locked in friendship and love, and you are their world. You are the air they breathe. And now, in this moment, you understand ... everything.

Part Two:
Solid Visions

The Shaman: When The Spirits Get Faces

> Look ahead.
> You are not expected to complete the task.
> Neither are you permitted to lay it down.
>   —*The Talmud*

An Open Letter to Transgendered Spirit-Workers

First, before I speak to you of what needs to be said, my sisters and brothers and sister-brothers and brother-sisters, please understand that I am one of you. I am no outsider. I was born female and male in one, I have lived as both, I look male now (clothed, at any rate) but I am and have always been the sacred third inside, no matter what my body was doing at the time.

Second, please understand that when the Gods and spirits took me and killed me and rebuilt me and brought me back and told me that I was a shaman now, their apprentice and tool, one thing was made clear: A shaman always serves a tribe. Without a tribe, they are nothing. And my tribe, I was told, is all of you. Transsexuals, both transwomen and transmen. Genderqueers. Cross-dressers of whatever stripe, fetishistic or otherwise. The normal-looking ones who have an inner female or male so strong that they demand part of their life, especially part of their sexual life. The intersexuals like myself who look in the mirror and know what they are, and want the freedom to be that. The ones who just know, inside, that they are both male and female—not theoretically but intimately, to know with every fiber of your body that you have walked in the world and male and female and something in between. You are all my tribe.

Even if your life path pains or annoys me, you are my tribe—the drug-addicted street queen, the autistic tranny nerd with no social skills, the FNT—fucking neurotic transsexual—who is damaged into insanity by a harsh world—you are all my tribe. Even if you hate me, even if you think that I'm a loon, you are all my tribe. I serve you all, whenever you ask, as long as you acknowledge this in yourself.

But this letter is written to a subset of a subset of a subset, a tiny number of people. I don't even know how many there are of you out there.

To be a spirit-worker, to be called by the Gods and/or spirits to destroy your life and be reborn to serve others, to be ridden by spirits, to ally with them and serve them and be constantly harassed by them, to lose everything and gain this knowledge ... that's a tiny percentage of any population. I'm not talking about the folks who take a weekend class and shake a rattle, the ones who do it part-time, the ones who can say no to it. I'm talking about the ones who have no choice, for whom spirit-work has eaten our entire lives, the ones for whom saying no is impossible because we are already bound by this calling ... and, certainly, the ones who are seeing this calling come down the tracks at them like a high-speed freight train. I know that it can be terrifying. Believe me, I know.

But if you're transgendered, in *any* way ... and if you've been tagged by the spirits to be a spirit-worker ... you have a double load on you. Transgendered people in the rest of the population have the option of denial. They can ignore their feelings, purge their secret wardrobes, throw away those sex toys, censor their thoughts, bury half their soul in the basement. It's not a wise choice, in my book, but they have the option. We don't. When we are drafted, we give up that privilege. We must deal fully and completely with our gender issues, as quickly and as honestly as possible. It is the first thing on our training, before any drums or rattles or chanting. If we do not deal with it, nothing will go right for us until we do. Period.

If you are not dealing with—and fully living—your sacred third gender, then everything that the Gods and spirits will do to you will be about forcing you to come to terms with this. If you resist, if you keep putting it off, things will just get worse and worse. This, too, I tell you from experience. I will also tell you that as soon as you start working to come to terms with it, things will improve, and they will keep improving as you being to fully live it. While this may also be true for transfolk who are not spirit-workers, please understand that when I say that things will just get worse for you, I mean that you are inevitably risking your life.

Understand that being a spirit-worker means that your life is fair game for meddling, if things interfere with your work. In fact, if anything interferes with your work, it will likely just go away. And since the first step for us is dealing fully with our gender issues, that means that blaming outside influences as a reason for not working with them is a bad idea. The Gods and spirits will not stand for that. What, you can't transition because your job wouldn't like it? Why, that's no problem. We can get that out of the way. There, you're laid off. See, now nothing's stopping you. What, you can't put on a skirt because of your spouse? Here, have some divorce papers. There, now you have nothing to lose. What, you can't do this because of your public reputation? How about a nice mental breakdown in public, right where everyone can see? There, now they all think you're nuts anyway, so you can do what you want.

I'm not joking. I've seen it happen, too many times. It happened to me. Any part of your life that will not support your job—and that includes this part of it—will go away. Clinging to it will just make it more painful when They pry it out of your fingers. If you keep resisting even in the face of all this, you will be given the final choice ... come to terms with your gender, or cease to live.

Why do we have to deal with this, first? Because it's a tool. Because it's a power. Because seeing things from both of those sides is an important part of learning to shift shape, to see from other eyes, to walk between worlds. While nontrans people can learn it in other ways, there's no question that we do have something special when it comes to gaining perspective, and I think there's even more to it than that, although that truth is elusive and arguable. But I, and other transgendered spirit-workers, have found that there are special powers and energies and techniques that only we can access. These will be your best tools, eventually.

Our situation is not modern. Any research about shamans and spirit-workers the world over will show unusual numbers of third-gender people. It's the one job where it's an advantage. It's the one area where research can't avoid finding us over and over, from Siberia to the southwest American desert. We transgendered spirit-workers have a long and very public tradition. Generally, when the oppressors wiped out shamanic cultures and tried to convert the shamans to "normal" behavior by their standards, it was us, the third-gender spirit-workers, who chose to die instead. There was no other option for us. There is no other option for us. We must be what we are.

What is it that we have to do, exactly? That depends on who you are. Certainly not all transgendered spirit-workers need to get sex changes, or alter their genitals. The trans continuum is a wide thing. There are those who are far to one end, and who may only feel the need to honor their nature occasionally with clothing and/or certain kinds of sex. There are those at the far end who feel the need to shift their physical shape entirely.

There are those in the middle who may go partway. What the Spirits want you to do is to *find your level and live it fully*. Explore your range of motion, step by step; go further until you hit the point where you get the message, "This is enough. There's no need to go further. This is who you are." You will hit that point, I promise you, wherever it might be. We all do.

So if it means that you need to change your body, then do it. Take the hormones, consider them shamanic mind-altering drugs (they are) that aid shapeshifting (they do). Get surgery, if that's what you need: consider it a blood sacrifice to the Spirits, like the Sanguinaria of the Roman *gallae*, like the Lakota Sun Dance. If you need to keep your body the same, but wear certain clothing, do it. If you need to ritually put on a skirt and take it up the ass, do it. If you need to carve a sacred strap-on phallus and thrust it into a willing hole of flesh, do it. If you need to change your name, change your look, change your body, change your life, do it. Do it all the way. Don't put it off. You don't have that privilege. Whatever point you fall on, honor it as an integral part of your life and your identity. It is who you are, and it is part of what makes you good at your job. Let no mundane reason stand in your way.

Then you have to live it, and live it publicly. The other option that you are forbidden is that of the closet. You don't have to tell every single person that you meet, but if it comes up, or they ask, you must answer truthfully. You need not make an effort to be seen, but you must make no effort to hide ... and if someone of this tribe needs you, you need to let them know who and what you are. This, too, is found in all the shamanic cultures that talk about us: we must be public about who and what we are, we must be visible, marked out, set apart, that we might be easily available to those who need us. That means that we are targets, which means that we must also be damn brave, and set an example.

One of my jobs, as a transgendered shaman who belongs to a Death Goddess, is to speak for the Dead of my tribe. And, my sister-brothers, my brother-sisters, the Dead of our tribe are angry. They rage, they weep, they cry out. They rage because we are being killed in the streets, because we are turned away when we seek food and shelter and work and health care, because we are ridiculed and often unloved, because we are exiled from our families and clans, because we are beaten down until we break and take our own lives. Because to live in our country is to live in a war zone. Our Dead are angry, and they demand this of us: that as much as we are able, we will do what has to be done to make sure that there are no more fallen in this war. In order to save each other, we must band together and take care of each other, because alone we go down. Hear their cries, if you can. If you are going down this path of serving our tribe, their cries should be audible to you. The Dead are not so hard to call up, if you dare listen. This must not happen again, they say. Hear them.

The numbers of our tribe are growing. More children are born with intersex conditions every year. More teens are evidencing transgendered behavior every year. Like the intersex frogs in the Potomac, affected by pesticide runoff, we swim in a toxic brew of poisons that is, ironically, making more of our tribe. Look for the scientific evidence; it's there. But beyond that, our tribe needs more spirit-workers, of any tradition, to serve them, to take care of our living and our dead. We are needed more than ever, and that's why we're getting drafted in such numbers.

We are needed, my sisters and brothers. Don't fear this *wyrd*. Embrace it.

It's not like you have any choice, anyway, so you might as well. And besides, you are so desperately needed.

For the ancestors of our tribe, for our Dead, and for those yet to be born,

–Raven Kaldera

For the past decade and a half, since I've been writing about transgender spirituality, I've been going about giving workshops on it. When I'm there, I don't lecture. I tell these stories to people, in ways that they'll remember and take with them. I wear my embroidered skirts and I drum and I sing, and they remember. But a couple of years ago, people started asking for a new kind of story. After I'd finished telling them about Agdistis and Lilith, Dionysus and Shiva, Turquoise Boy and White Shell Girl, they started asking for my story. What brought me to this point? I was taken aback the first time I was asked. The second time, I had my story ready. After all, if the shaman is a myth, I'm living it. I live it every day, every moment, in everything that I do. This isn't, in my mind, a story with the weight of the Gods, but it is the one that I have to tell.

When I was a small child, a strange noncorporeal woman came to me, in dreams and when I was awake and alone. She told me that I was hers, and took me places and taught me things. I never saw her true face. Later, in my teens, I went through the diagnosis of my intersex condition, the repression of my gender dysphoria, dead people and the spirits of plants continually speaking to me, and many years of illness that culminated in an actual near-death experience from hemorrhaging. During that experience, I saw my Goddess's face for the first time, and She was half beautiful woman and half rotting, skeletal corpse. She took me apart like a butchered animal and put me back together ... differently. When I woke up the next morning, I knew that I had to transition soon. Immediately. As quickly as possible.

During the next several years, I went from female-of-center to male-of-center. I don't say female to male, exactly, because I was never all the way to the one side, and I didn't move all the way to the other one ... or rather, I didn't stay there. I believe that in order to reach that middle point, you have to be like a pendulum. A pendulum, when pulled to the side and let go, seeks the middle. It is in the nature of the pendulum to seek the middle, but it never goes straight there. Instead, it swings to the far side, and then back to the first side (but not quite as far) and then back to the other side again (but not quite as far) and so on, until it comes to rest in the center. It may take many swings to get there.

That's the way that it works with gender identity. In fact, if the transfolk who read this book could only take two things from it, the second (after the we-are-sacred thing) would be this one: that in order to find that middle ground, you have to experience, as fully as possible, the two ends, and then move to the middle with that knowledge echoing in you. If you don't spend enough time on either of the ends, it will take significantly longer to get to the middle and be comfortable, not agonized, about it. That time can be public or subjective, it's the intensity that counts, not the exterior. For some people, nothing will be "enough" except for physical and hormonal changes; for others, merely being repeatedly seen as one gender or the other by some people under controlled circumstances is enough. This is a long, slow process, however. It can take many years, and is impossible to rush.

Once I passed the midline and swung to the far side (the first and furthest I ever swung to male), growing a beard and body hair and losing my breasts, being seen as clearly male in public, my Goddess leveled other taboos on me.

Instead of the transgendered female shamanic taboos, social and sexual (dressing as male, not being sexually penetrated, etc.) I got hit with the male sexual taboos for my tradition. These included wearing skirts as part of my ceremonial costume, wearing jingly bells, and rediscovering ritual penetrative sex ... the way that a male-bodied person would. I wasn't required to do full drag or pass as female again; the point was to mix gender cues just enough to read "not fully male or female in some way" to outside eyes.

I read a lot, and I learned things. I learned that my experiences were not anomalous. I learned that this sort of thing happened to people all over the world ... and that there was never any going back. I learned that the shamanic tradition that I got dragged into, the northern European tradition of my ancestors, used to have words for this: *ergi, argr*. I learned that the shamans who crossed gender didn't just do it for symbolic reasons. It gave them power. The anthropologists only talked about social and symbolic power; they didn't get it. They didn't understand that the title "walker between worlds" was literal, not symbolic.

There's another part of being a shaman that most people in our culture forget. It's especially ignored by those who romanticize the idea of being a shaman, or think that they want that job.

There was a time when I used the word "shaman" casually. There was a time when I, like so many spiritual seekers, compared shamans to all sorts of people, and all sorts of people to shamans. That was a long time ago, although not so long ago as the beginning of this book. Even then, it was following me, shadowing me, stalking me, herding me. Finally it came and got me. The Gods and spirits surrounded me, claimed me, killed me (literally), and brought me back very different. From that time on I was a shaman in the classic sense—a servant to the Gods and a friend and ally to many spirits.

Being a shaman is not like what I, in my ignorance, thought it would be like. It is not about personal spiritual empowerment; it's about being a tool of the Gods whom I serve and the spirits with whom I am allied. It is not about following one's personal bliss; it is about being a public utility for any tribe member who knocks on your door and needs help. It is not about doing fancy magic spells; it is about coaxing, propitiating, bargaining, and sometimes begging other Entities to do things that you can't. It is not about your own highest good; it is about being a sacrifice for the good of your people. It is not about having an epiphany, a little depression, and a few psychic experiences; it is about being tormented by spirits for years into illness or madness, coming all the way up to the door of literal death and, hopefully, not actually dying, although the chance is there. It is not about being cool and spooky; it is about working day after day with no clock and no retirement, often to the point of exhaustion, helping all the ones with their hands held out, even though there are too many to help and too much to do, until your time is up and you leave this lifetime.

It is not about me.

That's the unglamorous part, the part that modern Westerners who buy all those rattles and drums don't want to see. In many traditions, being chosen by the spirits as a shaman is nonconsensual. You don't get to take it for yourself, and attempting to reject it will result in madness and/or death. Modern people don't like to think about spiritual paths that are nonconsensual, thrust upon you by relentless greater forces, where you must learn to swim or sink and die. To the modern spiritual seeker, any spiritual or psychic experience should be open to any sincere person who works at it, and those who don't want to go there should be able to walk away.

We transgendered folk know better about that, anyway. Shamanism aside, we know intimately about being handed a path we didn't choose and probably didn't want, that will make people think we're crazy, that may force us to give up large portions of our lives, that may require us to do extreme things to our bodies, that will make us into new and different people, and that we can't walk away from without the risk of madness and potential death. That sort of thing sounds all too familiar to us. We get it, down to the marrow of our bones. When traditionally-gendered people protest about the unfairness of having spiritual change pushed on them by the Universe, we give them The Look. Usually we don't say much, though. There isn't much that can be said, besides "Kid, you have no bloody idea."

At first, I figured that was why there has been such a high percentage of transgendered people among traditional shamans in so many cultures. It certainly isn't true across the board; some cultures don't have third gender roles, and it's often important for their shamans to breed normally and to pass on the shamanic genes. But of all professions past and present (with the possible exception of prostitutes), the one with the highest proportion of gender-transgressors is that of spirit-worker, whatever word may be used for it in any given culture. It must be, I thought to myself, because gender transition offers such a good vehicle for shamanic transition.

Then I actually went through the shamanic transition, complete with "shaman sickness", and discovered that there was far more to it than that. First, there was the confusing issue of the "shamanic death". For real shamans, this isn't merely metaphorical, or social, or even personal-transformative in nature. It's physical. Some come down with serious illnesses, others go mad for a long time and come very close to suicide. Some get both. Why would the Gods and spirits do this to someone? The truth is strange and subtle, and has to do with the relationship of the physical and astral bodies. (For a really good primer on the relationship of the physical and astral bodies, read Joshua Tenpenny's essay on Body Congruence in the Solid Visions section of this book.)

The shaman's command of altered states—referred to in some popular books as "techniques of ecstasy"—basically comes down to mastering a variety of ways to achieve different states of consciousness at will. These are states which, if they were thrust upon someone, would give them a condition of temporary insanity. The shaman learns to bring them on, stay in control, and use them to work with the Entities of other planes of existence. Sometimes control of these states ends up being learned through being afflicted with them; the first classic difference between the shaman and the madman is that the shaman comes through the sickness saner than most people.

The first and most basic insanity/ecstasy state is dissociation from the physical body to such an extent that the astral body detaches partially or entirely, floating in the meat puppet but not being connected to it. While this is not a healthy state to live in all the time (again, see the Body Congruence article), it is one that the shaman needs to learn to induce and control at will in order to shapeshift, travel between worlds, and journey out of the body. Gender-based body dysphoria, creating an anatomical difference between the physical and astral bodies that inevitably drives them apart, is an effective (if painful) method of assuring that the connection between the two bodies is "loose" enough to make the shamanic techniques easier. While other pathologies can and do create dissociation (such as abuse or chronic painful illness in childhood), gender dysphoria ensures that we are used to our two bodies being shaped differently, doing different things simultaneously, and giving the brain/mind two separate sets of stimuli. Unlike abuse victims, we are "wired that way". In other words, our particular form of suffering makes us better able to be spirit-workers, were we to be called by the spirits to do this thing. It's no wonder that they so often choose from among us. Shamanism is the only job for which gender dysphoria is actually an advantage, if a difficult one.

Of course, learning to control something is very different from being controlled by it. One of the first things that I had to learn was how to be both all the way in and all the way out of my body, not just the sort of half-in half-out disconnection created by a lifetime of gender dysphoria. One needs to be in the car to drive it, or else one needs to be out and walking. Being half in means that you don't go anywhere. To that end, I had to learn to be entirely in my body in a way that I hadn't been since early childhood. Changing my body and finding my proper physical level, bringing my flesh significantly closer to my astral form, was a great help with this practice. Even if there isn't going to be any physical transition, plumbing the spiritual and psychic layers of one's own transgendered nature is a great help with learning how to do this right.

That's why dealing with one's gender issues, to the greatest extent possible in every direction, is the first thing that the spirits make a newly-claimed transgendered shaman do ... at the point of a sharp stick, if necessary. (Considering how painful the subject is, it's sadly often necessary.) The ability to master the basic skills of spirit-work depend on it. We have an advantage, but first the spirits have to force us through our self-imposed walls. Make no mistake, they will do it. That's the reality behind the open letter that I wrote and put on my website.

But back to the issue with Death, and bringing the eventual shaman within a hair's breadth of it. This isn't just any old near-death experience. It's orchestrated by the spirits in charge, and they have a hand in how it goes. When I read the accounts of traditional tribal shamans (especially from the subarctic area whence comes my own tradition) I noticed that the dismemberment vision is surprisingly frequent. It was one of the "tags" that helped me to figure out my own experiences and put a label on them. That dismemberment isn't metaphorical, it's literal. The spirits change, mold and refit our astral bodies, making them even more different from our physical ones. We are refitted in a great variety of ways, depending on our inborn gifts and wiring, and the purposes that the spirits have in mind for us. This kind of retrofitting can apparently only be done to a person in the kind of great extremity created by being close to death.

There's more to the shamanic third-gender path than just a loose physical-astral connection, though. If you live the taboo fully (taboo being used in the sense of "thing that is mandatory or forbidden that gives you more power") you get, well, more power. Lots more. There seems to be a spiritual groove in the Universe, a sort of narrow detour off of the "ordinary" third gender spiritual path, that lends a huge amount of mojo to your personal power, will, ability to move the Universe in your direction. In order to access this taboo which my ancestors called *ergi*, you need to A) be a living public archetype of the third gender shaman, B) be openly sexually transgressive in ways that are gender-inappropriate for your birth role, and C) be willing to be a social outsider.

Some of us, of course, were doing that already.

If you haven't been chosen by the spirits to become a shaman (and for that, you should probably be grateful rather than disappointed) then your exploration of this path will go as the Universe says that it will go, personalized just for you, at the best pace you can travel given any resistance you might be working through. Still, if you consciously work with controlling the connection between your various bodies, it can be useful in other ways.

I once spoke about transgender spirituality at a trans group in another state, and afterwards a transwoman came up to me, wanting advice. She was in training to learn Traditional Chinese Medicine, and the elders who were teaching her had no idea what to do with the concept of sex reassignment. Their main worry seemed to be that the removal of her testicles would affect her overall health, because in TCM the gonads are the repository of the *jing*, the essence that keeps our bodies holding to the correct pattern of functioning.

She wanted to know if there was anything she could do to keep her *jing* while getting rid of her testicles.

I asked the spirits, and the answer came clear and bright. *Jing* was energetic, not physical, right? "Do you have an astral uterus and ovaries?" I asked her. She blinked—I suppose no one had ever asked her that before—and said, "Well, yes, of course!" I told her to work on becoming aware of the *jing* energy in her male organs, and slowly moving it over, bit by bit, to be held in her astral body where the ovaries should be. I warned her that it would be a slow process, but she had six months before her surgery. I also suggested that afterwards, she work hard on keeping a good connection between her two bodies in the gonadal area.

This anecdote shows that transfolks who are energy-workers can learn—and teach—things about the gender of energy bodies that may be missed by energy-workers who aren't yet fish discussing water, as it were. Most opinions on the gender of astral bodies fall into two camps: either that they are, of course, boys or girls just like "all" humans, or that they have no gender. The reality is, as any transperson can tell you about flesh bodies, not nearly so simple. Astral bodies can be strongly gendered, vaguely gendered, or not gendered at all. They can have characteristics that are male, female, both, or neither; they may echo their physical envelopes or be completely different. They may also change, at will or willy-nilly.

You know. Kind of like the Gods. After all, that part of us is closer to Them, isn't it?

When faced with the question of gendered gods, spirits, and astral selves, I think that a lot of the folk who revert to either pole are simply shying away from the giant tangled mess that is our, and their, inheritance around gender. Thinking about where it might fit, through that mass of tangles, is intimidating. Even looking at that question is intimidating, and a simple one-size-fits-all answer is comforting, if inaccurate. We, however, know better, because we have no choice but to know better. Sometimes having no choice can be a good thing. It can force us past our fears, and take us places we never would have had the courage to explore.

Middle Ground

Kenaz Filan

I know many trans people who truly were born in the wrong bodies. If they had been born with an innie instead of an outie (or vice versa), they would have been perfectly contented, "normal" boys or girls. My case appears to be a bit more complex. Near as I can tell, my gender isn't misplaced so much as fundamentally broken. If I had been born with a female body, I'd likely be a large woman with a shaved head and a great deal of resentment about the expectations and limitations that came with being female.

Many people find that a very difficult pill to swallow. Once upon a time we had two boxes labeled "male" and "female." Now we have two extra boxes labeled "MTF" and "FTM." While they are still controversial, they have received the coveted Physician's Seal of Approval. Doctors believe that transsexuality exists (well, most of them), and if you don't you are an anti-science bigot. People who feel they belong in the "none of the above" box don't have that medical imprimatur. We're just attention-seekers or performance artists. The idea that someone might want to change their gender is less threatening than the idea that someone might want to live outside those gender roles.

It's interesting to note how much power we give our medical and scientific establishment. For years, people with CFS and fibromyalgia were whiners and malingerers because there was no Official Diagnosis. If the doctors can't put a name to your condition, you must be making it up. Once we burned people who spoke inconvenient truths. Today we just ignore them, because after all they disagree with the Best Scientific Minds, and so they must just be crazy or faking it. The establishment has only grudgingly accepted transsexuality for a decade or two; today a few of them are discovering that perhaps the old rules of "you're either a boy or a girl, or maybe you're one who wishes you were the other" don't always apply. Maybe in a decade or two we'll be in a place where the existence of third-gender people is accepted in mainstream Western science.

It's also interesting, and a bit depressing, to see conflicts among transfolk as to who the "real" transsexuals are. I can understand why an MTF might not feel a lot of kinship with a mundane straight guy who occasionally likes wearing lacy lingerie at a BDSM club. (Of course, I can also see why an MTF might not feel a lot of kinship with many of the nuttier and more dysfunctional MTFs I've encountered.) But I'm not sure it is useful to draw hard, fast distinctions between "cross-dressers" and "transsexuals." I've found it more helpful to describe all gender-variant people as folks who have an 800-pound gorilla in their living room. Some of us can keep our gorilla happy by occasional cross-dressing. Others will have to live full-time as trans; still others have a primate who will only be pacified by surgery and hormones. I'm not sure it is productive to turn gender dysphoria into a contest to see who has the biggest and most spectacularly dressed gorilla.

I'm less surprised by the hostility some lesbians have toward MTFs. A lot of second wave feminism is based on determinist gender politics. When you throw transfolk into the mix, you suddenly call the whole structure into question. And, to be fair, there are plenty of straight guys who will put on a dress if they think they have a chance of seeing naked boobs. (Anyone who has ever been in a chatroom knows that all too well.) I'm not sure how you determine who does or does not deserve to be in "female" space, nor do I have any illusions that those boundaries will be respected by the folks who would cause a problem. It's not an easy issue, and the fact that both sides are currently screaming at each other and flinging accusations around isn't making it any easier.

When I started my gender journey, I felt more uncomfortable with male roles than my male body. To a large extent that is still true. While I wouldn't mind looking a bit more androgynous, I have no particular desire to replace my penis with a vagina, nor do I lay awake at night wishing I was Paris Hilton or Raquel Welch. (In fact, I've come to realize that I am as uncomfortable with highly feminine roles as with highly masculine ones.) I don't identify as "female" so much as "not male", but trying to explain Third Gender to the mundanes takes a lot of time, so I generally go with the "transsexual" label when people ask why I'm wearing a dress. (Perhaps someday our society will find a place for ladyboys and eunuchs...)

By playing that role, I'm able to get the hormones which alleviate my rage flashes and depression. I'm able to present in a more feminine way in the workplace, although I have to follow certain guidelines: it's not so much that I "pass" as that I look like I'm trying to pass. Coming in with the shaved head exposed is a no-no; far too masculine. Since I don't wear wigs, I have to do headscarves. This has led to a few funny moments; I get lots of attention from Orthodox Jewish men and have been mistaken for a nun on at least one occasion. I have tried doing "boy drag" on a few occasions while job hunting, and found that living full-time while presenting male is profoundly uncomfortable and leaves me feeling exhausted and short-tempered in very short order. I may be forced into that position for a period if the economy doesn't pick up: I'm trying to keep myself cheerful by calling it an exercise in gender play rather than selling out. If I think of it as an ordeal to be overcome, it becomes an interesting game. Otherwise, it's just depressing.

Being third gender gives me a different perspective on gender politics. I've lived in both a testosterone- and estrogen-driven body, and don't feel particularly driven to deny either state of being or write it off as a cosmic mistake. This allows me certain insights into what drives men and women. Ideally, living between genders would allow me to act as an ambassador between the two. Unfortunately, I haven't yet seen many traditionally gendered people who were particularly interested in that service ... or who cared about gender issues at all.

I think that indifference is one of the reasons why I've been tasked to live as third-gender. I'm supposed to make people think about what it means to be male/female. I'm supposed to make them question how gender plays out in their life, and offer them ways in which they could be freed from the tyranny of the Great Binary, but at times it feels more like I'm pissing into the wind. I'm trying to explain to them how their lives are ruled by the roles they were born into, but they can't hear it or don't want to. Sometimes I feel like I'm falling down on my job; at other times I remember prophets are rarely honored until after their culture kills them.

In my ideal world, people would start to question how much of their identity is being spoon-fed to them. They would ask questions about how much of who they are is defined by their bodies, and how they could transcend or expand upon those definitions. They would quit trying to split everything down the middle: good/evil, black/white, male/female, etc. They would begin to understand that the world is a more varied and wonderful place than that, and so are they.

One of the deities who works with me is the Norse trickster god Loki. To me that is a huge part of Loki's nature: pointing out the complexities when someone wants to run for the warm, comfortable and simple. It's not a coincidence that he is both mother and father, or that he is perceived by many of his followers as androgynous. Loki isn't good with boundaries or "thou shalts." He is no more interested in fitting into one gender than he is in playing one side of the great Jotun/Aesir war ... and, of course, he pays a terrible penalty for his refusal to be pigeonholed into a neat little category.

The Blooming Lotus of Womanhood
Joni Kay Rose, M.Div, CHT

Excerpted from Over the Gender Rainbow: My Long Journey Back to Womanhood

I once knew a Buddhist lay teacher who was very feminine, with long blond tresses. Despite his appearance, people came from long distances to listen to his wisdom. Years later, I returned to find that the teacher had become a woman ... and now her talks were more brilliant than before, and more people than ever came to hear her speak. As a male teacher she had been like a budding lotus. As a female teacher she is now the lotus in full flower.

Avalokiteshvara, or Avalokita for short, is the Bodhisattva of compassion. She is said to have been born out of a beam of light from the third eye of Buddha Amitabha, the Buddha of radiant light, when He visited this planet and realized it needed more love. Avalokita is androgynous, sometimes appearing as a male deity, but more often as a feminine one. In China She is known as Kwan Yin, or Gwanyin, becoming Kanzeon or Kannon in Japan. In Vietnam She is Quan Te Am. In Tibet, and possibly elsewhere in Central Asia, Avalokita is known as Chenrezig. Usually He's a male deity there, but even by Buddhist standards He has a great many feminine traits. In fact in the thangkas or paintings He often looks like a goddess.

Ordinarily Avalokita is said to be a Bodhisattva rather than a fully realized Buddha. In other words, He is a deity who is learning His true nature. He works very hard to save all beings from suffering, according to legend. One day Avalokita believes at last He has freed all beings from suffering, or will shortly complete this monumental task. So He takes a nap to get His beauty rest, but when He awakens He sees now there are more suffering beings than ever.

In despair Avalokita breaks down and cries, real feminine tears of compassion for all the suffering beings in the world, so many that He now despairs of ever saving them all. Thus in this time of despair Avalokita's true feminine nature comes out. The deity weeps until the tears create a lake. Out of the lake of Avalokita's tears a lotus springs up and blooms, and out of the lotus blossom a beautiful young woman springs forth. She is Tara, the female Buddha of compassion, and She tells Avalokita that She will help Him liberate all beings. Together they vow to go on with this work.

Some legends speak of this as the birth of Goddess Tara, yet Tara is immortal. She is a Goddess, Bodhisattva, and Buddha all in one. She has always existed, I am certain. Perhaps this is just Her first appearance to Avalokita.

While most of us who worship Goddess Tara have come to Her through Tibetan Buddhism, her name is Indo-European, not Sino-Tibetan. This suggests that She was known to Tantric Buddhists in Northern India before Buddhism came to Tibet. While the name Tara is usually considered Sanskrit in origin, it is a feminine name that is found in many different Indo-European speaking nations.

As the Bodhisattva of compassion, for eons Avalokita struggles to liberate all beings, yet Her true femininity has too often been veiled as She attempts to disguise herself as a male. Perhaps She fears that the other Buddhas will not respect Her if they know Her true nature, yet if they are truly the enlightened beings they are said to be they will welcome Her as their sister in the Dharma. Finally after She breaks down in tears of compassion for the suffering of all beings, the lotus blossoms fully, and the Buddha of Compassion reveals Herself in full flower of womanhood. Avalokita is the budding lotus; Tara is the lotus in full flower.

Since the male deities can no longer disrespect Her, they try to persuade Her to become male so She may become a full-fledged Buddha. Tara responds by saying there are already plenty of male Buddhas. She will become Buddha in female form.

At every moment Tara is realizing Her true nature as a female Buddha. In Her divine transition from Bodhisattva to Buddha, She also springs forth in Her true feminine form. Thus She shows all beings the feminine pathway to Enlightenment. May She be revered throughout the universe!

To live genuinely as our true selves: this means leaving behind mindless conformity and denial of our true nature. It requires us to find our own path, to walk the road less traveled. As children, most of us are indoctrinated with a set of dogmas that we're supposed to at least pretend to believe. Often we're assigned a religion, and we may be pushed into a particular lifestyle and occupational choice. Assumptions are made about our sexual orientation, and from the moment of our birth we're assigned a gender, with the assumption that we'll identify with that gender all our lives.

Ultimately each of us, transgender or not, face the same two choices: we can try to be who we've been told we're supposed to be, or we can be the person we know in our heart of hearts we're meant to be. We can listen to external authority, or we can listen to our own inner guidance. We can live our truth, or we can live a lie. All of us, including me, face these choices every day of our lives.

Even though the majority of people may be quite happy with the gender they were assigned at birth, can any of us afford to let others tell us who we are? Not only our gender, but also our religion, our values, our occupation or profession, and our identity as persons are of concern in this respect. If any of us allow others to tell us who we are, regardless of how we feel in our hearts, what then is left of our identity?

In my gender journey there have been many who've helped and supported me. Some were transwomen or transmen; others non-transgender people who tried to understand our cause. I wish I could say thank you to every one of them, as I couldn't have made it without their help. I've sometimes had non-transgender people tell me they think I've been brave to face my inner truth. I appreciate that they're not trying to be condescending, yet I really don't think of myself as brave. I was terrified when I went in for surgery, both times. Going before a judge to have my name and gender changed was scary too. Even using the ladies room, much as I take it for granted now, was once traumatic. I did these things only when there was no other alternative, no other direction I could go with my life.

While meditation and prayer remained central to my life, at times I've found myself coping with ambivalent feelings about Buddhism. I feel grateful to be part of a religious tradition with no patriarchal father-god: Buddhism has always been beyond god the father, and 2000 years before Darwin and Wallace, Buddhist have recognized that the universe in constantly evolving, with no need for a creator deity to bring life to the level of chaos that we see around us. I also have an ascetic side that repeatedly had drawn me toward Buddhist monasticism.

Yet in practice, Buddhism is still a patriarchal religious tradition, and there remains much prejudice toward women and sexual minorities even though there are no scriptures to justify such prejudice. Yet can I not find much of value in it anyway? After all the religions I'd studied previously, it was Buddhism that brought me to the Goddess, who is everything to me.

During the spring of 2008 I attended the annual Conference of the International Foundation for Gender Education, which was held in Tucson. It was the first time I'd attended a transgender conference in several years. Visiting with my former friends in Tucson made it doubly exciting. My workshop entitled *Life after Life: Transsexuality and Reincarnation* wasn't terribly well attended, but did attract several very enthusiastic participants. After discussing some of the ramifications of past-life memories to transgender persons, I regressed the attendees to their most immediate previous lives, to help them see what they could learn about themselves through hypnotherapy.

Past-life recollections aren't a special gift acquired by spiritually advanced people. Most of the subjects of past-life regression are just ordinary people who happen to have such memories. Often the main reason is that we died traumatic deaths in our previous lives that may take lifetimes to get over. Great spiritual leaders like Thich Nhat Hanh, the Dalai Lama, or the Rinpoche I studied with in Arizona, even though they may have had many rebirths, are actually less likely to remember previous lives if they died at peace with themselves and hence have no emotional baggage to bring with them into their present lives. Perhaps, if I die peacefully in this time, I may not even remember this life after I'm reborn once more.

The only halfway effective argument I've seen against reincarnation is that though some people may seem to have memories of a previous life, the recollections aren't their own, but come from other people through the collective unconsciousness. According to this argument, my memories of living and dying in Europe during the early part of the twentieth century aren't really my own. I've somehow acquired them from the other woman who had these experiences.

This leads to the question as to where "I" stop and others begin. In contrast to Hinduism and other religions, Buddhism teaches that there is no immortal, unchanging soul to reincarnate. Rebirth involves a coming together of similar aggregates to re-create a somewhat similar, though by no means identical, personality. So it almost becomes a semantic question whether or not the European woman and I are the same person. We're not the same person exactly; yet neither are we two distinctly different people.

For that matter, in what sense was the baby boy born in Cleveland in 1944 "me"? Or the youth growing up in New Jersey, was that the same person as the woman I am today? Or the young man growing into middle age in California, in what sense was he the same person as the woman I am today? The "I" who lived as a male in those days is no more the same person I am now as the woman living in Europe before that. There is a sort of continuity, but the transformation over time has been so radical that in a sense I really am no longer the same person.

While I question whether past lives can explain homosexuality, as some authors have suggested, it does go a long way to explain transgenderism. While some people seem inclined to remember mainly lifetimes in their present ethnicity and gender, others recall lives in faraway countries, sometimes of the "opposite" gender from who they are now. This proves that sex and gender aren't immutable, since many people have lived as both sexes. In a sense, over many lifetimes we're nearly all transsexuals. This can help explain why some people feel out of place in our birth sex. Since we may anticipate a future incarnation also, it helps prepare us. If we aren't able to transition in this life, we may look toward a future rebirth in our gender of identity.

Of course there are many people who disbelieve the evidence for reincarnation, just as there are many people who refuse to believe in transsexuality. Since I've tended to be a skeptic myself regarding supernatural phenomena, I can partly understand. Regarding transsexuality, though, I'm convinced that if people really got to know our people they'd understand our true nature. Our bodies, particularly our genitalia, do not determine our identity. Likewise with reincarnation, though it may be a little harder to convince some people, we need to understand that every one of us has an identity that transcends the body we're currently manifesting in. Attempts to explain away this reality only create more confused thinking.

My second workshop at the IFGE Conference, entitled *Late-Blooming Flowers: Coming to Womanhood after 55,* was better attended. We discussed the reasons why people delay transitioning from male to female until late in life, and some of the difficulties this delay can create. We noted that many people delay their transition because of fear, denial, self-hatred, guilt, shame, or other negative feelings. Still, as we noted, in the end we find we cannot find happiness until we live as our true selves. Unfortunately, as I pointed out from personal experience, the delay can make our transition more traumatic, as the continuing testosterone damage to our faces, hair, vocal chords, and other parts of our body is difficult to reverse. Yet we can still serve as role models for the transsexual community.

This workshop too came from as place deep inside me. How many decades had I delayed my own transition, treating my urge to dress *en femme* as an addiction to be overcome? Even in 2000, with a new millennium at hand, still I wondered what I could do—go to Twelve-Step meetings, undergo hypnotherapy, even consider taking testosterone—to stop dressing up. It was 2001 by the time I finally acknowledged my femininity as an essential part of me.

Even then I continued to hope that, since taking testosterone wouldn't be a good idea, maybe reducing my testosterone might cause me to lose interest in women, and hence in women's clothes. Until then I'd let the testosterone ravage my body, right up until my surgery in 2003, so that I've had to live with the resulting damage ever since. As recently as 2005 I'd spent six months living as a male, as though somehow, if I couldn't completely overcome my feminine desires, I might at least sublimate them into my male self. It was doomed to failure.

Finally, in 2006, I embraced the only alternative I had left. At last I came home to my true feminine self, knowing that I am a woman, 24/7, no more and no less. I finally realized that the essence of womanhood doesn't depend so much on what I have or don't have between my legs as how I look, act, speak, think, and above all feel. Like a beautiful bird at long last liberated from its little cage I flew high into the clouds, and joyously came down as rain on my true home.

It's been several years now since I had the dreams of my future life. Even now I pray to manifest a female rebirth in about thirty years. Thus, by the grace of my Goddess, my womb will be restored so I can live as a normal woman once more. I pray that I'll live in a good female body in a country where women are respected.

This, Goddess assures me, is to be the century of the woman. Within thirty years, as I prepare for my next birth, women will advance in all professions all over the world, achieving at long last our place of equality and power. No longer will being born female be considered being shamefully "low-born," as it still is in some countries. No longer will women need to feel afraid for our lives and our safety. No longer will we be expected to define ourselves according to the men in our lives. Women will advance freely into the highest offices in all lands, not riding on the coattails of our husbands, but rather on our own merits. More and more, I shall feel proud to call myself a woman.

To be reborn in Her image, Goddess cautions me, I must learn to be wholly compassionate. I must learn to overcome anger and impatience—still a challenge for me even now—and learn to think and feel as She does. I must learn to feel motherly toward all living beings, as She does. Meanwhile, I'm grateful to be able to live full-time right now as the woman I've all along known I'm meant to be. Beneath all the disappointments, medical bills, and bureaucratic red tape, one thought keeps coming to my mind. "I'm Joni now, 24/7, I'm Joni Kay Rose. I've become the woman of my dreams, and I love it!" Free at last, thank Goddess, free at last! All praises to the Venerable Supreme Goddess, in whose image I pray to be reborn.

Oh my Goddess, I cry out to You
in the name of my forsaken people.
From the ladies in the secret spas
to the girls who walk the street each night,
all those who struggle just to pay the rent
and try to find enough to eat each day,
while always hoping for a little surplus
to buy their hormones any way they can.

Oh my Goddess I cry out to You
in the name of my forsaken people.
In every country in the world we struggle
against discrimination and oppression.
While from the police we find no safety;
just more harassment and intimidation;
and our poor sisters, thrown in jail with men
like gentle dolphins tossed into a tank of sharks.

Oh my Goddess I cry out to You
in the name of my forsaken people.
We who do no harm to anyone:
Why do they persecute and rape and kill us?
Why do they ridicule us so?
Because we live our truth they fear us.
For we are living proof that all their concepts
are nothing more than lies and mass delusion.

Oh my Goddess, I cry out to You
in the name of my forsaken people.
May I live to see the day the world
shall finally cease to scorn and mock us
but instead once more shall honor
the special gift of wisdom that we offer.
And our great bridge of rainbow light
Shall help bring peace and justice to the world.

Sacred Stories
Silence Maestas

An important element of a transgender identity is a personal story of becoming. These identity narratives are stories that have been shaped in private, composed of all our memories, thoughts, emotions, and sensations. When we are lost, we sing these songs around personal fires to remind us where we came from. Every time a new chapter of the story falls into place, we become better able to find order in the chaos that often dominates our lives. Our stories are more than just a chronology of how we got from one point to another; they are living maps that describe who we have been, who we are now, and who we might become.

Stories are important to people who don't live a fully heterosexual, gender-normative life. Whenever we get together, we talk about our coming out stories, about when we "first knew", and about the twists and turns that brought us to where we are. Each story is unique, but there are many common themes. Confusion, fear, and rejection often figure prominently in these ongoing dramas, but so do joy, acceptance, and, finally, peace. This community of outsiders prizes stories of becoming. We bond around these shared experiences, getting to know each other and ourselves better each time we express them.

Maybe even more than the stories of becoming told by lesbians and gay men, the stories told by transgender people are essential to who we are. Since we've had to justify our reality to others—and ourselves—we also have to come up with a few coherent truths. We need a firm sense of ourselves in order to make sense of a life that feels nonsensical, or explain actions that might look insane or misguided to those around us,. In the story cycle of our lives, this struggle for Self is one of the main themes. (I'll use the capitalized 'Self' to refer to a deep and fundamental part of our being, of which we may or may not be aware.)

How have we handled this struggle? Challenges come at us from every side. Family, religion, place of employment, the public school system, health care providers, fair-weather friends, and unhelpful bystanders complicate efforts to work out who we are and what, if anything, we're going to do about it. This internal work might be the hardest part, but the Self-recognition gained provides the strength to face the external work. With luck, our personal gains will be enough to carry us through the trials the world throws at us.

No one creates a personal story in the same way. For some, a fully recognized identity has always existed, regardless of exterior markers. Other people come to recognize themselves more slowly, collecting bits of information over the years, placing childhood experiences in a new light, carefully feeling out who they might be in relation to other people. A brilliant "aha" moment might finally put a name to a half-understood identity, but at the same time create more questions than it answers ... and sometimes it takes a risk, a stab in the dark, to find out exactly who we might be.

A sense of Self that is strong and (hopefully) getting stronger is the narrative voice in our story. That's the prize won for having wrestled all the questions into submission, either by answering them or learning to live with them. With some sense of Self in place, we can begin to tell our story. When did my Self first speak to me? How did my Self feel when I was a child? How did my Self feel when my heart was broken for the first time? Has my Self always been honest with the people around me? What have I been afraid of hearing my Self tell me? With work, these questions can be answered—and are often revised at a later time. Our stories are not static because we are not static. Bodies and minds change, and our stories must shift to accommodate new information. Our epic narrative is as organic as the shells we live in.

Seeking our story is the same as seeking our Self. We are our stories, made up of all the joys and terrors of being human; whether we like it or not, we belong to our history. It's probably no coincidence that the first books published by transgender and transsexual people were autobiographies. (The same is true for gay people; even now, coming out stories make up a major part of lesbian/gay/bisexual fiction and non-fiction.) We seem to have a deep need to tell our stories. The sensationalized attention often given trans people is certainly enough to make the writers of these autobiographies want to speak for themselves, but even those who don't write memoirs may have a desire to orient themselves through a sequence of years that were likely confusing and difficult.

Stories have been used as way to teach and remember. This art has been used to pass down cultural and spiritual truths to new generations, giving them knowledge about their history and place in the universe. Many of these stories have come down to us as the myths of various cultures, but teaching stories still play a vital role in religious and spiritual traditions today. Whether written, sung, or shared in ritual, these stories link the present with the past. Both teller and listeners are oriented in time and space.

Telling our stories orients us, too. Even if we're our only audience, we achieve the same ritual goals as the tellers of sacred stories do. We find our place in space and time, and give ourselves meaning. The biggest questions answered by myths—where did we come from, where are we now, where we will go from here—are the same questions that are answered by our self-created myths. Our lives and all within them become an entire cosmos, and it's up to us to articulate the story cycle.

Telling our stories of becoming is a holy act, and we should remember this. Giving voice to our experiences makes them real. We literally create something out of the intangible stuff inside our heads; that's pretty powerful magic. Our personal myths grow and evolve over time. Clarity and truth grow each time they are told, and thus does a little more order come into our private universes.

And my story? I'm still trying to work out the details, and the telling changes each time I recite it. I hesitate to commit too much to paper because I'd hate to be locked into a single form without the option to revise it at a later time. Even the process of writing it down is challenging; I have to choose which of several truths to speak about. I can say this much: my transgender becoming started a very long time ago, possibly in my mother's womb, or maybe when my carbon was still floating in the atmosphere. I was arranged and oriented according to divine intent, and it was Their hands that brought me to a more complete knowledge of myself. Without that guidance my identity would have continued to hibernate, not fully in one world or another. My body's voice would still be drowned out by distress and sadness continually seeping up from my unconscious. I didn't know why I was always unhappy; I just knew that nothing in life ever brought me calm or lasting satisfaction.

Technically I fall on the FTM spectrum by virtue of being (as far as I know) biologically female, and because I have moved from identifying as a woman to identifying as something-other-than-a-woman. I don't feel like I have much in common with the other people grouped here. For one thing, I identify as third gender rather than as firmly male or masculine. My body is only comfortable with a masculine presentation (at least in public) and while I have some freedom with that, I have to stick to a more rigorous dress code than I used to. The part of my thirdness that I am most comfortable with the world seeing is me as a feminine young man.

My transgender identity, and indeed my identity as a human being, is bound up in my spirituality; whatever story I tell about myself is also a story about my Gods. Working to find comfort that brings together body, heart, presentation, spirit, and action has made me much stronger in my faith. Whatever changes and choices I make allow me to more fully manifest Their presence in my life. I am loved by a chaos God and servant to a death Goddess, and it is my humble honor to carry Them into this world through my slippery third nature. The Gods are shifty beings with countless faces. The more sides I see of Them, the more I come to know myself, and thus are our stories woven together.

I am a spirit-worker, which means I am is at the disposal of the deities and spirits I serve. Without a doubt, my Goddess finds my multiplicity useful, though I don't fully understand how. The spirits around me find my transgender nature appealing, and I have used this to my advantage when encountering them. While it's hardly necessary to be transgender in order to be in service to the spirit world, knowing that I am adds weight to my conviction that I belong to this path. For me, my thirdness is a way that my Work becomes physically manifest; I believe that I bring the worlds together by existing somewhere in between.

Though it was the goddess Hela was the one who made me aware of the extent of my queer nature, it was Loki who first began to open me up to possibilities. The Norse deity Loki is a shapeshifter and sex changer. The ecstatic relationship we share was at first very gendered; I actually rejected Him early on because He was much more masculine than the Goddesses I had worked with and loved up to that point. As our relationship has grown deeper over the past several years, I have come to love Him from all my aspects, and he shifts in complement to me. Together we have cycled through many aspects of religious love. Our fluid, multiple natures create endless potential for love, ecstasy, and desire, and I am honored to have the potential to offer my God so much of myself.

My spirit-work manifests most significantly as devotion (and let no one ever say that devotion isn't work!) My thirdness gives me tools on the devotional path I could never have imagined. I have been able to fall in love with my Gods as a woman, as a man, as a sacred Third, and as a human being. Love is the foundation of my life and my spiritual discipline. It is the fuel that drives my spirit-work, it is the language I use to communicate with the spirits, and it is the way I break the boundaries in and around me. My capacity for love and ecstasy—and thus for spiritual service—is exponentially increased because I have so many hearts to love from.

Even if our transgender nature is hidden, from the world or from ourselves, it shows up clearly in the eyes of the Otherworld. The Gods recognize and remember us, and the spirits see us for who we really are. I imagine if a transgendered person is involved in any meaningful spiritual practice, they will naturally be led to self-honesty through the transformative power of spirituality. Anyone looking to escape their true self through the power of religion is going to be disappointed. The Gods will not "cure" us. They will, however, make us more real.

Body Congruence
Joshua Tenpenny, LCMT

The theory of Body Congruence begins with the premise that existing simultaneously with our physical body we each have a body comprised of subtle energy, roughly the same size and shape as the physical body, anchored to the physical body but distinct from it. I will call this the "astral body" for the purposes of this article, but it may also be called the subtle body, the soul, the spirit, the energy body, the body of light, or a variety of other names.

It is not necessary to be able to perceive the astral body to use most of the techniques described in this article. Your internal sense of who you are and what you "really" look like will usually match the astral body very closely. It is often the body you see when you dream about yourself. If you have no experience manipulating the astral body, most techniques can be done quite effectively by using imagination and persistence. As with most skills, while some people are naturally gifted at this, almost everyone can do it to a certain extent if they try. In some of my descriptions, I do not make a clear distinction between psychological constructs and energetic phenomenon. I do believe there is a distinction, but in practice the techniques work very similarly.

Two Bodies, Two Souls

Both traditional Chinese medicine and ancient Greek philosophy recognize a distinction between the bodily aspect of the soul which perishes with the death of the physical body, and the heavenly ("astral") or eternal aspect of the soul which can exist beyond death. If a person has an "out of body" experience of some kind, this is "astral body" I am referring to is what they travel in while the physical body remains at rest. It is also the body that may travel on to the afterlife after the body dies, and if a ghost remains it is the remnants of this astral body. The "aura" is a diffuse energy field which surrounds the astral body like the atmosphere of a planet. The bodily aspect of the soul is the bio-energy which sustains the physical body. It is inseparable from it on a cellular level and animates the tissues. Without it, the flesh will rot and die.

The connection between the physical body and the astral body is much more flexible. The physical body can maintain basic metabolic processes without the astral body, and the astral body can move beyond the physical body under certain circumstances. Even so, these two bodies have a very strong natural affinity for each other. In a state of optimal health, they work together to maintain homeostasis and balance, and naturally bring themselves into line with each other. As the physical body grows and changes, the astral body naturally adapts to match it. Even though it is more malleable, changes in the astral body can also influence the physical body, generally via small neurological or biochemical alterations, affecting the metabolism, immune response, sexual response, and the chemical aspects of mood.

No one is ever in a completely optimum state of health, and substantial incongruence between the astral and physical bodies can occur. This generally occurs in one or more of the following ways: similarity, connection, stability, and definition. While transgender is primarily an issue of dissimilarity between the astral and physical bodies, other aspects of incongruence can arise due to a variety of related and unrelated factors. I will describe each one individually, but keep in mind that they often occur in combinations.

Similarity

When the physical and astral bodies are in perfect congruence, they look very much alike in shape, form, and essence. Transgendered individuals almost all have an astral body that reflects some aspect of their internal conception of their gender, although it may be more or less hermaphroditic than that internal conception. This is one of the few types of inherent dissimilarity. (Other inherent dissimilarities involve being not-quite-entirely human, and that is beyond the scope of this article.)

In general, lack of similarity is the most obtrusive type of incongruence, causing a great deal of vague discomfort that may be hard to pin down if the individual isn't aware of their astral body. Dissimilarity between the bodies can manifest as severe discomfort with the physical body and general awkwardness moving around in it, and a general lack of identification of "self" with the "flesh". There can be an urge to create alternate personas with costuming or cross-dressing, and there is often a strong desire to modify the physical body. Sexual functioning is frequently compromised, as good sex is an energetically powerful experience that requires physical body and astral body to work in harmony.

Dissimilarity may also arise over the course of a person's life when there is a sudden dramatic change to either the astral or physical body, as a result of emotionally traumatic injury, or in response to a physical change that the person is unwilling to fully accept. Adolescent growth spurts routinely cause a period of dissimilarity which resolves naturally in most young adults. For a transgendered person, the changes of puberty may be the first time they experience feelings of dissimilarity between their body and who they know themselves to be. This can cause substantial emotional turmoil which may not resolve until the person finds a way to express their inherent gender.

Dissimilarity may be caused by rapidly gaining or losing weight. A person who thinks of themselves as "fat" no matter how much weight they lose often has an astral body that is stuck at a heavier weight. The loss of a limb or other body part may cause dissimilarity, especially if the loss is sudden or traumatic or happens during a period of mental dissociation. The remaining presence of an astral limb after the physical limb is gone may contribute to the phenomenon of "phantom limb syndrome".

The most basic method of dealing with an inherent dissimilarity is acknowledging its existence. For most types of dissimilarity, this is an emotionally challenging experience, so I will give a set of exercises for that. It may be very difficult, but it can dramatically improve your ability to understand and handle the problem. This is a delicate process that may need to be done in stages. Do only as much as you are comfortable with, and come back to it in a few weeks. (Or years—however long it takes.) Don't force yourself through it.

First, become familiar with your astral body. You don't need to be able to "see" it in the occult sense (though if you can, do that instead of this visualization). Sit quietly and try to visualize the "real you". Let the image come to you, without judging that image or comparing it to your physical body. In most cases, this is what the astral body looks like, and the image has a strong feeling of rightness and realness to it. If nothing happens, spend a few minutes making a mental space for that image to be inviting it to come when it is ready, and then put the exercise aside for at least a few days.

Once you have an image of your astral body, imagine moving around in that body and going through your daily activities in that body. It should seem comfortable and real, not like a wild fantasy. Work on this until you become comfortable with that image. Can you look in the mirror and see that body? If not, imagine it. Look into the mirror inside your head, and see your real self reflected there. (Transgendered folks wrestling with issues of who they are and what they want to become may want to check out Kate Bornstein's *My Gender Workbook*.)

The next step is to become familiar with your physical body as it is. Again, try not to judge it or compare it to anything else. Just look at it, touch it, explore it. Start with area that are emotionally neutral to you, and then move on to ones that have stronger positive or negative associations. If certain areas are very difficult for you and don't want to go further, don't. Take some time to integrate the experience, and come back to it at a later date. Don't attempt to like the body you see and try to feel comfortable in it. You find that happening all on it's own, but you may find you are growing even more aware of how uncomfortable you are with your body. You may even feel uncomfortable with your sense of what your astral body looks like. You may not be feeling what you think you are supposed to be feeling. Whatever your response, acknowledge it without fixating on it. Just accept that this is the body you are in at present, and it is different from your astral body. It is natural for that to be profoundly uncomfortable.

Doing both of these exercises almost always has a very strong effect on someone with substantial dissimilarity between their astral body and physical body, but it can be hard to predict what that effect will be. Some people find that when they appreciate each body for what it is, they can find forms of expression that satisfy both. If unresolved trauma contributed to the dissimilarity, this exercise may bring the person to a place of healing where the dissimilarity resolves itself. However, when the astral body has a strong inherent difference that cannot be resolved with the physical body, it is likely to cause ongoing distress unless effective coping strategies are developed.

Many transgendered people choose to resolve this dissimilarity by altering the appearance of the physical body. Temporary alterations such as hairstyles and clothing are commonly used, but some transgendered people use surgery and hormones to bring their body into closer alignment. Any of these techniques may be very successful, only partially successful, or entirely unsatisfactory, depending on the individual. The degree of dissimilarity does not reliably indicate what level of physical adaptation the person will need to feel comfortable.

For a transgendered person, dissimilarity can also occur after physical gender transition. If their astral body has adapted to their physical body as it was before transition, it may habitually hold that old form even after the body changes to a more comfortable form. This is more likely to occur with surgical changes than with hormonal changes. In hormone therapy, the body actively participates in a gradual process of physical change, and change happens only to the extent that your physiology allows. Surgical modifications are very sudden, and modify the body in a way that physiological processes cannot.

Resolving this type of dissimilarity requires reshaping the astral body to match the physical. This can be done with visualizations opposite to the ones described above. Look at your physical body, then close your eyes and picture yourself. Is it the same, or do you still see the "old you"? Imagine your physical body as it is, going about your daily activities. Stay present with whatever emotions come up. Keep working on this until you become comfortable with it. Touch your body while looking at it. Feel the shape of your body and say to yourself, "This is how my body is. This is what I look like." Don't let judgments about whether your body is good or bad come into this. You don't have to like it. Just acknowledge that it is real.

In some cases of incongruence, consciously reshaping the astral body can be useful. This is very beneficial when the difference is due to some sudden injury, or emotional trauma that has made the astral body unable to adapt. When the dissimilarity is due to something inherent to the astral body, it may be possible to reshape the astral body either to match the physical body or to a "middle ground" between them, but this is not a permanent solution. The functioning of the astral body will be impaired, and it may quickly return to its natural shape. Reshaping the astral form is an advanced technique, and best done with the assistance of someone with skill in this type of shapeshifting. If you would like to try reshaping on your own, begin by strongly imagining the intended form. Then using your hands and strong focused intent, sculpt the astral body into that shape. If the intended shape is one you have a strong affinity for, or your astral form is very malleable, this may happen fairly easily, but for most people this takes a great deal of practice and natural ability.

Connection

In a congruent set of bodies, the physical and astral are tightly connected at many points, and exchange energy freely. In a poorly connected set of bodies, there is a general feeling of disconnection to the physical world, and energy does not flow freely between them. Dissimilarity, not surprisingly, can cause disconnectedness. So can chronic physical pain or chronic emotional trauma from a young age, especially if accompanied by feelings of lack of control. The abuse of drugs and alcohol can cause disconnection, especially if used to "escape" reality. Hallucinogens and numbing drugs such as opiates are particularly dangerous in this way. In a similar fashion, disconnection can be caused by psychiatric problems of the sort that interfere with one's interface with reality—schizophrenia, severe depression, etc. And, of course, when a person is in the process of dying, the astral body disconnects from the physical.

Disconnection can manifest in a high pain threshold, to the point where the individual may not notice when they are injured. Disconnection can lead to poor digestion and a weak immune system. It often shows up in sexual problems where the person prefers to go off into their own world during sex rather than being present for it. They may think of their genitalia as an independent entity which they have little control over. People whose bodies are poorly connected tend to go easily into trance, but may find the state hard to control and they often have difficulty coming back out of it. They may appear "spacey" much of the time.

One common result of poor connection is a general disregard of the physical well-being—not bothering to eat properly or at all, ignoring the need for sleep, ignoring illness or injury until it becomes too severe to ignore. In some cases, there is thrill-seeking behavior of the sort that flippantly risks life and limb. There may even be self-injuring behavior. Sometimes these things can be used as a distraction from whatever pain has caused the disconnection, but often they seek these experiences because it they need that level of intensity for anything to feel real. Unfortunately, this is a behavior that tends to escalate, with bigger and bigger thrills needed to create the same effect. They may find a socially acceptable outlet for this in dangerous sports such as mountain climbing or skydiving, or they may prefer bar fights and reckless driving.

People who do a lot of spiritual or magical work that requires altered states and trances, journeying out of the body, or possessory work can also end up with a very loose connection between their bodies. This is particularly likely if the person's spiritual practice is very strongly focused on the spiritual to the exclusion and devaluation of the physical world. Strong connection can be maintained by spiritual practices that involve the physical body, using the physical and astral together rather than independently. Engage all the senses in your spiritual practice, using movement, touch, chanting, incense, clothing, and physical objects. Make the physical sacred.

If the disconnection is caused by physical or psychic pain, it is rarely productive to attempt to establish a connection until the source of the pain has been addressed. Sometimes this just isn't possible, and in that case disconnection and its associated problems may be preferred. It is perfectly reasonable to not want to be fully present in a body that causes you constant pain, or even constant annoying discomfort. However, if you have made considerable progress on the issue, or are in a place where you are better able to cope with it, establishing a better connection can be an important part of the healing process.

To reestablish connection in a lasting way, it is vital that you like and respect yourself. Not everyone with poor connection has this problem, but for those who do, establishing self-worth is the first step. You must want to be healthy and want to be in your body. Also, if you've been using drugs, alcohol, self-injury, sex, or any other activity to numb the pain and distract yourself from the problem, it is generally more effective to focus on those behaviors rather than working directly on astral connection.

Valuing the body and the physical world, and faithfully working at a regime to keep the body healthy and give it regular pleasure (massage, dance, walking, good food, whatever works for you) is important in retraining the mind to accept reconnection. Yoga, Tai Chi, and certain martial arts are very powerful tools for learning to use the body and energy together. Connecting deeply to earth-energy through the body, perhaps with the aid of the land-spirits, can help as well. For gender dysphoria or other issues of dissimilarity, the mapping techniques described in the dissimilarity section are also useful for strengthening connection. Connect the parts that are most congruent, and "map" the others to body landmarks and/or physical objects that can be carried on the body. Other good tools to help with connection are mindful touch, eye contact, and focused breathing with a sympathetic partner or friend.

If it has been determined to be appropriate—i.e. it won't traumatize the individual further—the astral body can be deliberately "anchored" in the physical body. This can be done through mindful touch with the intent of "locking" the two bodies together, perhaps accompanied by mindful breathing and eye contact. The five lower chakras of the body should make a very strong connection if everything is working correctly. (The upper chakras primarily connect the astral body to the outer cosmos, and do not anchor strongly to the physical body.) The acupuncture meridians can also be used for specific points of connection.

Establishing a solid connection between the astral and physical bodies may be necessary in an emergency, for instance if someone has gone into trance and is having trouble returning. Sharply pinching the upper lip can be effective in this case, as it is a connection point for the front and back energy channels. Any quick sharp pain may do the trick, the way you would slap someone who was out of control or losing consciousness. If the person has come out of a trance and is having trouble getting seated in their body, it may also help to pour cold water (ideally salt water) on the head and the back of the neck. Eating, changing clothes, or taking a shower may also help.

Stability

The physical body doesn't change quickly, though it will age over time, or become ill, or have accidents, or be altered with drugs or hormones or surgery. The subtler aspects of biochemistry and neurology may shift more quickly, but the basic physical form stays the same from minute to minute. Most people's astral bodies are also stable and keep the same form over time, with only slow and gradual changes. Some people, however, have astral bodies that shift and change rapidly, perhaps from day to day or hour to hour. Some may even be constantly moving and shifting and flickering in ways that the physical body can never replicate. This creates a continual state of incongruence between the bodies.

Constantly shifting or unstable astral bodies are rare, but usually fit into a handful of known causes. Gender-wise, the sort of transgendered individual who has a shifting astral body is often the sort with a fluid gender identity that may shift and change in response to different situations. (This can be an addition to the problems of dissimilarity and disconnection.) Someone with multiple personality disorder (now known as Dissociative Identity Disorder) will generally have an astral body that shifts when a new personality takes control. Some spirit-workers do a lot of astral shapeshifting for their work. This may lead to instability in their astral body, but it is likely their talent for shapeshifting derives from as inherently unstable astral body, rather than causing it. People with strong spiritual affinities to animal souls may continually shift their astral bodies between their animal and human forms. Many genetic psychic vampires have inherently unstable astral bodies, with many fine strands coming out through the aura.

An unstable astral body can sometimes manifest as someone who "isn't what they seem" on the outside, or who can chameleon into different personas for different situations. Some have a good deal of control over their shapeshifting; others don't, and may not even be aware of it. If stability is the only issue, and it's not causing any problems, then don't worry about fixing it. If there are problems, fortunately it's one of the easier incongruences to learn to control. Simply imagine and visualize the desired form, or energetically sculpt and mold the astral body. An unstable astral body is generally very easily shaped in this way. Holding the astral body stable in one form may be more challenging, but repeated practice and mindfulness will help. A shapeshifting astral body can be a real gift if you know how to use it properly instead of letting it run amuck on its own. The more control you can learn, the less it will trouble you.

Definition

Most people's astral bodies are well-defined, in that they seem solid, with clear edges and a definite shape. Even a very unstable form is generally well-defined, flexible yet solid. A few people, however, have astral bodies that are limp or blurry, dissolving around the edges. Like a cloud, their form has no clear edge. This is never a good thing. In most cases of a persistently poorly defined astral body, there is a poor sense of self, and there may be lifelong psychological dissociation. The individual usually has poor boundaries with others, and others' opinions and feelings; they may not be clear on where they stop and someone else begins. They may have sexual dysfunction when the person has only a vague understanding of what goes on "down there". They generally have difficulty with psychic shielding, because that requires putting a firm boundary around the edge of the aura. For that matter, they may have trouble with energy work in general, because energy flows sluggishly through them and their astral "limbs" may not be strong or well-formed enough to channel energy precisely. A person with a poorly defined astral body will tend to have weak vital energy, because without a healthy boundary, the poorly defined astral body tends to continually leak.

The vital energy can be depleted to the point where the astral body can't hold itself together, due to malnutrition, prolonged sleep deprivation, serious illness, or severe emotional strain. In these cases, the astral body is weak and thin, hanging in a thin aura that contracts closely around the body, and the *chi* of the physical meridians is also low. There may not be any psychological factors present in cases of severe physical exhaustion, but if this is the case, the boundary should firm back up again if the physical problem is resolved. Habitual use of narcotics or certain other drugs can also cause the astral body to blur at the edges, and this may not resolve itself if the person gets sober.

Except in these extreme cases, psychological factors are a primary cause of poor definition, and the individual may need to get professional psychological assistance to build a sense of self and deal with their boundary issues. Physical and energetic techniques can help the process, but will not create lasting change unless the psychological factors are addressed. The best thing the person can do to directly improve definition is to mindfully run their hands over their entire body on a daily basis, perhaps when bathing, with the intent of smoothing and solidifying the edges of themselves and getting a sense of who they physically are. If definition is the primary problem, this exercise might be challenging but it should also be empowering. If they can't do this exercise at least once or if it causes them distress, there is some other factor at work that should be attended to first.

Almost any type of massage or bodywork will help with developing an awareness of the physical body and its edges, which may help define the astral body edges as well. This works even better if it is done mindfully by an energy-worker massage therapist who can help solidify the astral body as they work, perhaps describing it to the client as they go along. Additionally, if the individual is inclined to learn energy work, they can start with shielding, which can help them learn to create (if only artificially) clear edges and prevent excessive energy leakage. Techniques that make them more aware of their astral body can be beneficial, but only if they are naturally inclined to that sort of work.

There are many different ways to build up low energy if this is part of the problem. Some people find a great benefit from being in nature, especially lying on the earth and connecting with that energy. Some people can supplement their vital energy by passively absorbing it in high-energy places such as music concerts, although many people with low energy will find these places overwhelming and exhausting. A few people have the skill of drawing energy directly from another person but this is not appropriate to do unless the other person volunteers. Energy treatments such as Reiki can supplement the vital energy, like a transfusion, but aren't a replacement for one's own vital energy. The Chinese practices of Qi Kung are very effective at strengthening the astral body, and are easily learned by individuals who are not energetically sensitive.

Eating a whole-food diet with live foods is almost universally helpful for low energy. Eat vegetables as fresh as you can get, straight from the garden if possible. These are full of vital energy, but it dissipates fairly quickly once the vegetable is picked. Fresh unpasteurized milk is hard to obtain, but a great source of vital energy. Directly from the animal milk has as much vital energy as blood, and unlike blood, it remains quite vital for a day or more provided it doesn't get very hot or very cold. Also very beneficial are foods that are still alive, such as sprouts, active-culture yogurt, and any fermented foods that have not been pasteurized.

In general, body congruence is an important, if much overlooked, issue of both psychic and physical health. It is important for practitioners of any kind of bodywork, energy work, or psychic healing to understand it in depth and be able to tell what sort of problems their clients may have with it. On the other hand, it is also important for practitioners to be humble about whether they can help the situation, or whether they should even try. If the person has complex or deeply rooted psychological concerns, it is irresponsible to assume you're your compassion and intuition are a substitute for training and experience in psychological counseling. Be supportive of the person's emotional experience, but ensure the person has appropriate psychological support.

Also remember that attempting to resolve problems of body congruence is not something a practitioner does *to* a client. It is something that they try to aid a client in doing for themselves. In all cases, the client's needs, desires, abilities, and current life situation must be taken into account. Body congruence issues don't happen without a reason, and they may not be ready to cope with that reason yet. Patience and caution is necessary; it is not something that can be forced out of season. If nothing else, the information can be given and planted like a seed that has the potential to grow in the future.

Epilogue

I'm finishing this second edition nearly ten years after I finished the first one, and the question that reverberates in my mind is: are things any different now? Yes and no. On the one hand, some hard-won milestones have appeared since that time. On the other hand, some things have become even more complicated.

The efforts of intersex activists have seriously reduced the number of infant genital mutilations, although they are not stopped by any means. International attention has been given to the issue, and more and more doctors and parents are being educated about it. Various procedures have been set out for the medical field and a certain amount of lip service has been given, but as of now there is no way to enforce these protocols.

In the meantime, there has been a decade of GLB and transgender groups jumping on the new intersex situation without a clear understanding of the problems involved. The letter "I" was stuck onto the end of the acronym—as in "GLBTI"—in many cases without actually having any intersexuals in their groups, or giving much thought to the needs of potential members with intersex disorders. By definition, of course, the only intersexuals who came into GLBT groups were ones who identified as nonheterosexual, or who were transgendered to one extent or another.

However, this was not an identity shared by all, or even most, individuals with intersex conditions, and some resented what they considered to be a medical label associated with sexual-preference and gender-identity demographics. On top of that, some parents of intersex children were uncomfortable when they looked for resources about their newborn's medical problem, and came up with references to the GLBT community. While there are no documented accounts of parents actually choosing to have their child surgically modified in order to avoid the terrible fate of being queer, some intersex activists did panic a bit, fearing that it would happen. As a result, some activists and medical personnel worked out the Disorders of Sex Development label as something too "medical" for anyone to claim as an identity, and "safely" separated from the GLBT community. They hoped to phase out both the outdated "hermaphrodite" and the now-controversial "intersex" labels.

This move has made those activists who strongly identify with the GLBT community, and with intersex as an identity, feel angry and alienated. Intersex people fall variously along the spectrum from one side of the split to the other. (Me, I just shake my head whenever I see euphemizing of a stigmatized identity, because I know that in every case, euphemizing the stigmatized eventually stigmatizes the euphemism.) It will be interesting, and educational, to see how it all turns out.

Of course, the GLBT communities all meant well when they stuck the "I" on the end of their acronym. They were trying to be inclusive, making space for the handful of loud intersexuals (like myself) who openly identified with the rest of the letters. They had little information on the political and social needs of intersexuals, besides the work of a vocal few who were speaking out against infant genital mutilation. *Sure, no problem, I'll be against genital mutilation and promise never to do it to the children that I might (but statistically probably won't) have, and I'll promise to work toward loosening society's mores of gender; now we're meeting this group's needs, right?* This attitude was exacerbated by the fact that most intersexuals weren't real clear on what needs a movement should be adding to the list.

Some of the more specific goals of more recent intersex activists do resemble the goals of transgendered activists—for example, the idea of creating a database of friendly and understanding medical personnel, and doing mass education of other health care professionals in order to increase that number. (It's been noted that in many ways the needs of both the transgender and intersex demographics are less like those of sexual-preference groups and more like those of disability groups, but that's a different book.) In these areas it does seem as if it would be less work to hitch both horses to the same cart, so long as minor but important differences are not discarded in the process. However, we still need to clean up the mess from the homophobic/transphobic response to the last attempt to integrate us. No, it wasn't fair, but it happened, and both communities need to think about what can be done to repair the damage.

The past decade has also seen an explosion of transgender activists and resources, as well as an explosion of younger transgender people. There are not only significantly more transsexuals between the age of 16 and 22, there are more people in that age category (and others) who are openly identifying as third gender on the near side of transsexualism ... and sometimes the far side. Some, admittedly, are doing it for political reasons (one remembers the "political lesbians" of the 1970s and how little time that lasted), or in some cases pure rebellion, but they will either outgrow it or grow into it, and any amount of deliberate gender crossing is good for people's perspective in the long run. Some are legitimately finding themselves as third gender not because they don't like social roles, but because their deep body-centered self is somewhere in the middle, and would be no matter what social roles and programming we had, and that's just the way it is.

In some rare cases, we are now seeing children as young as 10 or 11 being aided in transition by supportive parents; the number of transsexual teens who transition as soon as they are out of high school has risen drastically. Those of us whose generation wandered around until our thirties (or later) before transitioning are looking wistfully at them, but it's good to know that all our work paid off and it will only grow from here. The growing transgender demographic is snowballing, and while the frightening murder rate may be a backlash, it is also a sign of how much influence we are gaining as a phenomenon.

It has also been gratifying to see the Transgender Day of Remembrance, set for November, spin out into a worldwide phenomenon. The dead of our tribe are being accounted, remembered, and celebrated; as people who are often cast out from our own families, we need all the sacred ancestors that we can get. We light candles and call their names, and hopefully inspire each other and our allies to stay alive and to protect each other.

On the other hand, at a recent Day of Remembrance, a transwoman came up to me and noted that this event, with its tone of sadness and mourning, was the only holiday our people have. "Find me another one," she told me. "A joyful one." I'm still considering the possibility, and I throw it out to all of you ... perhaps a holiday in the springtime, full of possibility, with parades of people carrying sacred figures that lie between male and female, a public showing and reverence of transgender bodies, transgender desires, transgender gods? A libation of pomegranate juice and a blessing of our amazingly different rainbow of lives, all bound in the sacred Third space?

It's true that Stonewall was started by drag queens (and one drag king) but Gay Pride is, and should be, an inclusive holiday for the entire GLBT spectrum. Transfolk need their own culture that is not dependent on that of GLB folk who, however much they may support and love us, in the end may not fully grasp our particular needs. Transgendered people are the least acceptable tail end of the GLBT movement, the ones who wait in the shadows when every bill is proposed, wondering if we will be sacrificed yet again for the "normalcy" required to get it through. We deserve to have our own celebratory culture holiday that is not just about death. We deserve some balance to our mourning. Let there be joy. I await the ideas of my creative tribe.

Most important, the discussion of transgender spirituality has also grown. When I started writing the first edition of this book, no one was talking about it except for me and a couple of others who touched on it. *Transgender* and *religion* were words that people hardly dared to combine in one sentence, except perhaps to complain. Today, transfolk are writing about it in droves, including people in religions that I have no experience writing about. This is a joy to my heart. I want to see us taking our sacred roles in older faiths and carving out our own places in newer ones. I want to remind my brothers and sisters that faith in something greater than you can provide that anchor, that buoyancy, that light in the darkness when everything is at its worst. We need that, as much or more than anyone else.

Take it, my sisters and brothers. It doesn't have to cost more than it gives, if you choose wisely, if you remember that you have the right to pick and choose. It doesn't have to cost much at all ... and oh, the payback. Really. Listen to your shaman. It's worth every doubt.

But I still believe,
Yes, I still believe,
Through the shame
And through the grief,

Through the heartache,
Through the tears,
Through the waiting,
Through the years,

For people like us
In places like this,
We need all the hope
We can get,
Oh, I still believe.

−Tim Capello

Appendix: The Intersex Flyer For Parents

Please copy this flyer and distribute it to anyone who is pregnant, is considering becoming pregnant, or who works in the OB/GYN field. As an act both of gender subversion and of compassion, make piles of copies and put them in the waiting rooms of OB/GYN offices. Copy it and use it as many times as you like; I'd rather have it go out everywhere than lay any claim to it. Spread the word.

"Congratulations! Is It A Boy... Or A Girl..."
And What To Do If It's Not So Clear
(The Truth and Reality About Intersex Children)

We all want the best for our children, and none of us want our children to suffer, but sometimes we can't always agree on what "the best" actually is. If you're the parent of a child born with an intersex condition, you may not be sure what is right for your baby. This information was written by real intersexuals, those of us who live and cope and manage with our conditions all the time. We feel that you deserve to know what it's like for us, and what it might be like for your (current or potential) intersex child. As parents, you deserve the real truth, straight from the source. We'll try to answer your questions here.

Questions and answers about intersex children:

1. What is intersexuality?

Intersexuality is a group of medical conditions called "Disorders of Sexual Development (DSD)" that blur or make nonstandard a person's physical sexual characteristics. These include Klinefelter's Syndrome (XXY chromosomes), congenital adrenal hyperplasia (CAH), and other rarer syndromes. People with these conditions were once referred to as "hermaphrodites" or "pseudohermaphrodites", but since these terms tend to make people think of mythical figures, we prefer the term "intersexual". This is about medical conditions, not myths.

Some intersexuals are born with genitalia that are "ambiguous", meaning not completely male or female. Others are genitally normal at birth but develop mixed secondary sexual characteristics at puberty. One of the rarer conditions, a form of CAH, involves endocrinal salt-wasting and these children may need steroid medication.

Intersexuality is more common than most people think. Statistics on the number of intersexuals that are born vary from 1.7% of the population (for all intersex conditions) to 1 in 2000 (for those born with ambiguous genitalia).

2. What do you mean by "ambiguous genitalia"?

Ambiguous genitals can take many forms. The male and female genital characteristics can be combined in many different ways, or there can even be no external genitalia at all. Almost none have both a functional penis and a functional vagina, however.

3. What is the traditional medical treatment for a child with ambiguous genitalia?

The traditional treatment is for the doctors to decide from a predetermined checklist what sex your baby should be, and then surgically modify your child to resemble that sex. We disagree with this treatment for a variety of reasons.

First, the deciding factor tends to be ease of surgery ... in other words, the pediatric surgeon's convenience. Over 90% of intersex children as are assigned to the female gender because "it's easier to make a hole than to build a pole", to quote some pediatric surgeons. Often, the deciding factor is penis length. If the medical personnel feel that your child's penis is not big enough, they will remove it and assign the child to a female sex. We feel that since intersex children have been affected by both male and female hormones before birth, it is impossible to tell what sex your child will identify as once he/she is old enough to talk about it.

Second, the surgeries are not very good. Operating on infant-size genitalia is not an easy thing, and procedures such as clitorectomies (removal of the clitoris) often leave the individual with no sexual sensation later in life. In addition, scar tissue can build up, leaving an appearance that is not cosmetically good. Doctors often claim that they can create "perfectly functional" genitalia, but to date only one study has been performed to do a followup, and it does not look good for their claims. (Dr. David Thomas, a pediatric urologist in Leeds, England, did a follow-up study on 12 intersexuals surgically "assigned" as girls; all had surgery that was unsatisfactory in some way and in 5 of the 12, the relocated sexually sensitive tissue had withered and died.) Many of us, as adults, suffer from intense anger and depression due to lack of genital sensation. Post-surgical intersexuals can also be more prone to urinary tract and other infections.

We realize that it may feel difficult and uncomfortable to think about your child's adult needs, but babies do grow up (we hope!) and become adults, and all adults deserve the ability to make their own decisions about their bodies. We ask that you please leave your children this ability.

Third, when artificial vaginas are constructed in children, they need to be "dilated" to keep from closing up. This involves the parent being forced to insert a plastic "stent" or phallus into his/her baby's genitals on a daily basis for a long time. In any other context, this would be considered sexual abuse, and indeed many of us are psychologically and sexually damaged by this procedure. For that matter, asking a small child to expose their genitals repeatedly to crowds of doctors, interns, and medical students, which often happens on check-up visits, is also damaging.

Fourth, there is no real health or safety reason to operate on infant genitals solely for reasons of gender ambiguity. Any reconstructive surgery that needs to be done can be done with much, much better results at or after puberty, when the area is adult-sized. Some doctors claim that allowing a child to grow up with ambiguous genitals will lead to that child feeling suicidal. In fact, there is absolutely no proof of this. (No such studies have been done on most intersexual conditions; the one small study that was done by Dr. Justine Schrober on the quality of life of 12 men with very small penises found that they were doing fine and many had supportive partners.) However, many of us as adults have become suicidal due to unsatisfactory surgeries and our treatment at the hands of the (still experimenting) medical community.

It probably seems uncomfortable to think about having to raise a child who isn't normal in some way, and you may worry about your child's feelings while growing up, but please believe us when we say that it is easier to face childhood being a little different than to face adulthood with parts that don't work right and can't be repaired.

4. What do I do if I have a child with ambiguous genitalia?

Please do not let the doctors operate on your child unless there is a real medical emergency, such as a blocked urethra or other urinary or bowel trouble. Make sure that they understand your position on intersexuality before your child is born, so that no trouble will arise. In at least one case, doctors operated on the child anyway without the knowledge or permission on the parents. Please don't let this happen! Your child's genital tissue must remain unmarred until they are more physically mature.

5. What sex should I raise my baby as?

You need to make your own decisions regarding how your baby is to be raised. We, as intersexuals, were generally able to decide what sex we felt ourselves to be by puberty. This means that you, the parent, not a team of doctors, can and should make the decision about your baby's sex ... as long as you remember that the child, grown up, will make the final choice. Some of us do change sex later in life, and you should do your best to be open to this possibility. There is no scientific evidence for the medical community's claim that we will stay whatever sex we are raised. We are not blank slates; we simply do not have the means to make our wishes known in infancy. Although consulting the doctors involved can give you useful information to help you with your choices, only you can decide. However, you can have support for your choices; see the list of groups below.

6. What should I tell my child about his/her condition?

As soon as your child is old enough to understand, you should explain things as clearly and simply as possible. Your child should never feel ashamed of his/her medical condition. Many of us suffered terribly from the secrecy and shame surrounding our intersexuality; our parents either refused to explain why we were put through painful surgeries and/or fed hormones at puberty, or they taught us that it was shameful and that we were never to speak of it. In some places, it was common for hospitals and doctors to destroy the medical records of intersex children, in order to prevent them from finding out how they were "abnormal". However, most of us figured it out anyway. Honesty is the best policy.

Keep your child's medical checkups regarding their condition to a minimum, and chaperone to make sure that he/she is not used as a guinea pig or educational display. Learn as much as you can about your child's condition, and do not let yourself be made to feel stupid, incompetent, or incapable of making decisions. When your child is approaching puberty, it might be best to carefully discuss the possibilities and what they might entail. This might work best in the framework of family therapy, preferably with a gender specialist. Your child must be the final arbiter of what is or is not done to his/her body, and your job is to discover and advocate for his/her choice.

Finally, we strongly suggest that you join a support group. You are not alone, and neither is your child. Contact the networks listed below to find out if there is a group in your area, or if you should start one. You might also think about a support group for your child, so that he/she can know that they, too, are not alone. It's a good thing for them to meet adults with their condition, who can reassure them about life.

7. Can an intersex person live a happy, fulfilled life?

Yes! Although no official studies have been done (we're all waiting for them), our anecdotal evidence suggests that intersexual children who are raised in a loving supportive family with no surgical intervention until they wish it, and with parents who do not make them feel ashamed, are well-adjusted and happy, often with loving spouses/partners. (Other studies done on children with other disabilities have shown that the child's level of adjustment depends less on the severity or social obviousness of the disability and more on the presence or absence of loving family support.) It's those of us who had more intervention, not less, who are more likely to have psychological and sexual dysfunction today.

The parent of an intersexual has been blessed with a very special and gifted child, who requires a lot of patience and love. You will need courage to stand up for your child's real needs, but you are the only advocates who really care for your baby. We hope that in reading this, you will be able to make decisions about your child's treatment that truly work for their well-being and not some abstract illusion of social "normality".

8. Where can I find out more about intersexuality?

Organization Intersex International http://intersexualite.org
ISNA (Intersex Society of North America) http://www.isna.org
Bodies Like Ours http://www.bodieslikeours.org
Androgen Insensitivity Syndrome Support Group http://aissg.org
Accord Alliance http://www.accordalliance.org
(DSD-oriented liaison with the medical field)

Bibliography

Athanassakis, Apostolos N. *The Orphic Hymns*. Missoula, Montana: Scholars Press, 1977.

Bly, Robert. *Iron John: A Book About Men*. New York, NY: Perseus Books, 1990.

Bolen, Jean Shinoda. *Goddesses in Everywoman*. New York, NY: Harper & Row, 1984.

Bolen, Jean Shinoda. *Gods in Everyman*. New York, NY: Harper & Row, 1989.

Califia, Pat. *Public Sex*. Pittsburgh, PA: Cleis Press, 1994.

Conner, Randy P. *Blossom of Bone*. New York, NY: HarperCollins Publishers, 1993.

Downing, Christine. *The Goddess*. New York, NY: The Crossroad Publishing Company, 1981.

Eliade, Mircea. *Shamanism*. Princeton, NJ: Bollingen Series, 1964.

Eliade, Mircea. *The Two and the One*. Chicago, IL: University of Chicago Press, 1979.

Evelyn-White, Hugh G. *The Homeric Hymns and Homerica*. Cambridge, MA: Harvard University Press, 1914.

Fiedler, Leslie. *Freaks: Myths and Images of the Secret Self*. New York, NY: Simon & Schuster, 1978.

Frazer, J.G. *Pausanias's Description of Greece*, Translation. New York, NY: Biblo & Tannen, 1965.

Frazier, Sir James. *The New Golden Bough*. Garden City, NY: Anchor Press, 1961.

Graves, Robert. *The Greek Myths*. Harmondsworth, Middlesex, England: Penguin Books, 1955.

Graves, Robert. *The White Goddess*. New York, NY: Farrar, Straus, and Giroux, 1948.

Kiefer, Otto. *Sexual Life in Ancient Rome*. New York, NY: Dorset Press, 1993.

Hamlyn, Paul. *The New Larousse Encyclopedia of Mythology*. Middlesex, England: Hamlyn House, 1959.

Harner, Michael. *The Way of the Shaman*. New York, NY: Bantam Books, 1982.

Hirschfeld, Magnus. *Transvestites*. Amherst, NY: Prometheus Books, 1991.

Ions, Veronica. *The World's Mythology in Color*. Secaucus, NJ: Chartwell Books, 1987.

Knight, Richard Payne. "A Discourse on the Worship of Priapus (1786)". Republished in *A History of Phallic Worship*. New York, NY: Dorset Press, 1992.

Miller, Richard Alan. *The Magical and Ritual Uses of Herbs*. Rochester, Vermont: Destiny Books, 1983.

Paris, Ginette. *Pagan Meditations*. Dallas, TX: Spring Publications, 1986.

Pomeroy, Sarah B. *Goddesses, Whores, Wives, and Slaves*. New York, NY: Schocken Books, 1975.

Teish, Luisah. *Jambalaya*. San Francisco, CA: Harper & Row, 1988.

Stone, Merlin. *Ancient Mirrors of Womanhood*. Boston, MA: Beacon Press, 1979.

Vermaseren, Martin. *Cybele and Attis*. London: Thames and Hudson, 1977.

Walker, Barbara G. *The Woman's Encyclopedia of Myths and Secrets*. San Francisco, CA: Harper & Row, 1983.

Williams, Walter L. *The Spirit and the Flesh*. Boston, MA: Beacon Press, 1986.

Wright, Thomas. "The Worship of the Generative Powers in the Middle Ages in Western Europe (1866)". Republished in *A History of Phallic Worship*. New York, NY: Dorset Press, 1992.

About the Author

Raven Kaldera is a troublemaker. He is an organic farmer, homesteader, Northern Tradition Pagan *ergi* shaman, astrologer, psychic vampire, herbalist, pervert, FTM intersexual, founding member of the First Kingdom Church of Asphodel, and author of too many books, stories, and articles to list here. One author friend has referred to him as "frighteningly prolific". Another called him "an activist for everything that he is". He is absolutely determined to change the world as we know it, and last he checked, was actually making a little headway. Raven lives on Cauldron Farm with his MTF wife Bella, his FTM partner Joshua, and random assorted housemates and refugees. 'Tis an ill wind that blows no minds.

CPSIA information can be obtained at www.ICGtesting.com
Printed in the USA
LVOW091324090312

272334LV00002B/149/P